Women, Islam, and Identity

Gender and Globalization
Susan S. Wadley, *Series Editor*

Other titles in the Gender and Globalization series

Bodies That Remember: Women's Indigenous Knowledge and Cosmopolitanism in South Asian Poetry
Anita Anantharam

Family, Gender, and Law in a Globalizing Middle East and South Asia
Kenneth M. Cuno and Manisha Desai, eds.

From Patriarchy to Empowerment: Women's Participation, Movements, and Rights in the Middle East, North Africa, and South Asia
Valentine M. Moghadam, ed.

Hijab and the Republic: Uncovering the French Headscarf Debate
Bronwyn Winter

Imperial Citizen: Marriage and Citizenship in the Ottoman Frontier Provinces of Iraq
Karen M. Kern

Jamaat-e-Islami Women in Pakistan: Vanguard of a New Modernity?
Amina Jamal

Lines in Water: Religious Boundaries in South Asia
Eliza F. Kent and Tazim R. Kassam, eds.

Policing Egyptian Women: Sex, Law, and Medicine in Khedival Egypt
Liat Kozma

Super Girls, Gangstas, Freeters, and Xenomaniacs: Gender and Modernity in Global Youth Cultures
Susan Dewey and Karen J. Brison, eds.

Transforming Faith: The Story of Al-Huda and Islamic Revivalism among Urban Pakistani Women
Sadaf Ahmad

Women, Islam, and Identity

Public Life in Private Spaces in Uzbekistan

Svetlana Peshkova

Syracuse University Press

First Edition 2014

14 15 16 17 18 19 6 5 4 3 2 1

∞ The paper used in this publication meets the minimum requirements of the American National Standard for Information Sciences—Permanence of Paper for Printed Library Materials, ANSI Z39.48-1992.

For a listing of books published and distributed by Syracuse University Press, visit our website at www.SyracuseUniversityPress.syr.edu.

ISBN: 978-0-8156-3373-0 (cloth) 978-0-8156-5305-9 (e-book)

Library of Congress Cataloging-in-Publication Data

Peshkova, Svetlana.
Women, Islam, and identity : public life in private spaces in Uzbekistan / Svetlana Peshkova. — First edition.
pages cm. — (Gender and globalization)
Includes bibliographical references and index.
ISBN 978-0-8156-3373-0 (cloth : alk. paper) — ISBN 978-0-8156-5305-9 (ebook)
1. Muslim women—Uzbekistan—Social conditions. 2. Women's rights—Uzbekistan. 3. Social change—Religious aspects—Islam. 4. Women—Identity. I. Title.
HQ1735.27.P47 2014
305.48'69709587—dc23 2014029021

Manufactured in the United States of America

Contents

Acknowledgments

Help and assistance from numerous people and financial support from several institutions made this book possible. My deepest gratitude goes to the women, men, and children who opened their homes, hearts, and life histories to me in the Ferghana Valley and Tashkent in Uzbekistan. I apologize if I have failed to represent your lives adequately, but each one of you is at the heart of this book and an important part of my identity and scholarship.

I have benefited greatly from discussions with undergraduate students and colleagues at the University of New Hampshire and Syracuse University, which helped me to learn how to write accessible ethnography, to stay excited about teaching anthropology, and to think about new, interesting projects. The two anonymous reviews from Syracuse University Press as well as feedback and emotional support from my dissertation adviser, Robert A. Rubinstein, and my mentor, Abdullahi A. An-Naim, enhanced my ability to write and rewrite this book. I thank Susan Wadley, Deborah Pellow, Sandra Lane, and Hans Buechler, who taught me by example that human stories, gendered and unique, are worth being taken seriously. Special thanks to Susan Kennedy, Alecia Bassett, and Annie Barva for copyediting the manuscript at different stages. I am also very grateful to Catherine Goodard for her excellent indexing services.

I used my dissertation research during 2002–2003 as the background for the book's narrative; it was made possible by a Claudia DeLys Grant from the Department of Anthropology and a summer research stipend from the European Union Center at the Maxwell School of Citizenship and Public Affairs, Syracuse University. My ethnographic research in the summer of 2011 was sponsored by the International Research and Exchange Board through the Individual Advanced Research Opportunities Program and the University of New Hampshire's Graduate School through the Summer Faculty Fellowship. Fundamental to the conclusions I advance in the manuscript, this research provided new materials and experiences that challenged my assumptions about history, gender, ethnographic research, and myself as an individual.

In the fall of 2011, generous support from the American Council of Learned Societies provided me with invaluable time for analyzing ethnographic materials and writing the bulk of this book. The Center for the Humanities and the College of Liberal Arts at the University of New Hampshire provided funds to finish the manuscript and revise it. There would be no book about women, Islam, and identity in Uzbekistan and their public life in private spaces without the university's ongoing support.

This manuscript would also never have been possible without support from my family and friends. My mother, Valentina Peshkova, taught me that women can become successful professionals against all odds in any place and time, whether the Soviet Union or the United States of America. My father, Alexey Peshkov, taught me that there are always two sides to a story, whether the story about Russia's war in Afghanistan (1979–89) or a story about personal relationships. My son, Alex, was a part of my research in Uzbekistan and this book even before he was born. He taught me how to love and care for others, not only for myself and my ideals. Since he has come into my life, everything I do and write is done so through the eyes of me as his mother. My friends Erin and Andrew Sharp, Lori Lee, and James Tucker helped me to start and finish this book and become a better person and scholar in the process. Other friends—they know who they are and what they have done for me, even if I failed to recognize it at the time and don't identify them specifically here—continue to make my life enjoyable and remind me that it is full of surprises.

Women, Islam, and Identity

Introduction

Personal Notes, Leaving Tashkent, August 2011

I leave the Tashkent airport's passport control behind. Clean shiny tiles. Bright lights. I cannot read the words on the monitors. All I see are reflections of the lights and myself. I feel cold—the air-conditioning and fear. What if this is not over? The plane. I need to get on it. Then I can exhale. A woman comes up to me, "Are you okay?" I cannot talk. Trying not to cry, I nod. She walks away.

Trying to escape the monitors that act as mirrors, and the blinding lights, I walk into a duty-free store. Aimlessly I look around. Liquor and snacks. The salesperson behind the counter is saying something. I cannot hear her, but only my heart rattling inside my throat: lub-dub, lub-dub, lub-dub. *Pressure is growing in my ears. Nauseated I am going deaf. I hang on to reality with a word: the plane, the plane, the plane. I cannot faint now. I need to get on the plane.*

The salesperson comes up to me. I realize that she is the same woman who asked me if I was okay. I read her lips, "Are-you-okay?" Not again. I am leaning on the shelf; the tears start running down my checks, onto my nose, and down my neck. Uncontrollable. I cannot hide them under the oversized sunglasses. She looks confused. I turn my head to the right, away from her. I see toys. My son. I need to focus on my son. He loves "stuffies." I need to get him one. I move toward the toys. She follows. I see a distorted dog with a big head, small body, and huge eyes. Distorted twice through my tears. I point at the dog. "My son," I begin but cannot finish the sentence. My voice breaks. She picks the dog up. I nod. I pay at the register.

"Where is Sochi?" I whisper, trying to ask her where the correct gate is. She knows I am lost. "[Just] a minute," she replies and leaves the store for a moment and comes back in. Her hand pointing to the right, she says, "That way." As I am leaving the store, she adds, "He will like this dog," and tries to smile. I turn toward her and try to force a feeble smile and nod. She is kind.

I turn right and walk through an unbearably long corridor; it's never ending, closing in on me on both sides. I stumble upon a little girl crawling on the floor. Her parents are looking at their tickets. Two little boys in yarmulkes next to them are arguing over a toy. Then, another desk—another checkpoint. "This way to Sochi!" a woman officer yells. "Are you going to Sochi?" I realize this question is for me. No one else is around. I nod. "Come on, hurry up," she adds. I turn my head. A long, bright corridor with lights and mirrors looks back at me. It looks so clean that I feel dirty. The officer looks at my boarding pass and passport, frowns, "Take off glasses." Satisfied, she checks me in. "Go ahead."

More gates, officers, touching, pushing, and rushing. My legs are getting weaker. But I need to hold it together a little longer. I have to get on this plane. It has to take off. I have to get to Sochi. I want to see my son. "Are you going to Sochi? Come on! Get on the bus," someone says.

I am in the bus, surrounded by young men, probably migrant workers. I breathe in their sweat and smoke mixed with the cool evening air. They must be going to Sochi, the home of the 2014 Winter Olympics, to make money. They have no idea what I just went through. Or maybe they go through it every time they go to or leave Russia.

The runway. The officer waves at me. Why me? I inhale and bite my lips. He waves again. I move closer. He looks at my boarding pass and points up the stairs into the plane. Women first, I realize, as I follow another woman. At the entrance to the plane, the flight attendant offers me a seat in the business class. Why? Maybe my large sunglasses. I am the only one wearing them so late in the evening. Maybe I look too lost and too different from others. She leans toward me and says, "Fifty dollars." I take a seat in the business class, the first row. "Unlimited drinks," she adds. "Good," I say while sliding the money into her hand.

I am inside the plane. I brought my body that far. It is about 10:00 p.m. The plane is an hour late. I wrap my arms around myself. Waiting is killing me. I want to see my son! I want out of this country! One by one, the men from the bus pass me by on their way to the economy-class cabin. None of them gets an offer to move into the business class.

I look at the floor, then at the flight attendant, then at the door. Soon, I tell myself. Almost. We are all accounted for. A border guard checks the plane's papers. The door closes. The usual talk by the pilot and the flight attendant. The plane moves. Seems like nothing and no one can stop me now, and . . . we are airborne. I exhale.

The Subjects of This Story

In the Soviet Union's Socialist Republic of Uzbekistan, Tursun-oi was a Communist and the head of a silk factory.[1] During perestroika, she left the party, privatized the factory, and became a successful businesswoman. In the late 1990s in Uzbekistan, newly independent from the Soviet Union, she retired and became a religious teacher and leader. Tursun-oi is one of many individuals in post-Soviet Central Asia who have reoriented their life toward Islam as they understand it. She is among a few who have felt a need to share their understanding of *pravelinij* (correct) Islam, or *Allah yo'lida* (God's way), with others by teaching them how to be, in Russian, *nastoyashiye Musulmane* (truly Muslim) or, in Uzbek, *mosolmonchiliq*. In an interview in 2002, Tursun-oi described the feelings that accompanied this rela-

1. In this book, the characters' names are pseudonyms. In these names, the ending *-hon*, which indicates an individual's sacred descent, is accidental and not meaningful. The ending *-opa* communicates a level of social respect or age difference or both.

tively new vocation: "I teach students at home. I teach them Islam. My students respect me, and they are so happy and so joyful that they can study with me. Before I read *namoz* [ritual prayer], I always say, '*Alhamdulillah*' [Thank God]; I say, 'Thank you, Allah, for my life!'"

Another woman, Jahon, while effecting change in others through the spiritual support she offered them, also felt passionate about her mission of teaching others how to lead a "correct" Islamic life. During one of our meetings in 2011, she reminded me that this "correct" Islam was built on "love [toward] each other" and was "not about difficulties" but "should be easy and beautiful."

In a 2003 interview, Jahon described this "correct Islam" as "the new" and not "the old" way of life:

> Of course, if you want to do it the old way, to live not *po-Islamski* [Islamically or in accordance with Islam, *mosolmonchiliq*], do it! But I want to see you as Muslims, and I have to show you a good road, the right way, God's way. God has given you children, and you should raise them Islamically. . . . You can have money in this life, but you may not have a chance to have another life. The money is for this life. For the next life, you should know Islam and teach your children [about] Islam, give them a chance to live Islamically. If you do this, then your children will be respectful. They will be good people. Only do it with *sobr* [patience]; [then] they will have *sobr* too. You should give them Islam first and then give them money and earthly goods. Do not spend all your money on clothes. Buy knowledge. Buy books [about] Islam [for them] and scientific books. Help them get knowledge. They could use this inheritance later. You could use it, and your kids could use it. The books will stay with you and them forever. The clothes will wear off.

The old and new ways Jahon described did not coincide with a normalized division of Central Asian history into Soviet and post-Soviet eras. The old way did not end with the disintegration of the Soviet Union, nor did the new way begin at that time. These ways are not temporary or spatially bound but represent ongoing and inescapable yet not uniform processes of change in individual lives. For some Central Asians, such as Jahon and Tursun-oi, this change is taking place in terms of their understanding of Islam. It is a moral change indexed by the virtues of love, respect, patience, studiousness, care for the self and others, mutual help, responsibility, and goodness. Both material and spiritual, inseparable and corresponding, this change means reorienting individuals toward a "good" Islamic "road," toward "the right way." This right way is about valuing some material-spiritual needs and corresponding desires over others and about valuing some ways of thinking, feeling, and acting over others.

This ethnography is focused on particular individuals, including Tursun-oi and Jahon, who claim to be "truly" Muslim and to facilitate the process of changing into better humans those people who surround them (for a persuasive case in favor of case studies, see Flueckiger 2006). These individuals' actions, experiences, life histories, and statements about being "truly" Muslim and about "correct" Islam are the threads woven through the narrative. Some of them teach about "correct" Islam. Others embody "correct" Islam by providing pastoral care and officiating at various *meropriyatiya*, social events that include ritual components claimed to be traditional and Islamic. Yet others become healers or educate their family members about Islamic piety. Despite different approaches, the protagonists' self-formation into "truly" Muslim humans and the forms of knowledge they create and promote in the process lead to social change. In order to enhance our analytical understanding of social change in the region, I describe some of these experiences and actions and provide a relational analysis of individual self-formation and concomitant emerging knowledge(s) leading to social change.

Religious knowledge(s), behaviors, and sensibilities created and embodied by the book's characters are not detached from their physical bodies. These individuals need food and shelter and want to be loved and respected and healthy. They struggle to shape their lives in a context of daily worries about their families' economic security and physical well-being and safety. This environment enhances and hampers some of their actions, dreams, and choices. Therefore, although this book tells the stories of particular individuals, they are not the only characters in it. To tell their stories is to tell about others around and with them; the land that they live on; their ability to create solutions to the daily problems; illnesses and frustrations they experience; their memories and future plans. Their spouses, parents, children, and grandchildren as well as other unrelated men and women they meet at work, at the market, and at various administrative offices are parts of their social-historical and natural environment. Each individual's self-formation into a "truly" Muslim human happens while interacting with this environment.

Research

The individuals I write about here live in a fertile Central Asian oasis famous for cotton cultivation, the Ferghana Valley, currently part of three sovereign countries: Uzbekistan, Tajikistan, and Kyrgyzstan. Muslim armies conquered Central Asia, including the valley, in the early eighth century. While integrating existing local practices and beliefs with those brought by the conquest, Sufi sheikhs, spiritual leaders and scholars, facilitated the nomadic and sedentary local peoples' gradual conversion to Islam. For instance, a cult of Muslim saints "replicated" already existing "patronage networks," while the locals came to understand an existing veneration of sacred places in terms of Islam (Khalid 2007, 22). Through the "dual process of localizing Islam and Islamizing local traditions," Central Asian communities eventually came to see "themselves as innately Muslim" (Khalid 2007, 22).

In the nineteenth century, the Russian Empire conquered a large part of Central Asia, which at the time was known as Turkistan, the territory that bordered Siberia to the north, India and Iran to the south, Mongolia to the east, and the Caspian Sea to the west. In the 1920s, the region was incorporated into the Soviet Union. After seventy years of being a part of the Soviet Union with its proclaimed state atheism, in the early 1990s Central Asian republics, including

Uzbekistan, became independent countries, and Islam became an important part of the new countries' national(ist) ideologies.

Uzbekistan's current population is about twenty-nine million, 80 percent of whom self-identify as Muslim. Among them, being Muslim is understood and enacted in a variety of ways. There are "secular" Muslims, the individuals who self-identify as Muslim but either do not believe in God or understand their atheism or secularism in terms of being "good" Muslims, different from "bad" Muslims, who zealously express and share their faith in God (McBrien and Pelkmans 2008, 89). In addition to Muslims, there are Christians, a majority of whom self-identify as Russian Orthodox, as well as some Protestant converts and devotees of Hare Krishna, who are a statistical minority in Uzbekistan. Among them, piety is understood and enacted in different ways as well (see Peyrouse 2007).

In 2001, a research interest in Islam and its role in post-Soviet ideologies and people's daily lives led me to Farg'ona Vodiysi, a province in Uzbekistan's part of the Ferghana Valley.[2] There, in the city Hovliguzar (a pseudonym), during visits in 2001, 2002–2003, and 2011, I spent time interviewing, observing, sharing stories with, and learning about "correct" Islam and how to be a better human from women such as Tursun-oi and Jahon.[3]

When I first met these women, some of them self-identified and were referred to in their communities as *otinchalar*. The word *otincha* (with the plural ending *lar*) is a colloquial version of the term *otin*

2. From here on, I use the name "Ferghana Valley" to refer to Uzbekistan's part of the valley.

3. In 2001, I interviewed close to two hundred individuals, both women and men. During 2002–2003, my research included thirty women. I focused on five of them. I gathered the ethnographic material through interviews, participant observation, and collection of life histories. I interviewed five male religious leaders. From 2003 to 2011, I kept in touch with my contacts in the valley through email and phone calls. In 2011, I interviewed twenty individuals, including four women leaders I focused on and one male leader I had befriended during my previous research.

or *otinby*, which in Uzbek means "teacher." I was told that a younger woman could be referred to as *otincha* and an older one as *otinby* or *otin*. In the summer of 2011, some of the women I am writing about insisted on being referred to as *otinlar* rather than *otinchalar*. According to Tursun-oi, *otin* is the "more respectful" and "official" term, which signals one's education in religious matters above a rudimentary knowledge of prayers and ability to recite the Qur'an.

The word *teacher* neither captures the religious knowledge that these women provide nor describes the role they play in social change in their communities. In this book, reflecting a decade of changing lives and terms, I use the terms *otincha* (pl. *otinchalar*) and *otin* (pl. *otinla*r) interchangeably. Regardless of the terms, these women's social significance exceeds social roles ascribed to them, including teacher or practitioner officiating at ceremonial gatherings. They are local leaders committed to intentionally and purposefully changing themselves and their families and communities into better human beings.

Women such as Tursun-oi and Jahon are leaders who do not head public protests. Not overtly political, they effect incremental changes by connecting social transformation to individual moral change, which begins with learning about a universal ethical paradigm provided by God from the beginning of times and encapsulated in the Qur'an. I refer to this process as learning *how to do the right thing* in order, using Paul Rabinow's phrase, to have a "*life well led*" together as a community (2003, 7, italics added).

These women insist that a long-term, less-obvious change is more sustainable than an overnight radical one; such change is aimed at the cause, an individual self, and not at a symptom, the social. They believe that immoral individuals create social immorality, not the other way around, and that in order to reverse this process the change has to start with the individual. In 2001, one of these women said, "The rest of the world knows very little about . . . our *otinchalar*. You should tell them." In the hope that I can kindle appreciation of small incremental individual changes that lead to larger social changes, this book about individual lives and their social effects is my direct response to her request.

Women as Individuals

Several scholarly works discuss social activism of Muslim women in different sociohistorical contexts, including women leaders and preachers in the Arabian Peninsular, Egypt, Bosnia, China, Iran, Syria, Pakistan, Turkey, Nigeria and Indonesia (e.g., Abbott 1942; Afsaruddin 2002; Ahmad 2006; Bringa 1995; Gillette 2000; Hafez 2011; Hegland 1997; Hoodfar 2001; Horvatich 1994; Kalmbach 2008; Mahmood 2005; Peshkova 2009b; Saktanber 2002; Sule and Starraff 1991; Van Doorn-Harder 2006). Several scholars write about women religious teachers and leaders in Uzbekistan and Central Asia (e.g., Constantine 2007; Fathi 1997; Kamp 2006; Kandiyoti and Azimova 2004; Kramer 2002; McBrien 2009; Rasanayagam 2010; Sultanova 2011). This book builds on some of these works but also differs from them.

Existing studies of Central Asia too often conceptualize individuals as subordinate to the strictures of their families, communities, societies, countries, and religion, focusing on what is shared with others and not on human creativity or on their selves (e.g., Alimova and Azimova 2000; Corcoran-Nantes 2005; DeWeese 1994; Fathi 1997; Nalivkin and Nalivkina 1886; Snesarev 1974; Sultanova 2011; Tabishalieva 2000; Troitskaya 1929; Zhilina and Tomina 1993). I seek to reverse this trend. Rather than writing about and analyzing individual lives along the lines of essential categorical identities, such as "Muslim women" or "Uzbek or Central Asian or post-Soviet women," I focus on these women's uniqueness and demonstrate their differences. Taking a lead from Nigel Rapport (2003, 15), I assemble the data in a way that highlights the details of their lives, decision making, choices, desires, and dreams and that demonstrates that these lives cannot be reduced to "imperative statuses," such as gender, nationality, ethnicity, religion, epoch, and locality. Regardless of whatever categorical identities can be (and in everyday life are) assigned to these people, they are creative individuals. While construing their destinies *despite* and *in relation to* others, they are able to think on their own terms and "pursue [their] own goals independently of the goals of a group or community" (Sokefeld 1999, 418).

Zooming in on and sharing these women's unique stories allow me to make their visions of social change and their attempts to affect this change "filmable."[4] At the same time, I hope the book's characters do not seem like still photographs of idealized stoic and moralizing Muslims but can be seen as complicated and pragmatic human beings, with histories of pride and selfishness, who are capable of both caring for others and treating them unfairly. Some of their statements and actions are contradictory. Parts of their stories are inconsistent. Yet this is exactly what makes these individuals human, each one of a kind impossible to replicate.

By theorizing an individual not as an example of the social but as a fundamental and essential entity that creates the social, the approach I adopt in the book has humanist, scientific, political, and ethical dimensions (as in Rapport 2010, 22). Such focus affirms the irreducibility and value of human life, whether this life is lived in the Ferghana Valley, the United States, Sudan, or New Zealand, in the eleventh, fifteenth, nineteenth, or twenty-first century. This focus also allows for more nuanced generalizations and consequently for a more accurate social analysis.

Although there are plenty of differences among the people I am writing about, myself, and the reader, there are universals beyond imperative statuses that we all share. These universals include our personal uniqueness (Rapport 2010), our capacity to change, our interaction with our environment (physical, social, or virtual), our physical bodies with complex neurological systems, and our *real* selves (Marranci 2006, 2008).

4. This notion comes from Professor Michael Freedman, personal communication to the author, September 2001.

The Personal

In line with my intention to write the book about individuals who create the social, I invite the reader to accompany me on a journey to the valley to do anthropology as an individual experience beyond just the application of a set of ethnographic methods. Ethnographic research includes not only taking notes, surveying, and systematically observing or interviewing others, but also experiencing the personal—physical discomfort, selfish desires, ethical compromises, and longing for recognition and redemption. Glimpses into my—the researcher's—private life and my personal struggle with fear, attachment, pride, and guilt that accompanied this research and writing will help the reader to recognize my—the researcher's—biases and to interrogate the ethics of my research (on the importance of the researcher's reflexivity, see Chiseri-Strater 1996; Chodorow 1999).

Claims to objectivity, often "based less on the nature of the research encounter than on the objectifying rhetoric of reporting norms" (Davies 2008, 8), motivate anthropologists to exclude their emotions and feelings from the data collection, analysis, and writing about the research. As a result, ethnographic writing can hide as much as it reveals. Yet emotions, thoughts, and actions are inseparable (Jackson 2010). As a result, much of the analysis and writing is rooted in the researchers' personal histories, insecurities, and experiences. Personalizing ethnographic research can admittedly be overbearing and detract from the focus and substance of the research itself. But depersonalizing it equally haunts ethnographic accounts, which avoid admitting that they too are the products of human beings who are creative and fallible, capable of memorizing and failing to remember, and who make, reflect, and challenge their normative contexts.

I include myself in this book as a part of the human landscape of this study, present ethnographic research and its findings through storytelling, and integrate academic and personal perspectives on the material (for more on this approach, see Behar 1993; Ellis 1993; McNamara 2009). The Ferghana Valley *within* me—memories and feelings about the people I have met and about their stories—is also a part of ethnographic material. When used together, my personal experiences and the stories about the book's characters' lives "enliven" each other and open up possibilities for the reader to experience and critically evaluate the process of collecting data and the conclusions advanced in the book (Narayan 2007, 138). Finally, for future ethnographers, such a representational approach offers a way of learning about research and its mistakes in order to do better both ethically and theoretically.

Theoretical Points

In terms of representational style and theoretical analysis, I draw particularly on two of Rapport's concepts: (1) life project, "a kind of self-theorizing and self-intensity that affords an individual life a directionality and force," and (2) existential power to be and become (2003, 34, 75). I also adopt Saba Mahmood's theory of "ethical agency" (2005, 35) and Gabriele Marranci's definition of Islam as "a map of discourses" and of culture as "a part of nature" (2008, 149, 92). I take the term *discourse* to refer to the broader "range of discussions that takes place within a society about an issue or set of issues" (Conley and O'Barr 1998, 7) and not as a totalizing force articulated by an impersonal state (Foucault 1980). Marranci's (2006) theory of identity and concept of individual self, discussed later in the book, are two additional important concepts informing the book's analysis and conclusions. In more than one way, this ethnography is a purposeful assemblage of various materials, including others' and my experiences, stories, memories, and theoretical arguments. Through combination and synthesis, not just an application of existing theories, I craft a theory in the following chapters.

My central analytical argument is that *theoretical analysis of the role of religion in social change (in post-Soviet Central Asia) should start with an individual who creates social relations through what I call "relational existential power" and who is not constituted by these relations but informed by them.* This argument was initially seeded by a significant number of works' attempt to explain social change by addressing Islamic revival, renewal, and Islamization in post-Soviet Central Asia (e.g., Babadzhanov 2002; Fathi 1997; Khalid 2007; Roy 2000; Ye'or 2002). Although these analyses certainly contributed to my understanding of social dynamics in the region on the brink of the twenty-first century, in this book I propose a different approach to understanding the role of religion in social change.

Following Marranci, I take contested definitions of "how to be human and consequently who is human" (2009, 145) to form a conceptual kernel of this change. A number of scholars observe that some of these contested definitions in the region are manifested in diverse ways of being Muslim (e.g., Louw 2007; McBrien and Pelkmans 2008; Rasanayagam 2010). I find this diversity arresting; it illustrates that something of significance is happening, enabling these differences. Drawing on Rapport's (2003) alternative anthropology of power, I propose to explain this "something" not in terms of social forces, complex histories, or a post-Soviet "rebirth of Islam," but in terms of *relational existential power*, which individuals exercise in the process of creating the social (on "the rebirth of Islam," see Babadzhanov 2004). This power is animated by a "practice of individuality," understood as "a human perceptual and cognitive norm" and "an act of will," put into effect by individuals *in relation to* each other (Rapport 2003, 29, 48–49).

The argument I advance contains the seven propositions inferred from the ethnographic material. These propositions exemplify a practice of individuality and summarize each chapter's theoretical significance: (1) The process of self-formation, achieved through human interaction with surrounding environment, is necessary for an individual life project to unfold; this process leads to social change. (2) Social relations and history do not determine individuals but affect them in significant ways. (3) Individuals create liberatory and nonliberatory discourses on rights and duties that lead to social change. (4) Individuals develop knowledge about a relationship between human and divine worlds by increasing self-knowledge through a practice of thinking, feeling, and acting, which results in a cognitive opening that leads to individual moral change. (5) While interacting with and in relation to the human and nonhuman environment, individuals are not constituted by but create discourses on religion. (6) Individual existential power to change the self and others is relational; the actions of others do not determine this power but inform it, and personal faith in God does not negate it. (7) Individuals create the society and state by pursuing their life projects intentionally and purposefully.

A Map

This book includes seven chapters. Each chapter begins with a proposition and my personal notes describing the journey to and from the Ferghana Valley. I start in chapter 1 with Tursun-oi's life history, an account about an individual who diligently created and daily experienced social history. This chapter sketches out a theory of individual self-formation incorporating God, history, and society. The second chapter describes changes and continuity in the lives of a male healer, Tahsir, and one of his followers, Nainahon. Their lives exemplify individual creativity and social history's effects on individual lives. In chapter 3, we learn how Jahon's and Nainahon's visions of gender dynamics contest accepted notions of "liberation." These unique visions reflect social dynamics but are not determined by them. Chapter 4 demonstrates the pedagogical importance of didactic storytelling (*masala*), an essential element in educational and ceremonial settings, and points out its role in individual self-formation.[5] Chapter 5 explores a different understanding of "national Islam" as "personal" Islam by focusing on changes in the lives of the book's central characters (from 2003 to 2011) and their connections to social changes occurring in Uzbekistan. Chapter 6 intro-

5. *Masalasi* is usually translated from Uzbek into English as "an issue." I translate it as "didactic storytelling" or "a didactic story." The word *maslahat* can be translated as "telling stories"; it is a process. I use a Russified version of *masalasi*: *masala* (sing.) and *masalas* (pl.).

duces the concept of "relational existential power" and its challenges to existing understandings of "the social" in the Ferghana Valley and beyond. In chapter 7, I tie together individual stories in order to critique the prevailing understanding of the (Uzbek) state and individual ability to effect social change. All of the chapters support my central argument about importance of an individual in creating social relations and change.

Religion, the Uzbek State, and This Book

In post-Soviet countries, religion is married to politics and nationalism. In Uzbekistan, the "ideology of national independence," although centered on Islam, endorses imaginaries of religious pluralism by emphasizing an historical peaceful coexistence of several faiths and provides models for Muslim citizens' moral behavior (Adams 2010, 4, 198; see also Rasanayagam 2010). Through this ideology, the Uzbek state effectively authorizes "politically correct," "traditional" forms of Islam that do not challenge the government and elites' understanding of political stability (Louw 2007; Papas 2005).[6] As a result, the concept of citizenship in Uzbekistan links the religious and the political, whereby a good citizen has to have politically correct sensibilities, knowledge(s), and behaviors (for more on religion and the nation-state, see Asad 1999).

In Uzbekistan, being Muslim and devout in general is also intimately connected to economics and social prestige. An intensity of religious devotion can increase one's social standing or land one in jail. One can also extort a bribe by accusing someone of spreading religious propaganda in the "traditionalized" but secular Uzbek state.[7] Religious devotion is not the only thing an individual benefits

6. "Neighboring Afghanistan is . . . an example of the civil conflict and society and economic devastation wrought by alien forms of Islam," explained Islam Karimov, president of Uzbekistan (quoted in Rasanayagam 2010, 108).

7. As Professor Marianne Kamp told me in personal communication, May 14, 2010.

from or suffers for. She has to be careful about getting too rich, too critical of the government, too famous, too well traveled, too close to the ruling elite, or too talkative to strangers. As I discovered during my last visit to the Ferghana Valley in 2011, one also has to be careful about asking such questions as "What is Islam?" and "How much Islam is enough, or how Muslim can one be in Uzbekistan?" unless one talks to religious leaders and academics approved by the government.

During the first decade of the twenty-first century, Uzbekistan was less accessible to independent researchers than any other post-Soviet Central Asian country. Between 2001 and 2011, I went there four times. Never afraid of people with whom I spent time and learned from, I was always anxious about the Uzbek law enforcement agencies. Their representatives, although claiming to speak on behalf of the government, which claimed to speak on behalf of the people, exercised social control through surveillance, intimidation, threat of imprisonment, and horror stories about torture and death. "Our people have no rights; we have no democracy here," an official at one Bureau of Internal Affairs branch in Uzbekistan told me in 2011. "No one is safe here [in Uzbekistan]; from oligarchs to ordinary people, we are all like ants. They [the state] can crush you like an ant, and no one will notice," said a businessman from the valley the same year. In order not to be crushed like ants, locals have to be creative.

I had to be creative in writing this book. The individuals I focus on are engaged in activities prohibited legally by their government. Although I informed the participants about potential risks and about how I would use information they shared with me, and they still consented to be interviewed, I do not want to provide information that might cause reprisal against them by the representatives of the Uzbek state. At the same time, in order to do justice to the stories shared with me, I want to be precise and detailed. As a result, I have to write a narrative that obscures information about research participants yet still provides a valid ethnographic account. I have resolved this quandary by (1) using pseudonyms for all individuals and the places where they live (but not all the places mentioned in the book); (2) creating composite characters, places, and stories; and (3) writing parts of the book as creative nonfiction (as in, e.g., Narayan 2007).

Although the book's narrative is definitely mediated, it is *not* fictional. Crafted from the ethnographic material, it refers to real, living, and breathing human beings whom I knew and touched; cried, laughed, ate, and lived with; learned from, felt for, lied to, detested, or loved (cf. Haraway 1988). I hope that other storytellers at other times and places will offer necessary correctives to this book's narrative.

Full Disclosure

My desire to tell this story with great care is also politically motivated. I am not a dispassionate observer geographically and emotionally detached from the Ferghana Valley. I grew up in the Soviet Union believing in the values of socialist redistribution, free health care and education, and international solidarity among unique Soviet nations. I was enchanted by possible post-Soviet freedoms and disenchanted by the post-Soviet states' violence, as were some people I met in Uzbekistan. Like them, I continue trying to achieve my goals and pursue my dreams despite economic chaos, changing borders, and others' attempts to control my life. Therefore, no matter what my current geographic location is—the United States or Russia—I cannot, as Daniel Varisco (2005) argues regarding anthropological representation, write Uzbekistan and these people out of my life or write myself out of this story.

I feel compelled to tell this story for three reasons. The first reason is that there is a shortage of political, journalistic, and academic critical discussions of and limited knowledge about the everyday lives of people as *individuals* in Central Asia and the Ferghana Valley. For example, in 2011 US presidential hopeful Herman Cain demonstrated this lack of knowledge by referring to Uzbekistan as "Ubeki-beki-beki-beki-stan-stan" and dismissing the "gaffe" and the country as unimportant (Gharib 2011). In order to get attention, individuals populating post-Soviet Central Asian states have to experience or carry out antigovernment uprisings, ecological damage, and human rights abuses. These actions and the analytical labor that goes into their representation lead to the second reason for telling this story.

Central Asia—the Ferghana Valley in particular—is often described as an epicenter and a primary target of "Islamic" militants, extremists, fundamentalists, and terrorists (e.g., Lahoud and Johns 2005, 139; Charlick-Paley, Williams, and Oliker 2002, 32–33; Peimani 2002, 75). In such accounts, not only the territory and people but also the name "Ferghana Valley" can connote danger and terror, which are no longer regional but global (Masylkanova 2010; Yemelianova 2010). They reach as far as the United States, where in 2011 a young man from Uzbekistan, Ulugbek Kodirov, allegedly devised but failed to carry out a plan to assassinate the president of the United States, Barack Obama (J. Reeves 2012).

Human rights abuses, too, are prominently associated with Uzbekistan in the media and scholarly works (mine included). Although the displacement of the loci of danger and terror from the (Uzbek or Muslim) people to the (Uzbek) state is important, focusing on danger does not help us to understand and appreciate individual lives and social change in the valley and the country. Following other scholars who write against this discourse on danger (e.g., Heathershow and Megoran 2011; M. Reeves 2005), I challenge the reduction of Uzbekistan to danger by focusing on, describing, and analyzing local individuals' roles in creating the social.

The third reason to tell this story is my personal discontent with what I call the "state of the post-Soviet state." Not limited to Uzbekistan, this state is manifested in political and economic corruption, psychological and physical violence, multiple emerging and entrenched forms of social hierarchy, and the absence of a larger ethical paradigm. Therefore, inasmuch as I write this book against the discourse on danger, I also write it against discourses praising post-Soviet freedom and democracy. While writing against these discourses, I am careful not to substitute for them a discourse of fear as the main emotion structuring the lives of local people in Uzbekistan and characterizing the state of this post-Soviet state.

Jeffrey Sluka, Noam Chomsky, and David Price (2002) call on anthropologists to become witnesses and get directly involved in public debates about human rights. While keeping in mind that our witnessing is "an act of interpretation" and that "a hyper-desire to be relevant" may be too selfish, too inconsistent, and too socially constructed (Rabinow 2008, 36), I see this book as a form of action aimed at understanding the state of the post-Soviet state and at changing it.

Public Life in Private Spaces

I spent a majority of my time in the valley observing and participating in public life that takes place in private spaces. This social life created by individuals in people's homes has fascinated many scholars and state agents in different places and different times, including the Uzbek government during the first decade of the twenty-first century. This interest was not new. After imperial Russia conquered parts of Turkistan in 1865, the agents of the imperial security services were charged with finding out if subversive activities were taking place behind the closed doors of individual homes. They defined public life in private spaces as the "meetings and gatherings plotting a great conspiracy[,] [which] are explained customarily in the event of disclosure as constituting . . . clubs and sometimes prayer meetings" (Miklashevsky 1924, 243). Yet, the agents lamented, it was "impossible to establish the existence of anything by witnesses, as not one Moslem will testify against another" (Miklashevsky 1924, 243). In the end, neither imperial Russia nor the Soviet Union later could fully control social life in people's homes. This inability has continued to make the Uzbek government anxious since the Soviet Union's dissolution.

For instance, in the early 2000s representatives of the government and official religious leadership condemned public life in private spaces, including some popular propitiatory rituals officiated by *otinchalar*, as sites of conspicuous consumption and dissemination of "not traditional" forms of Islam (Kandiyoti and Azimova 2004). In

Hovliguzar, some women who officiated at such ceremonies during 2002–2003 came to criticize them in 2011. Yet they continued insisting on the importance of social gatherings and religious education at people's homes; they continued making them happen.

The *mahalla* (neighborhood) committees, one mechanism of the Uzbek government's social control of private life in public spaces in the early 2000s, were expected to report to local National Security Service (Sluzhba Natsionalnoj Bezopasnosti, SNB) offices about social activities in their neighborhoods and about visiting foreigners (see Bogner and Human Rights Watch 2003; Massicard and Trevisani 2003). I was told that representatives of these committees collected from religious teachers unaffiliated with the state signed statements promising not to teach minors. Yet even after signing such statements, the same teachers informally carried on teaching others, including minors, about Islam, some by defining their instruction as "tutorship." Existing criticism and social control of public life in private space, however successful, could never eclipse its vibrancy.

The Last Visit

In order to document changes and continuities in the lives of my friends and acquaintances, I went to the valley again in late June 2011. I thought that independent ethnographic research on Islam in Uzbekistan was challenging but not impossible. The day after my arrival in Uzbekistan's capital, Tashkent, I registered with the Office of Visas and Registration (Ofis Viz i Registratsiji, OVIR), which is affiliated with other law enforcement agencies, such as the Bureau of Internal Affairs and the SNB. To maintain a low profile, I traveled back and forth between Tashkent and the valley.

When initially planning my research in 2011, I decided not to audiorecord interviews. But once I was in the field, my memory could not cope with the amount of information I was receiving. Because ethical protocols and theories often change in response to the real circumstances being described (Horwitz 1993), during the last week of research, with the participants' consent, I audiorecorded interviews. I transcribed these interviews, translated them into English, and then deleted the audio files. At Internet cafés, using a portable modem lent to me by a friend for the duration of the visit, I uploaded interviews into my online mailbox and deleted them on my computer. Some notes I typed directly into Google Docs (which claims to store users' notes securely online). I audiorecorded my personal notes and observations and asked a friend in the United States to audiorecord observations I shared with him on Skype.

Near the end of my 2011 trip, despite my attempts to keep a low profile, officers from the Bureau of Internal Affairs and the SNB detained me and some of the participants of the research, confiscated my computer, voice recorder, and camera and erased the remaining data. During my interrogation, one of the SNB officers told me that I asked the wrong questions about Islam and met in the wrong places with the wrong people, all Muslim in their differing ways. The officer's report about my last visit to the valley became the foundation of an obscure online article penned by Rauf Zuvaidov (2011). In it, Zuvaidov refers to me as an "English Mata Hari with a Russian passport in Ferghana" and depicts my independent research as a subversive activity.

At the end of the summer of 2011, I returned to the United States with fragments of data, including some recovered pictures and the stories and files I had emailed to myself prior to detention. I felt overrun with guilt for overestimating my ability to carry this project through and to protect research participants from law enforcement agencies. Regret is a regular affliction of ethnographic research. If only I knew then what I know now, I would have asked different questions and would not have said some things that I did say, paid closer attention to what was said and what was left unsaid, and spent more time with some people and less with others. I would, should, and could have, but I had to write this book with the material and the feelings available to me.

Language

Although Uzbek is the national language of Uzbekistan, Russian continues to be popular in the country and the region. After the Russian imperial conquest in the late 1880s, knowledge of Russian assured social advancement. For much of the twentieth century, the territory of Central Asia I am writing about was a part of the Soviet Union, where Russian was the primary language of educational instruction, and native languages were secondary to it. After Uzbekistan's independence from the Soviet Union—a process known as the *Mustakilliq*—the importance of Russian diminished but did not disappear. During the first decade of the twenty-first century, two factors ensured its use in the region and sustained its status as the language of the socioeconomic and political elites: (1) Russia's active participation in regional economic, political, and social affairs and (2) local people's ongoing migration to Russia to perform seasonal and permanent work (see Sahadeo 2011).

I conducted research in Russian mainly in the city settings, where the majority of people were still familiar with the language. I was able to use Russian often but not always. Many older women in their seventies, eighties, and nineties did not speak or understand Russian, and ceremonial events I attended were conducted mainly in Uzbek. As a result, even though I studied Uzbek for eight months during 2002—2003, I often asked for translation and clarifications from the people around me or used two interpreters: a teacher of Uzbek and Russian from a local college in the valley and a teacher of English from a local institute.

Throughout this book, the reader will see Uzbek, Arabic, Farsi, and Russian terms. The participants' code-switching from Uzbek to Russian intermingled with Arabic in a single sentence, situationally or topically, was not unusual (on such code-switching, see D. Abramson 2000). The adoption of Russian, Arabic, and Farsi terms in their daily spoken variant of the Uzbek language shows the complex social history of Central Asia, located on the Silk route, conquered by Muslim armies, and colonized by Russia. As a result of regional linguistic diffusion and borrowing, a number of Farsi and Arabic words, although slightly transformed, have become parts of Uzbek; they were Uzbekified, if you will. Therefore, their spelling may look odd to an Arabic or Farsi speaker. Some research participants, in particular those with an interest in religious education, used Arabic religious vocabulary in ceremonial contexts and in reference to their daily activities; they tried to imitate what they thought of as "proper" or "correct" Arabic pronunciation. I have consolidated all these terms in a glossary at the end of the book. In the glossary, I do not label the language from which each of the words was borrowed but do so in the text when appropriate to show how the research participants used these words and to demonstrate the code-switching. The glossary should help the reader navigate local linguistic diversity, which in itself not only demonstrates regional sociohistorical complexity but also exemplifies individual creativity.

Re-membering

History is multidirectional: it moves forward and backward, in parallels and in circles. History, by definition, is never still. For me, even in a dream, in a seeming suspension, there is no stillness. I always had difficulty creating a coherent linear historical narrative and even found an explanation of this narrative disability in my lack of patience. I attributed this difficulty to the social instability I experienced while "growing up Soviet" during perestroika in the context of the Soviet Union's disintegration. History happened then at a maddening speed; "the enemies of the Soviet people" became the heroes, while the Soviet heroes became villains. I had no choice but to rush to re-member history, substituting some parts of it with others, discovering and reshaping hidden parts, and hiding some obvious ones.[8]

8. By the term *remember*, I mean the individual memories existing in one's memory, but not immediately present in one's thoughts. The term *re-member* refers to a process of bringing individual memories into one's thoughts at the moment,

Although it was no easy task, this re-membering helped me to survive the transition from *Homo sovieticus* to *Homo postsovieticus* (see Gudkov, Dubin, and Zorkaya 2008). As a result, my history turned out to be formed of mismatching puzzle pieces. I re-member the Ferghana Valley in a similar way, as an incoherent, mismatched, and nonlinear story about other people's stories that I learned between 2001 and 2011, some of which took me by surprise.

simultaneously rethinking and reevaluating these memories by taking them apart, focusing on some of them and rearranging others. This is not always a conscious process.

I

Self-Formation and Social Change

Proposition: The process of self-formation, achieved through human interaction with the surrounding environment, is necessary for an individual life project to unfold; this process leads to social change.

A Friend in Hovliguzar, Skype Chat, March 2011

SVETLANA: Tell me honestly, should I come to Uzbekistan or not this summer?

NAVRUZ: Honestly, I want you to come. But I do not understand what your research is all about.

SVETLANA: I want to meet with my friends and acquaintances and learn about the changes in their lives.

NAVRUZ: I am asking because the government is very strict with *otinchalar*, with women who gather and read the Qur'an. You see, the [state's] control has increased. You need to be very careful with your topic.

SVETLANA: Of course.

NAVRUZ: You know we are always happy to see you.

SVETLANA: Old friends in Tashkent and Hovliguzar. I have nothing to hide.

NAVRUZ: Okay. I understand. Why are you asking whether you should come or not?

SVETLANA: Because of your [country's] paranoid *esenbeshnikov* [SNB agents].

NAVRUZ: Yes, we have some of those. But there is nothing to be afraid of. Only, when you come [here], do not go to their [the *otinchalar*'s] gatherings, do not be a part of the group, okay?
SVETLANA: Okay.

Leaving the United States, June 2011

At 8:00 p.m., we are finally airborne. This is our second flight. The first one took us from Boston to New York City's largest airport, JFK, named after the thirty-fifth president of the United States, John Fitzgerald Kennedy; this flight is taking us from JFK to Moscow. Our journey started at five in the morning on a bus to Boston's Logan Airport.

It is hard to describe JFK; it has everything but silence: a never-ending stream of human bodies and languages, including English, Russian, Italian, and Japanese, or was it Chinese, smiles and screaming, arguments and kisses, pushing and courtesy, hi tech and low tech, low security and password-protected Internet access points, Hermes and Bulgary next to McDonald's, loud TV and loudspeakers announcing that someone is late for a flight or has left a cell phone or an iPad at the security checkpoint or that someone is waiting for someone else at point X, Y, or Z. Some are sleeping, others eating, cleaning, patrolling, or talking on the phone, engaged in idle conversations about where one is coming from or going to. A child is crying, and feet are moving to and fro—high heels, sneakers, flip-flops, boots, canvas and leather shoes. And all of this is set in almost unreal bright florescent light and the barely detectable sound of air-conditioning.

We board the flight to Russia at about 7:00 p.m. and soon take off. My son falls asleep first. Then, while watching a movie, I doze off.

At about 3:30 a.m.—around 11:30 a.m. Moscow time—the plane comes alive. Tripping over and stepping on several sets of headphones, blankets, pillows, newspapers, and plastic bags on the floor, I go for a plane stroll. Sleepy faces, smelly toilets with water and urine splashed on the floor, fancy personal TVs with detachable control panels, which are also gaming joysticks, still playing movies—all enveloped in the smell of sweat mixed with home, occasionally covered by strong perfume and a light but detectable cigarette smell. Someone always breaks the nonsmoking rule on flights to and from Russia. The kids in the front row are still watching the ominous and omnipresent Tom and Jerry, *without much being lost in translation because there is almost no dialogue and plenty of violence that crosses sociocultural boundaries and territorial borders. I feel tired, barely able to keep my eyes open. The food carts are approaching again. . . .*

Then Moscow's Sheremet'evo airport; then another plane to Krasnodar, a city in southern Russia. After a seven-hour car ride with my father, we are finally in the Caucasus. I am leaving for Uzbekistan the next day. I am leaving my son with his grandparents in the Caucasus. This is difficult. I have never left him for more than three days. Agonizing over why one has to lose something to gain something, after a long conversation with my mother I fall asleep.

From Russia to Uzbekistan, June 2011

I am on my way into my past, flying from the Caucasus to Uzbekistan on a plane that belongs to Uzbekistan Airways. I feel anxious. Biting my nails. I am not sure why. Maybe it is my memories of survaillance, which led me to leave Uzbekistan abruptly in 2003. Maybe it is the insecurity of seeing others face to face after eight years. The pictures I share with those in Uzbekistan and my Skype conversations with them are always one step removed from the reality of wrinkles edging the corners of my eyes, pigmentation spots on my cheeks, gray hair, and dark circles around my eyes. I am getting older, and I am acutely aware of it. People remember me young and beautiful, and I would like to stay that way. Alas, gravity and time weigh heavily on our physical bodies; even if I still feel twenty-nine and sometimes behave as if I am eighteen, really I am almost forty.

I try to find something else to focus on. I look out of the window at the clouds. I focus on them. The clouds are like light purple cotton candy reflecting the light of the dawning sun. Some are almost transparent like ice and round like scoops of ice cream; others like boiling milk are rare and solid. In them, I see impenetrable and elusive mountains and canyons. In fifteen minutes, the purple turns into light blue and pink. Then some of the clouds turn bright white, while others have the color of condensed air, the color of nothing. The mystery and the mastery crafted with care and meaning. Shot through with gray, which slowly turns brown, the cotton candy turns to smoke. Moving on its own, this smoke morphs into smog. The smog becomes the ocean. The tide is rising into an eruption of wet snow, here and there melted under the bright sunlight into an abyss.

The earth is slowly floating below this storming ocean and its perfect waves. The closer the earth gets, the faster it seems to move. We fly over a land marked by freckles and a spider web of wrinkles. The shadows of the clouds are like age spots on the face of the earth. I realize that even while focusing on the land and clouds, I cannot escape the feeling of my aging body.

Fifteen more minutes. We are flying toward the sun, flying west toward "the east," toward the unreachable horizon, which is always ahead, both breaking from and merging with the sky. The clouds turn light purple again, with bright shiny lines embedded in them. In a few minutes, the light pink overwhelms the purple. The sun and the horizon are approaching. The fire and the water. The light and the smoke. Both colorful and colorless. I close my eyes. I can still see the sun. It bubbles and circles and turns into shapeless forms. I wait a minute and open my eyes. The clouds are below. The sky is ahead. Always. Everywhere. Its beauty arouses fear. Enriching and consuming, it is ready to carry or drop the plane. This sky is intricate matter and eternal ether, which was before and will be after this flight, this plane, and this trip. I close my eyes again. . . .

*We land late. I am in a long line of young, slim, and tired men and several women. They are mainly migrants—*gastarbeiteri *in Russian—seasonal workers returning to Uzbekistan from Russia. They travel to the Caucasus in search of a better, more stable income. There, some of them work at local markets or restaurants, while* *others do construction work. Three couples in their fifties and sixties are also in line. Maybe they visited the North Caucasus region of Russia, famous for its mineral water believed to have healing powers, or maybe they were just visiting relatives.*

Passport control takes about an hour, then customs. Another thirty minutes and I am outside. Tashkent's heat at 110°F feels overwhelming after the air-conditioned airport. I mix with the crowds of people waiting for arriving planes or getting ready for departure.

Meeting Tursun-oi

I met Tursun-oi in the summer of 2001 while researching women's reproductive health in the Ferghana Valley for an American nongovernmental organization. In the process, I became interested in the potential role of local religious leaders in changing local reproductive practices. At that time, I was not familiar with existing research about *otinchalar* (e.g., Fathi 1997; Gorshunova 2001; Sultanova 2000; Troitskaya 1929). I first heard about these women from a representative of a nongovernmental organization promoting women's legal rights. She highlighted the importance of religious leaders, noting that without their support any long-term sustainable changes in local reproductive practices were impossible. This comment led me to seek out religious leaders, both male and female.

Imams, male prayer leaders, were easy to find. They held a public office and represented official religious leadership sponsored and controlled by the Uzbek government. I met several of them. Women religious leaders had no public office; their leadership was unofficial. Meeting them required finding a gatekeeper, an individual with local knowledge of their informal networks. A local woman, a middle-aged interpreter working with me, Ismahon, became this gatekeeper. To my question about female religious leaders, she responded by first clarifying that two different words were used locally to refer to these women: one was *otincha*, a colloquial term, and the other *otinby*, a scientific term. She continued, "I have a highly respected teacher, Tursun-oi. She is an *otincha*." Then she suggested introducing me to her teacher. Later that week I met Tursun-oi.

Tursun-oi, in her early sixties, became my teacher too. My research interest, her position as a teacher and competence in religious knowledge, and our age difference of more than thirty years defined our relationship as one of teacher and student. Tursun-oi taught me about the meaning of being "truly" Muslim; she used to say that I was a Muslim who had not yet realized it. She wisely advised me about whom I should or should not meet and introduced me to other women who, like her, taught Islam but who also, unlike her, officiated at religious ceremonies. She taught me about motherhood, womanhood, the value of hard work, and the importance of family.

Gradually, while learning how to take her faith in God seriously, I came to better understand her mission, her life project. By listening to her stories, I learned more about Ferghana Valley and Central Asian history as well as about myself. She and her stories became an irreducible part of my own life project and personal history. But when I was first introduced to Tursun-oi, the first *otincha* I met in the valley, I could not imagine the role she would play in my life.

Life History

During 2002–2003, at least once a week for nine months Tursun-oi told me stories about her childhood, teenage years, and adulthood, about her children, marriage, parents, and students. These moments were the most intimate I shared with her. While telling these stories, Tursun-oi was no longer just a teacher, an older woman, or a religious leader. Her laughter and tears, her frustration and passion, mediated our differences on a very profound emotional level. I felt how she felt, maybe occasionally, imperfectly, and not fully, but certainly approximately—close enough to be able to empathize with her, to learn how to see the world through her eyes and how to see through her rhetoric to *inside* her stories.

Tursun-oi's stories were always aimed at a particular audience—in this case, the wider international audience to whom I promised to communicate those stories (Davies 2008, 199). In the stories, she fashioned herself as a character taking on different personas, including a loving child, wife, and mother, a public leader, and a pious individual. My critical evaluation of her stories was not different from my critical evaluation of other sources of ethnographic data I collected. Besides being ideological and an example of social construction, Tursun-oi's life history was incredibly enlightening for my understanding of public life in private spaces in the valley and the dynamic nature of individual life projects.

A Daughter and a Wife

Tursun-oi was born in September 1940 in one of the valley's *qishloq*s (villages). Her parents worked at a *kolkhoz* (collective farm) during the day. Her father was a local musician; in the evening and on weekends he was invited to various social gatherings. Her mother was a dressmaker. After working long hours at the farm, she made clothes on individual order. Tursun-oi and her daughters inherited her mother's legacy; they all were dressmakers.

In 1921, four years after the Great October Revolution in Russia, "the Russians" killed Tursun-oi's maternal grandfather. She was not sure why "he was [considered] an enemy of the [Soviet] people." In the family, they never talked about him.

Tursun-oi's mother was forty days old when her father was killed. Shortly after that, Tursun-oi's maternal grandmother remarried. Her new husband had children from a previous marriage; one of them became Tursun-oi's mother's husband when she turned fourteen. Tursun-oi remembered her mother saying that she was at first "afraid of marriage." Five years later, at age nineteen, she gave birth to Tursun-oi.

History happened. Tursun-oi was born. Some local people died naturally, and others were killed in the Great Patriotic War of 1941–45 (World War II). Tursun-oi was almost a year old when her father "was taken to the war." She was too little to remember that day. "He left home and never came back." Her mother never remarried.

She, Tursun-oi's paternal grandparents, and Tursun-oi waited for his return from the war. Tursun-oi's grandmother died and then her grandfather, but her mother and she continued waiting. They were still hopeful.

Life happened. The war ended in 1945. The Soviet Union was victorious but traumatized and in ruins. Some soldiers came back. Local people mourned and buried their dead, got married, and had children. Those who survived the war eventually rebuilt their lives and villages, towns, and cities; some created new families. Although their hope was fading away, Tursun-oi and her mother still waited for her father's return from the war.

Tursun-oi's mother became the family's breadwinner, a role customarily assigned to a man. A farmer and a dressmaker, she now became a businesswoman, making microloans to her relatives and neighbors. Her hard work eventually paid off. She became very successful, providing her daughter with financial security.

Several years went by. Tursun-oi finished school. She was "a very attractive" young woman, tall "with beautiful long hair," and had many suitors. Her mother decided that Tursun-oi should get married. "Let me marry you off, then I will look after your children, and you will be able to continue studying." Tursun-oi did not want to get married; focusing on a family would distract her from "getting more education." But her mother was a "strong-willed" and "wise" woman. Her decision was set in stone. Shortly after that conversation Tursun-oi married a cousin who lived in the city of Hovliguzar in the valley. After the wedding, Tursun-oi and her mother moved from their village to the city to live with Tursun-oi's husband's family.

"Because I led a correct life," Tursun-oi thought, "Allah was pleased [with] me and gave me a good husband." Her husband received "the highest [level of] education" and worked for the propaganda department in the city government and later for the "Gorkom and Obkom [Communist Party committees on the city and provincial levels]." "He loved and respected" Tursun-oi and repeatedly told her, "Do not get sick, please. I am afraid that you will get sick, and I will not be able to live without you a single hour."

The city life was "faster" and provided more opportunities. Tursun-oi decided to become a dressmaker, like her mother. Even though her husband had a good job, he had to raise his brothers and sisters from his father's first and second marriages because his parents had passed away. Tursun-oi wanted to have a job to help him.

By that time, Tursun-oi had four of her own children, each born two years apart: three girls and one boy. Several weeks after she had her last child, she went to a local "Dom Kulturi [Culture Center]," an important social and educational institution in the Soviet Union, to take courses on professional dressmaking. "This is how we lived. I was taking care of children and studying at the same time. My mother helped me with the children and house chores."

After finishing her studies at the Culture Center, Tursun-oi received an official certificate that enabled her to search for a job. She found one at a local *atel'e*, a dress shop specializing in tailored clothing. Russian dressmakers working at this dress shop helped Tursun-oi improve her dressmaking and designing skills. She remembered one of them, Olya, particularly fondly. She taught Tursun-oi how to pattern and cut out coats and dresses.

Tursun-oi was ambitious. She dreamed about a career as a designer. While working at the dress shop, she became a part-time student at a local institute. She could have gone to a more "prestigious" institute elsewhere, but her family was her priority; she stayed "close to home." While her mother took care of her children, cooked, and cleaned the house, Tursun-oi learned world history as well as how to teach Uzbek and speak Farsi. She also improved her Russian. "This is how it was then."

Meanwhile, Tursun-oi continued searching for her father. She contacted various veterans' organizations and eventually received a reply that he was "missing in action." Tursun-oi did not understand this response or accept it. "What does it mean, 'missing'? He was not a bird. He could not disappear without a trace." His physical body could not be in a nonplace outside of time. The hope that he could be found only extended the pain she felt in not knowing where and how to find him.

The Director

Tursun-oi's hard work, just like her mother's, eventfully paid off. First, she became a manager of "the weavers' unit" at a local silk factory. Later she became the head of the trade union at the same factory. Finally, in 1970 she was appointed the director of this factory. Tursun-oi felt both intimidated and proud. Such positions of authority often "came with bribes, but Allah wanted [her to have this position]."

As the new director, Tursun-oi hired the people whose work ethic she knew well and in this way formed "a strong team of women." The head manager, engineers, and the heads of the units were women. Although most of the workers at the silk factories were women, "some [unnamed] people" met with resistance Tursun-oi's directorship and her choice of women in leadership positions. Despite this initial opposition, her hard work was recognized and rewarded. She received different awards, including "the Socialist Competition Badge and a medal for distinguished labor."

Positions of authority in the Soviet Union came almost exclusively with Communist Party membership. Tursun-oi joined the party and became "a dedicated member" (unlike those who only paid their party membership dues). She left the party only after Uzbekistan's independence from the Soviet Union in 1991—*Mustakilliq*—when the party was disbanded. But this happened later.

Tursun-oi worked hard to make her factory exemplary in the Uzbek Soviet Socialist Republic. The factory became famous in the silk industry not only in the Uzbek Republic but also in other Soviet republics. Some of this success she attributed to the work ethic she inherited from her mother; much of it was certainly a result of the workers' and her "good team members'" daily cooperative work.

In the Soviet Union, the privatization process started at the brink of the 1990s. Tursun-oi was still the director of the factory. She supported this process by privatizing the factory and becoming its sole owner. The workers were let go. In what was by then the independent and sovereign country of Uzbekistan, Tursun-oi eventually "found new people and created a new good team of Russians and other different nationalities." Her new team, just like her old team, "worked very well together, as if [they] . . . were close relatives, like a family." They all helped to assure the relative financial success of Tursun-oi's private silk business.

In the late 1990s, Tursun-oi retired. The factory was transformed into small dress shops managed by her daughters. Meanwhile, she pursued another and in some ways more important and fulfilling vocation. She became a teacher of Islam. "I teach students at home. I teach them Islam. My students respect me, and they are so happy and so joyful that they can study with me. Before I read *namoz*, I always say, '*Alhamdulillah*.' I say, 'Thank you, Allah, for my life!'"

The Teacher

Tursun-oi "always respected Allah" and "always wanted to learn more about our tradition, Islam." Ironically, her secular education fostered her desire for a deeper knowledge of Islam. But in the Soviet Union, as a member of the Communist Party she was "afraid" because "the Soviet laws did not allow it." Despite these laws and her hesitation, Tursun-oi managed to pray occasionally at work and at home and to read some books about Islam, which were not easy to find. She even sneaked books about Islam into professional meetings and read them when nobody was watching her.

In 1992, her husband got a job at a local publishing house. He fully supported Tursun-oi's efforts to learn how to be a better Muslim. One day he brought home a new book about Islam. After reading it, Tursun-oi decided to seek religious guidance.

Her friend Gulchihra told Tursun-oi that Hovliguzar's Culture Center was offering a two-year program of Qur'anic Arabic (*al-fusha*). Tursun-oi's knowledge of Farsi and the Arabic alphabet, which she had gained during her secular education, was a great asset. She finished a two-year program in less than a year at the top of her group.

After the program, Tursun-oi's desire to know more about Islam amplified. She found a local *otincha*, who taught about Islam at her home. Dissatisfied with this *otincha*'s knowledge of Arabic, Tursun-oi went four times a week to a nearby city to get religious instruction from another *otincha*.

The more Tursun-oi learned about Islam, the stronger she felt a need to give her knowledge back to her community. "What else could I do with it? Take it to the grave? No." She decided to become a teacher, an *otincha*.

In every *mahalla* (neighborhood), there was at least one *otincha* who had memorized parts of the Qur'an and recited them at various ceremonies. Some of these women taught Islam and occasionally performed healing rituals. They also officiated at life-cycle ceremonies and led women's propitiatory ceremonies dedicated to popular female saints, mediators between humans and God, such as Bibi Seshambe (the Lady Tuesday) and Bibi Mushkil Kusho (the Lady Solver of Difficulties) (see chapter 2 for a description of these ceremonies).

Tursun-oi did not want to recite the Qur'an at ceremonies as some *otinchalar* did. She thought that many of them turned religious knowledge into a profitable business; for their recitations, they received a gratuity, which could take the form of money, food, fabrics, or other goods, from the families who invited them. Tursun-oi would have felt "ashamed to receive money for Qur'anic recitation." Instead she focused on self-education and later on teaching Islam to others at her home.

One day a woman named Hafizahon came asking Tursun-oi for religious guidance; she became Tursun-oi's first student. Then one by one other women came to her seeking knowledge about Islam. They had learned about Tursun-oi by word of mouth; someone told them, and they told others. The group grew like a snowball rolling downhill. Her oldest student was in her seventies, her youngest fifteen.

Tursun-oi also occasionally instructed local children. She did not publicize this fact and did not like talking about it because teaching minors was officially "prohibited." She even signed a document promising not to provide religious instruction to children, "but. . . ."

"One by one," new students came to learn from Tursun-oi. At first, she felt she "*had to* teach them Arabic and recitation of the Qur'an." But later she realized that "they also have to know shariat [the normative principles of Islam or Islamic law] and *hadislar* [hadith, the stories about and the sayings of the Prophet Muhammad and his Companions] if they want to live *po-Islamski*, in accordance with Islam. . . . They have to know so that they can go out and teach others."

Tursun-oi told her students that learning about Islam and changing one's life accordingly cannot happen overnight. According to her, this change starts with religious knowledge and happens in increments: "one step at a time" and one individual at a time. It takes time to understand the difference between "right" and "wrong." Hence, it is important to proceed "slowly."

In order to teach others how to be truly Muslim, Tursun-oi had to live as a good Muslim and always be "one step ahead" of her students, to know more than they did. She read books about Islam, one after another, summarized them, wrote down summaries of them, and then shared these summaries with her students. By increasing her knowledge, she increased theirs. Then her students would "go and tell others" and thus spread her knowledge.

In 2002, Tursun-oi was busy studying and teaching others four days a week. She had more than forty students. In the spring of that year, she felt increasingly tired. Doctors told her that she had high blood pressure and had to rest more. She took a short break from teaching, but in response to her students' persistent requests and a daily dose of high blood pressure medication Tursun-oi was teaching again in no time.

The students respected Tursun-oi and preferred her as a teacher to anyone else because she "decipher[ed] everything for them, every word." She taught them recitation skills and how to apply Islamic knowledge to such issues as modest dress, behavior around one's family members, children's upbringing, holidays, marriage, divorce, work ethic, and doubt in oneself or in God. The students told Tursun-oi, "We cannot call anyone else our *ustoz* [teacher]." Some of them "love[d]" her recitation skills. Others valued her ever-growing religious knowledge. Many enjoyed her teaching methods, including explanation and insistence on memorization and on making Islamic knowledge relevant to daily life.

Tursun-oi read many books. One of her favorites, *Hadith va Hayot* (The sayings and life of the Prophet Muhammad and his Companions), was written by Mohammad Sodiq Mohammad Yusuf, who after Uzbekistan's independence from the Soviet Union became the country's first mufti (religious leader entitled to provide legal rulings)—a spiritual leader for some Muslims and a political figure for others. Tursun-oi thought he was a very good writer and "a sheikh who suffered for his [religious or political] views." She heard some people saying that he was accused of helping an opposition movement in Tajikistan during that country's civil war (1992–97). The Uzbek state supported the other side, so he was arrested. Tursun-oi also heard that after his release he and his family moved to Saudi Arabia. There he opened a publishing house, wrote several books about Islam, and translated other scholars' writing from Arabic into Uzbek. He eventually led "an official delegation [of religious leaders]" from Saudi Arabia to Uzbekistan. Although Tursun-oi felt "ashamed" of her government, which "did not allow him to work here [in Uzbekistan], imprisoned him," and later "he became such an important man there [in Saudi Arabia]," she focused on his writing and spiritual leadership, not on his political views and activism.

Another book Tursun-oi enjoyed was *Mystical Dimensions of Islam*, by Annemarie Schimmel, translated from English to Russian in 1999. This book's stories—including the stories about famous spiritual leaders such as Rabia al-Basri (d. 801), "a woman known for her love of God," history of Sufism, and mystical poetry—greatly impressed Tursun-oi.[1] She shared summaries of the chapters with her students and friends.

1. Rabia al-Basri is considered to be a Muslim saint, an ascetic, born in Basra, Iraq, in the eighth century CE.

Tursun-oi believed that her ability to acquire knowledge was given by Allah and felt she had to share this knowledge with others. The Qur'an was central to her self-education and teaching. To master recitation of the Qur'an and to understand it as well as humans are able to do so were the goals that Tursun-oi set for herself and her students. She taught them proper pronunciation, corrected their mistakes, and emphasized the importance of understanding the recited passages.

Sacred Dream and Politics

One day Tursun-oi had a dream that established a special connection between her and Sheikh Baha al-Din Naqshband, born in the fourteenth century in the city of Bukhara. After receiving a confirmation of her "special connection" to the sheikh from Ruhshonoz, a local seer, Tursun-oi counted herself among the sheikh's disciples. The seer said that as a result of Tursun-oi's studiousness and moral commitment "to promote good and prevent evil," the sheikh chose her to receive his *barakat.* This indescribable supernatural substance conferring the ability to grant blessings to others can be inherited from parents or received from a spiritual teacher; it can materialize as health and wealth or personal happiness.

Because *barakat* makes things happen, it is powerful and marks those who possess it as special, unlike everyone else. Although all religious leaders in the valley "behaved as if" they had *barakat*, only some of them, such as Tursun-oi, "really" possessed it. She received *barakat* from the long dead sheikh in a dream and maintained it through her pious lifestyle, which included not only performing ritual prayers consistently and attaining a religious education, but also cultivating respectful relationships among the family members and dressing modestly in long dresses and large scarves.

Tursun-oi condemned in the strongest terms those *otinchalar* and mullahs (male religious leaders) whom she called "Wahhabisti" (sing. Wahhabist), defined as those who are inauthentic to the region's

Muslims.[2] They are "misguided" in their knowledge of Islam, and they see an emulation of the Qur'an to be the only correct way of being Muslim and "do not consider the *hadislar*" to be authoritative. Yet even though the Qur'an is central to Islam, "Islam is not [reduced to] the Qur'an." These Wahhabisti are also "political"; they call on young adults to resist the existing regime through protests and violence. Tursun-oi could not identify any one individual whom she considered to be a Wahhabist. She named no names, but she knew that "they are here, in the Ferghana Valley"; they were one of the reasons why "the president passed a law that prohibited teaching the Qur'an or Islam at home." Tursun-oi thought that in order to prevent the spread of "wrong Wahhabist knowledge" the government should institute exams for all existing religious teachers, including *otinchalar.* These exams would help to ascertain the level of their education and the kind of knowledge they promoted.

Unlike that of the Wahhabisti, Tursun-oi's teaching was "not political." She emphasized good Islamic living depending heavily on religious education and ritual prayer and not on political activism, and she warned her students that they should be careful of what they learn from others and repeat because talking about Islam as a political ideology has consequences, including imprisonment. Although teaching Islam at home was prohibited, "retired people" did not leave Tursun-oi alone. That is why she continued teaching even though she had "no permit to teach." She had only "a certificate for two years of [religious] education from the Culture Center."

One day Tursun-oi asked her husband if she should go "to the Bojxona [Customs Office] and apply for a permit [to teach at home]."

2. Adeeb Khalid suggests that the terms *Wahhabist* and *Wahhabi* originated locally in Central Asia, "in sectarian polemics among unofficial ulama even before the demise of the Soviet Union, [and] . . . [came] into discriminative use throughout the former Soviet space to denote any and all expressions of non-traditional Islam" (2003, 591). Johan Rasanayagam notes, "The label 'Wahhabi' can become a tool in local disputes to characterize parties as inauthentic or alien and therefore suspect" (2010, 239); as such, at times it is used in reference to non-Muslims as well.

Her husband replied, "Go, go, look for trouble," and advised against it. Tursun-oi also worried that if she were to register her home school, then she would "have to charge money for teaching." This would be "wrong and un-Islamic." She could not "take money for Islamic knowledge." As a result, she did not register her school. And because no one would give her "a permit to teach without charging money for classes," she continued teaching "without it."

At the time, Hovliguzar had a small number of state-regulated educational centers providing elementary Islamic education; none of them offered religious instruction to children. From time to time, Tursun-oi's friends sent their children to her to learn about Islam. Turning them away, Tursun-oi thought, "was not right." By now, her community, friends, family, and students expected her to share Islamic knowledge. She had their respect and trust and did not want "to let them down." Fully aware that "it is not permitted to teach children," she continued teaching to the best of her abilities because she felt she *had* to do it: "If you learn about Islam from childhood, you will live Islamically [all your life]."

Not only her community's respect but mainly her faith in God led her to interpret the existing prohibition of homeschooling Islam in a way that made it permissible, though unwise, for her to continue teaching. She believed that individual desires, including desiring knowledge, were not independent, but "God given." Therefore, a desire for religious instruction was beyond her or anyone else's control, the government's included.

Tursun-oi also believed that the quality of her existing knowledge about Islam allowed her to teacher Islam to others. Her knowledge was "not against the state" and not about "wrong beliefs." Hers was "correct" moral knowledge promoting respect, modesty, love, care of the self and others, and generosity. Therefore, she thought she was "helping the government" by providing some local Muslims with "correct" knowledge to counteract the "wrong" one, spread by other "ignorant or Wahhabist teachers." Even a local imam, an officially appointed administrator of Hovliguzar's central mosque, told Tursun-oi that he admired her teaching. He occasionally asked for her advice and sent students to study with her. Finally, Tursun-oi was not secretive about her teaching and was "sure that the *hokimyat* [city hall] knows what I am doing; they get information every day."

Her Parents

Two very important events happened in Tursun-oi's life at the turn of the twenty-first century. First, in 2000 her eighty-year-old mother died of diabetes. They "loved each other very much"; her mother was "the most beautiful woman, kind to others, honest . . . industrious and skillful," who "earned" God's love. Every little memory of her mother brought tears to Tursun-oi's eyes. She had to learn one of "the most important and difficult lessons" in her life—how to live without her mother.

Second, in 2001 Tursun-oi found out what happened to her father. One night she had a dream about him. In a couple of days, Ruhshonoz, a local seer, while acting as a medium, was able to set up a conversation between Tursun-oi and her father's spirit. Asking her to "stop looking" for him, to "wipe [her] tears" and "feel proud" of him, he told Tursun-oi that he was "a *shahid* [martyr] tortured and killed by the German soldiers" and "was now with God."

Now Tursun-oi's life history was somewhat complete. She knew where she came from, who her parents were, and what happened to them. Her mother was a "hard-working" and "wise" woman who remained loyal to her husband all her life but did not live to learn his story. Tursun-oi's father was a *shahid* who had died defending his family and his motherland. He was "a hero," not just "a soldier missing in action." Although she could not locate his physical body, she knew that his spirit was with God and that "he would be resurrected on the Day of Judgment."

The Students

Tursun-oi took her teaching of Islam seriously. She instructed her students to continue practicing recitation even if she was not available.

By means of *masala*, she taught not only her students but also community members who invited her to attend different *meropriyatiya* (social events with ritual components). Her didactic stories became famous. Relatives, friends, and acquaintances invited her over frequently: "Tursun-oi, please, come over, tell us *masala*s" (see chapter 4 for more on *masala*s).

Teaching others was a great responsibility. Tursun-oi thought she was a good teacher, an example for her students to follow. She always prepared before teaching by reviewing her notes and praying, asking God for guidance. She expected the same from the students and reminded them again and again, "If people invite you to such occasions as *iftor* [an evening meal] during *ro'za* [ritual fasting during the month of Ramazan], open your books and notebooks. Read them before you go so that you know what to tell people when they invite you. Prepare yourselves."

Jahon, in her early forties, and Zulfiahon, in her late forties, were Tursun-oi's favorite students. They asked her "many questions" and challenged other students. They had formerly studied with "one old woman" who "knew very little about Islam and Arabic" yet was teaching them "how to recite parts of the Qur'an." As a result, their pronunciation was "terrible." As Tursun-oi's students, they had to unlearn the "old woman's lessons" and "follow *tajweed* [standards and rules of recitation]." They gradually became her "best students."

Jahon recited the Qur'an "*cheroiliq* [beautifully]," but she was "hard-headed." Tursun-oi valued Jahon's dedication, passion, knowledge, piety, and "hard work to spread knowledge about Islam" among others, and she thought Jahon officiated at religious ceremonies in the correct way. She also liked Jahon's didactic stories. In short, Jahon reminded Tursun-oi of herself. But "Jahon recited the Qur'an like a man, too loud." Tursun-oi believed that "women's *awra* [modesty]" required a more subdued volume of recitation. Not without struggle, Jahon gave in.

Another of her students, Ismahon, recited the Qur'an in a very coarse manner but was very diligent. Dilbaropa, in her late fifties, a university professor, was a very good student and a hard-working woman with serious health problems. Karimahon, in her seventies, was the oldest student and had difficulty learning Arabic. She told Tursun-oi that she was losing her memory; nonetheless, she tried to do her best and used to get very sad and cry when she made a mistake. Tursun-oi felt sorry for her.

Zulfiahon was another student with a coarse voice, but Tursun-oi liked her because Zulfiahon was very knowledgeable, her brother was "a famous *qore* [reciter of the Qur'an]." She was also "a very traditional Uzbek woman" and "a respected *otincha*," active in her community. Zumrad, in her late fifties, like Karimahon, found learning Arabic to be challenging, but she was persistent.

Gulya, in her early fifties, was "a very simple Uzbek woman" and "a very good person." She was an *otincha* like Jahon and Zulfiahon and often presided over religious ceremonies in her *mahalla*. Hafiza was a young woman in her early thirties, a very good student, too shy to recite in front of other people. Shahida, in her early fifties, was unhappily married to "a drunk." Tursun-oi thought that Shahida was very kind and wanted to learn as much as she could about Islam. Her family life, though, occasionally prevented her from attending classes.

There were other students—in 2002, about forty of them. Some of Tursun-oi's students had started learning about Islam early on in their lives from their parents and other *otinchalar*. Others had started late. Some of them were *otinchalar*, and others were not. Some of them wanted to become *otinchalar*, and others simply wanted "to read" for themselves and to teach their families "correct" Islam. Her students had different needs and talents. Some were quick to learn Arabic pronunciations and correct rules of recitation. Others were better at explanation, while yet others had beautiful voices and recited the Qur'an with passion. Tursun-oi's students were of different ages and had different lives. Many of them were former professionals: an engineer, a university professor, a schoolteacher, a nurse, and traders. Others were housewives. But they all desired to learn more about how to be "truly" Muslim and so shared an *ustoz*, Tursun-oi, and attended her "home school."

Tursun-oi believed that there is no age restriction for learning about Islam. The majority of Tursun-oi's students were women older than forty, but not all of them. "Muslims should not wait until retirement" to become "truly" Muslim. Knowledge about Islam enables everyone—children, adults, and elders—to lead "better lives," she emphasized. One of Tursun-oi's students was about twenty-five years old. She was very busy at home with her children and in-laws and attended classes rarely. Another one was fifteen. She was finishing high school and preparing to take entrance exams to Imam al-Bukhari Tashkent Islamic Institute, named after the ninth-century theologian and scholar who authored the most famous collection of the stories about and sayings of the Prophet Muhammad and his Companions (*hadislar*). Other students whom she taught occasionally were ten to fourteen years old.

Tursun-oi's adult students had important roles to play in their communities' ceremonial life. Whether they were *otinchalar* in their neighborhoods or not, she encouraged them to volunteer to recite the Qur'an at the social gatherings, particularly in those cases when the attending *otinchalar* did not have the same level of knowledge the students had. In order to lead others, one did not have to be a particular age but only to have "*deen* [faith] and *illim* [knowledge]." Therefore, if there was no one to recite the Qur'an, her students should recite "the Word of God" even if they were the youngest at a ceremony.

The act of recitation counted as a *savob* (meritorious act) for the reciter, but "only if the Qur'anic verses were pronounced properly." The proper recitation also assured that the "*nur* [sacred light]" emanating from the Qur'an's sacred words, oral and written, filled the space where the women gathered and turned it into a sacred place. In such a qualitative different place, where the *nur* linked physical space and the divine world, individual women could make requests to God without religious leaders, practitioners, or saints' mediation; "in Islam, you can ask God anywhere at any time, especially during the prayer."

Historically, women in the valley did not attend mosques, and Tursun-oi believed that they had no need for it. As Muslims, they could communicate their requests to God without an imam's help. If they wanted to be a part of the "Muslim *umma* [community]," women needed to pray as a group. Where they did it was not important. They could do it at "*mazar*s [sacred graveyards]," numerous and popular in the valley, or at their homes while congregating with other women during ceremonial gatherings officiated by *otinchalar*. Because the majestic and miraculous quality of "the sacred word" transforms any place the Qur'an is recited into a sacred space, suitable for offering praises and communicating wishes to God, Tursun-oi could not understand "why some women fight this [the customary prohibition against women attending mosques or being imams]." According to her, these women were simply "ungrateful." They did not understand that "God *releases* us from *masjid* [mosque]; we do not need to do it as men do. Why should we do it?"

During our last meeting in 2003, Tursun-oi said that she wanted to visit the village where her mother was born to have an *ehson*, a ceremonial gathering to express individual gratitude to God and to make special requests in her memory, "*Hoda Holasya* ['If God wills' in Uzbek], *Insha'Allah* ['If God wills' in Arabic]."[3] During our first meeting when I returned to the valley in the summer of 2011, Tursun-oi told me that she wanted to be buried next to her mother. She remembered that before her mother passed away, she said, "I need air." Tursun-oi and her granddaughter lifted Tursun-oi's mother's head and laid it against Tursun-oi's chest. "Here [pointing to her chest], her last breath was on my heart."

Self and Identity

In order to become a better daughter, wife, director, teacher, and leader, Tursun-oi worked on her self persistently and purposefully.

3. By hosting such a ceremony, a household (not just its individual members) gains religious merit and blessing. *Ehson* also means "a good deed," "a moral act"; in the form of a good deed without feasting, it can also earn religious merit.

Social context and history informed but did not determine her desire and ability to self-form and to change others. Tursun-oi's choices and decisions, just as much as choices and decisions made by others, including her mother and superiors, created social effects. These effects in turn affected the outcomes of her ability to author her life. But without individual ability to self-form, to become and change or to stay the same, there would be no social effects.

My analysis of Tursun-oi's and other individuals' life histories and the social effects of their desire to become "truly" Muslim is informed by Gabriele Marranci's (2006) theory of identity. According to Marranci, individual identities are not by-products of social history and context. Learning about human and nonhuman surroundings through emotions, which are not subjective feelings but physical (bodily) responses to external stimuli, is central to the formation of human identity. "Although social interaction surely raises emotions," emotions have ecological rather than social ontology (2006, 51).

External stimuli in the environment cause emotional responses manifested as increased heart rate, sweat, and elevated blood pressure. We become conscious of emotions as feelings, such as fear or love. These emotions articulated as feelings become a part of our memory of emotions, which helps us to develop an individual "self."

Building on the work of Antonio Damasio (2000), Marranci (2006) accepts that consciousness and the self are not monolithic but divided into the core and extended consciousness, which correspond to the core and autobiographical selves. The core consciousness is a by-product of brain activities retaining information about how external stimuli affect an organism's internal state at a particular time in a particular space; the core consciousness gives us "the feeling of knowing" (Damasio 2000, 172, quoted in Marranci 2006, 45). The core self, then, is "continuously generated and time related . . . [as] we encounter an unending number of objects in our environment" (Marranci 2006, 45).

The autobiographical self—how we know ourselves historically—is intimately connected to memory; it allows us to reactivate selected autobiographical memories and the information retained in the core self. Without these autobiographical memories, we would not be able develop and realize our own historical and temporal continuity. Therefore, the self, "a product of complex neurological systems," is not an abstract analytical concept but really exists; without the self there would be no "reflecting subject" or "self-consciousness" (Marranci 2006, 45).

The understanding of self as real and different from identity is fundamental to Marranci's (2006) theory of identity. Identity is not a style an individual selects or a fluid or fixed state. Rather, it is "a delicately shaped machinery of our imagination," a process allowing "human beings *to make sense* of their autobiographical self [*sic*] and to express it through symbols, which communicate at an inner level feelings that are in other ways directly incommunicable" (Marranci 2006, 48, 51, italics in the original; see also Marranci 2008, 59). Symbols are storage units "filled with references to stimuli capable of provoking emotions which induce certain selected feelings," which, in turn, directly influence our minds and allow us to communicate what and how we feel deep inside (Marranci 2006, 48). Therefore, individual identity *can but does not have to change* as a result of social interactions. We are who we feel we are and not what others think about us because individual feelings (perceived and articulated emotions), not social relations, determine identity.

In light of this understanding of identity, changes in Tursun-oi's identity and in the identities of other individuals I am writing about cannot be fully explained in terms of Soviet and post-Soviet history and concomitant social dynamics in Uzbekistan. Both history and social context informed but did not determine their desires to lead a "truly" Muslim life and concomitant choices and actions. This desire was *their own*; it had an ecological and, according to them, transcendental—not social—ontology.

If we accept that the self is what I call "in-bodied"—located in a physical body—and, as Saba Mahmood argues, understood "in terms of the virtues and codes" of a particular ethical regime (2005, 32), then both a physical body and an individual's understanding of a particular relationship between human and divine worlds are necessary for self-formation and its social effects: the former is where one's desires reside and where choices and actions are formed, but the latter informs how the process of individual self-formation is understood and enacted. Therefore, a more nuanced understanding of the role of religion in social change in Uzbekistan requires a closer inquiry into and social analysis of "the architecture of the self" (Mahmood 2005, 166) and individual understandings of a particular relationship between human and divine worlds.

Self-Formation: From Capacity to Ability

In the process of collecting Tursun-oi's life history during 2002–2003 and analyzing these stories in the subsequent years, I came to appreciate a process of self-formation—of human individuation—essential to her understanding of what it means to be "truly" Muslim. This process underscored Tursun-oi's stories about herself and others and is similar to the process described in Marranci's (2006) theory of identity. The most critical element in this process, not elaborated in Marranci's theory, was Tursun-oi's faith in God, which informed her understanding of a particular relationship between human and divine worlds.

From our very first meeting, I struggled to incorporate Tursun-oi's faith in God into an anthropological analysis. To her, God was real, but not to me. God was a part of the (nonhuman) environment she interacted with that helped her to develop a sense of her autobiographical and core selves and therefore populated her memories of herself and her daily activities and future plans. Reflecting my prior theological training and the anthropological approach of not judging before learning about a phenomenon, I respected her faith. Yet because God was not real, physically or conceptually, to me, and there were not any *real* (physical) connections between Tursun-oi and God that I could observe and collect evidence about, which in turn would help me to evaluate these links, I could not include God in a relational analysis. In order to engage deeper with the architecture of Tursun-oi's self and understand better her self-formation as a "truly" Muslim human, I turned to Morton Axel Pedersen's (2012) concept of a self-relational individual. This turn required that I shift my analytical focus from Tursun-oi's social relations with others (how her reorientation toward God affected others or how others affected her) to her relations *with* and *within* her self.

Following Pedersen, I tried to see Tursun-oi as a self-relational individual, "the potentiality of relations" (2012, 60). Although I cannot explain why she thought of God as real and whether she had a definite intuition that God created all her choices and guided her life, she established relations with God (or, according to her, God established relations with her) on an intrasubjective level. As a part of what I call her "internal" environment, God became a part of her sense of self. Since identity is a process by which she made sense of her autobiographic self as a Muslim and expressed it through symbols, such as her stories, dress, rituals, and religious paraphernalia, her faith in God became a part of her surrounding (external) environment. These symbols, in turn, affected her self-formation, helping her to cultivate a particular Muslim self.

In this environment, Tursun-oi's actions to become and feelings of becoming "truly" Muslim—more Muslim than before—exemplified "relational transformation" within her self (Pedersen 2012, 63). This process did not substitute external relations with internal ones but shifted her focus from her relations with others to her relations with and within her self and with God. In the process, she learned that the latter relations were asymmetrical and hierarchical and required voluntary submission of human to divine world, and so she acted on this knowledge through her comportment toward her self and others; this was essential for living in a human community.

Before Tursun-oi shared with others her knowledge about how to correctly submit to God—before she refocused on external relations—she spent time learning about, in-bodying, and embodying God's ethical paradigm, which provided guidelines for individual self-formation through voluntary submission. She studied this paradigm by herself, with teachers, and through books, prayed regularly, and performed the hajj, the annual pilgrimage to Mecca during the twelfth month of the Islamic calendar. Both corporal and spiritual, inseparable and corresponding, this change within her self helped to reorient her life toward God, whereby relations between her self and God became stronger—intrasubjectively, within her. Her sacred dream and her communication with her father, among other things, validated her belief in God's control over her life. Getting a better understanding of God's justice—God's promise of rewards and punishments—strengthened relations between her self and God and increased her understanding and appreciation of the human potentiality for submission residing within her and within every other self. Her experiences of and feelings about self-relatedness, including her relations with God, were examples of and proofs that other individuals could rekindle or establish the same (or some) kind of relations intrasubjectively and then intersubjectively, with others.

When Tursun-oi was ready to share her understanding of becoming and being "truly" Muslim, while at the same time continuously cultivating her relations with God, she engaged others by reminding her audiences that they too had a capacity for ethical self-formation. They too could become better Muslims by learning how to do the right thing, to *develop* an ability to make correct choices and acquire correct actions. This understanding of human individuation was a direct result of the strengthening relations between her self and God as well as of her increasing knowledge, comprehension, and appreciation of God's ethical paradigm, encapsulated in the Qur'an and *hadislar*, whereby the former articulates the paradigm, and the latter offers its human understanding and embodiment as exemplified by the words and actions of the Prophet Muhammad and his Companions. This paradigm explained that God, the creator, gave humans free will to make choice and a capacity to learn how to differentiate between right and wrong, pointed out a particular (asymmetrical) relationship between human and divine worlds, provided guidelines for how to become "truly" Muslim, and offered examples of right and wrong choices and actions.

Tursun-oi's experiences as a Soviet leader and the knowledge she gained by studying at the Soviet schools and institutes and by reading books about Islam informed her view that those individuals who have a higher level of religious knowledge must explicate this ethical paradigm of the divine origin to other seekers of such knowledge. Once made intelligible, this knowledge would help one to develop better and closer relations with God and one's self, while evaluating and changing or finessing one's understanding of a particular relationship between human and divine worlds and the existing correspondence between one's beliefs, feelings, and actions. Hence, Tursun-oi initially looked for a teacher to guide her and later became a teacher for others.

From her increased knowledge of Islam and her personal experiences, Tursun-oi came to understand that the process of learning this universal ethical paradigm is a moral action rewarded by God because such knowledge, when applied to any given situation in daily life, guides and enhances individual ability to discriminate between moral and immoral actions and helps to make right choices. In the process, one can and inevitably will make a wrong choice, a mistake, which is a part of the learning process. As long as one continues trying to make right choices and perform moral actions, one will be able to learn from mistakes and make better choices the next time around. What matters in this process is individual "self-propulsion or movement," a force that springs from within an individual self (Rapport 2003, 33–34).

In Tursun-oi's understanding, this self-propulsion is a God-given capacity to develop, to be, and to become. This driving force has a transcendental not social ontology; created by God, it is *always already there*. Increased individual knowledge of Islam helps to actualize this self-propulsion: to act on it and to move toward God and then toward others because being "truly" Muslim is always participatory, intra- and intersubjective. Despite the prohibition of homeschooling and Tursun-oi's slowly failing health, this force propelled her desire and ability to continue teaching. Despite others and her self, she kept on moving toward being what she had to become—a better, more Muslim human.

Tursun-oi knew that developing individual ability to creatively apply knowledge about God's ethical paradigm in changing situations—what I call a *mastery of knowing and doing the right thing*—takes time. According to her, this process is slow but not impossible and, in a way, is inevitable because humans were created by God to be good and to have a *life well led* together with others.

Self-Formation as Social Transformation

In Tursun-oi's view, sustainable individual and then social changes come through an evolution, not a revolution. Women teachers and leaders like her have an important role to play in this process. "Our people are *avom khalq* [uneducated people]; [they] are mistaken in their practices. *Otinchalar* have to correct them. . . . We have to educate each other and the *avom khalq* slowly," she said in an interview in 2002. Once *otinchalar* have achieved a level of moral transformation, they will be able to "slowly" lead local Muslims (women, children, and men) away from certain practices that Tursun-oi defined as "un-Islamic" or "foreign" or both.

A leader does not just lead the followers away from something but also leads them toward something else. *Otinchalar*, according to Tursun-oi, should guide the *avom khalq* toward an Islamic lifestyle, toward a correct understanding, in her terms, of how to feel and act Muslim. She often disagreed with other *otinchalar* on how to be "truly" Muslim—for example, whether one can use mediators between human and divine worlds or whether one can venerate and cook at sacred places.[4] But she shared with them a desire to change her people through a moral evolution.

This evolution does not come easily; it is a never-ending persistent work on the self, on developing and exercising an ability to make

4. Tursun-oi's story about having a conversation with her father's spirit demonstrates that she was not consistent in her view of the use of mediators between human and divine worlds.

correct choices and actions. And as long as one is willing to continue trying, the change is in the making. In 2002, when I asked Tursun-oi, "How does one know that one is truly Muslim?" she responded, "You live like a true Muslim." It took me years to understand the meaning of this seemingly simplistic answer: to be "truly" Muslim means *being* Muslim, submitting voluntary to God's guidance by following the universal ethical paradigm, on an everyday basis. In Tursun-oi's view, being Muslim, knowing and doing the right thing, daily, is the process, not the goal. In this process, no human can attain perfection inasmuch as no human can have a personal relationship with God; a creature cannot know personally its unfathomable Creator, who can be known only through the *ayat*s (signs) found everywhere, including God's ethical paradigm encapsulated in the Qur'an, nature, humans, their actions, dreams, and feelings. According to Tursun-oi, being "truly" Muslim is also deliberate: an individual can make choices, learn from her mistakes, make choices again, and hope that the outcomes of these choices will result in God's justice and mercy.

Similar to Tursun-oi, other characters in this book desired to change their selves and their social context. After reorienting their lives toward Islam, the process that included establishing and cultivating their intrasubjective relations with God, they did not abandon the social context but instead plunged into it, understanding its potential to be reformed. Guided by a vision of society as a new space, neither completely innocent nor apocalyptic, yet purified and altered, a space that offers its own possibilities but imposes its own constraints, they seized an opportunity to change the terms of these constraints. This change was a long-term process that began with self-formation—a change within, intrasubjectively. Then, without abandoning their work on their selves, they tried to modify others purposefully and persistently, even while others modified but did not determine these characters' stories, visions, life projects, or desires for change.

2

Doing Our Part

The Social and the Individual

Proposition: Social relations and history do not determine individuals but affect them in significant ways.

Hovliguzar, Uzbekistan, August 2011

Ro'za *started this year on August 1. People who fast have an early breakfast, usually between 3:00 and 4:00 in the morning. They eat the evening meal,* iftor, *at about 7:30 in the evening. The month of fasting, Ramazan, ends with a huge celebration, Bayram Haid, also known as Eid al-Fitr. This year's Haid falls on August 31 or 30 (depending on the time zone).*

I wake up early. Today is August 11. I have to go to a downtown café, where I can use free Wi-Fi to Skype with my son, send some documents to my email box, and have a meeting with a friend who worked as an interpreter for me in 2003. She has a great command of Russian and Uzbek and helped me translate some of the interviews conducted in Uzbek into Russian before I could translate them into English. She also taught me about "Uzbek traditions" through her stories about her family and children.

I am staying with Rashida, my Uzbek language instructor during my 2002–2003 visits, who over time has become a good friend. She lives with her elderly father. Her husband is dead, and her daughter, whose room I now occupy, is married and now lives in another town. I sleep on the floor on a cotton blanket since Rashida does not have an extra bed.

On the way downstairs, I peek into her room. She is still asleep. Although Rashida and her father self-identify as Muslim, they do not fast. This is not unusual among the Central Asian Soviet educated elites, which she, as a professor at a university, is. So she has no reason to wake up early. I walk through the courtyard and look outside the gates at the street, a mixture of colors and architectural designs arranged along a road framed by tall sycamore trees, which create shade, much needed during hot summers, when outside temperatures can reach as high as 122°F. It is not yet that hot, but it soon will be. . . .

After I have a cup of Turkish coffee, I make my way to the Wi-Fi café through a local park. I have an eerie feeling that something is wrong. I've managed to stay in Uzbekistan for five weeks. A wedding here, a birthday party there, a trip to Tashkent and back to Hovliguzar, and then to the next town—I am always on the move. Nonetheless, today, I have a premonition that something is about to happen. Whatever the reason is, in my daily life I am always alert, hoping for the best, but preparing for the worst. While listening to an audiorecording of my last interview with Tursun-oi through the headphones, I stop to fix my sandals and look back. A young man is following me. He turns into another alley. . . .

I enter the café and order a glass of Coca-Cola. Two men, about my age, come in and take the table next to mine. They too order Coca-Cola. There is something odd about them. If they were friends, I would expect them to be having a more animated conversation. Or maybe I'm imposing my understanding of friendship onto them. They certainly are not rushing to put in the rest of their order. "This is not happening," I tell myself. "This is my imagination." I turn to my email and Skype. . . .

As I am finishing Skyping with my son, my friend arrives, looking exactly as I remember her. We exchange greetings and hugs and order ice cream. She shows me pictures of her children. Pointing to her youngest child, a son, she notes that her husband and mother-in-law were very pleased that finally she has given birth to a boy. This is not the first time I hear a story about a male child's value and a woman's responsibility to give birth to a son; if she fails, it is her fault, her deficiency. But this is no longer the case with my friend. She says she is happy. She says her life is now full and complete. I show pictures of my son and talk about my life. Although, according to local customs, I might have completed my duty as a woman since I have a son, my family is incomplete. I am single again. "Such is life," I state, trying to be assertive while probably sounding unsure.

In about thirty minutes, we decide to leave. She insists on paying the bill. The two men are still there. While putting my computer, pictures, and telephone into my bag, I glance at them. Their Coca-Cola is gone and they look like they are waiting for someone. I think I have nothing to worry about. We leave the air-conditioned café and step into Hovliguzar's fast-approaching midday heat.

My friend says that she is driving her brother's car and offers to drop me off to see Jahon and Tursun-oi one last time. "I am not [Michael] Schumacher [a seven-time Formula One World Champion], but I can drive," she jokes, and we take off. In a side mirror, I see a white car driving behind us at a distance, making the same turns we do. Am I imagining it? This is crazy! Am I being followed? Including the driver, there are three men in it. I cannot see their faces. I should have paid more attention to how the two men in the café were dressed.

We arrive at Jahon's mahalla [neighborhood]. *The children are playing on the dirt road outside Jahon's house. I look back, and I see the same white car. It does not turn onto Jahon's street and continues driving. We park on the side of the road and get out of the car. In a moment, a young man appears on the street walking toward us; he is neither one of the two men from the café. I am relieved but still mention this to my friend. She smiles and says that I am paranoid. "Why would there be surveillance? We did not do anything wrong," she says.*

Jahon comes out of the courtyard on the street. We hug by slightly touching each other's forearms, a greeting gesture that often demonstrates social proximity between women and their feelings toward each other, and exchange lengthy customary greetings. My friend apologizes to Jahon and me that she has to leave, but promising to stay in touch. We exchange hugs and lengthy good-byes, and she drives off.

While entering Jahon's compound, I tell her that I am leaving for Tashkent early tomorrow morning and won't be coming back to the valley. It is time for me to go back home, to leave Uzbekistan. So this is our last visit together. I also tell her, "I have a feeling that I am being followed." She does not respond. I wonder if she has heard me. She continues with the round of questions about my health and about my son and relatives, if anything has changed since our last visit about two weeks ago. I reply that we all are doing well and ask in return about hers, but, frankly, I pay little attention to her responses. My thoughts are back in 2003, reactivating memories of surveillance and fear.

After the round of pleasantries with Jahon's youngest daughter, I wash my hands in the courtyard. She then leads me into the guest room used for social events. This room has the only window with a street view. The rest of them have windows facing the courtyard. The house structure's focus on the family's internal social life is not unusual in the valley; it facilitates public life in private spaces.

I glance through the window on the street. I think I see the same young man. But at this moment Jahon's friend Zulfiahon comes into the room, smiles, greets me, and says that it has been too long and that I must come and visit her house today. This distracts me from the unsettling feeling of fear growing slowly inside me.

Jahon's daughter serves tea and snacks. These are for me since Jahon and Zulfiahon are fasting. I am hot and anxious, and drinking hot tea on a hot day doesn't help dealing with perspiration. Jahon's house has no air-conditioning. The draft coming from the street cools off the air only slightly. I ask Jahon if I can change my damp clothes. "Go ahead," she says and draws the curtains. I put on a fresh dark-green, loose, and soft dress. Jahon and Zulfiahon approve of my choice of dress, its length and color. Although they say nothing, I know that they did not like very much the short skirt and sleeveless T-shirt I was wearing when I arrived. This dress is also more suitable for visiting Tursun-oi, whose husband recently passed away.

Clothes matter. They refer to something other than themselves and communicate information; others read (into) an individual's sartorial practices. In Hovliguzar, clothes are symbols of moral or immoral character, good taste, family economic status, and good or bad citizenship. My friends in Tashkent advised me not to dress too conservatively to avoid any unwanted attention and not to wear a scarf while in the valley because a long-sleeved conservative dress that covers your calves and a scarf can be read now as a sign of over-zealous piety. According to my Tashkent friends' understanding of the state's contemporary interpretation of sartorial practices, there is a link between individual dress code and political ideology. A person dressed conservatively might be suspected of being too pious, pious to the extreme, an "extremist"—a step away from being a "Wahhabist."

Clothes. Suddenly it occurs to me that in early July, when her husband was still alive, I gave Tursun-oi a present, a black Badgley Mischka scarf. Women in mourning usually wear black scarves. I knew that. How could I have given her a black scarf, a bad omen? He died a couple of days after my last visit with her. What was I thinking? I brought a black scarf then. Am I now bringing surveillance by the SNB agents with me? What am I thinking? I should not go. But I cannot leave Hovliguzar without saying good-bye to Tursun-oi and without expressing my condolences. I have to tell her that I did not mean it, did not mean any of it, the scarf and the agents. I need to exonerate myself before being condemned. This is selfish; I know but cannot help myself.

A young man passes by Jahon's window. Is it the same man or my fear materializing as an apparition? It feels like déjà vu—the spring of 2003 all over again. I just changed my clothes. An idiot! What am I doing? How will the SNB agents interpret this change of dress? This is a bad omen too. This was a stupid decision. Clothes matter a great deal to me, particularly here, in Hovliguzar, and even more so today. Should I redress?

My thoughts, they are a multitude. I need to stop thinking. Whatever happens, I do not want to think about it now. But fear is powerful; it invades your self and makes you question your actions and intentions. It makes you investigate and interrogate your true feelings. As a result, you feel guilty, even if you have nothing to feel guilty about.

I did nothing wrong, and I did everything wrong. Don't I harbor antiauthoritarian feelings? I do. I DO think that fear of the popular uprising sustains the Uzbek state's vicious techniques of social control and that freedoms of speech, expression, association, and religion are VERY limited in this country. I AM biased against this state. I am guilty! And then the tape recorder and computer! Did I not read on the customs form that I have to declare all electronic devices? I am not stupid and know what this means, but . . .

Refocusing on Jahon, I realize that I missed some of what she was telling me but catch her half-sentence talking about Zulfiahon's sons, who are, just like Jahon's husband, working in Russia. "Many of our men do," adds Zulfiahon. I nod and talk about Central Asian migrants in Russia, then my son, life, teaching, and future plans. They respond, but I get what they say in fragments. Distracted by memories and still trying to resist the fear, a part of me is not participating in this conversation. Madness. My cheeks burn, then I feel a hot flash, followed by a cold sweat on the soles of my feet and the palms of my hands. My body, driven by my mind, is now out of whack.

Zulfiahon has to prepare the evening meal, iftor, *for her husband. She leaves. Jahon's daughter offers to take a picture of me and Jahon together and says that she will befriend me on Odnoklassniki .com (Classmates.com), a Russian social network website similar to Facebook. Before we leave for Tursun-oi's, I tell Jahon again that I think the SNB agents are following me. She looks undisturbed and tells me not to worry. "They always follow foreigners."*

When we leave the house, I see the same young man squatting at the intersection of Jahon's dirt street and the main asphalted road in the neighborhood. He notices us, stands up, and starts moving along the road in the same direction we do. Jahon asks local men fixing her neighbor's gates if that young man is local. "No," one of them replies. Now the smile leaves her face.

In order to know whether I am being followed or not, Jahon suggests taking a shortcut, a back street too narrow for cars to drive through. As we approach the end of this street, a white car meets us on the other side, with three young men inside. Now we know.

In front of Tursun-oi's house, Jahon tells me again not to worry and promises to pray for me, and, if questioned, to tell the SNB agents that I did nothing wrong. This is precisely what I am trying to avoid. I do not want the SNB officers to question my friends and contacts. But it is too late for Jahon and Tursun-oi.

I know I am doing nothing criminal, and, as Jahon says, the officers always follow foreigners. But they do not use three agents at the same time.

The Valley and Beyond, 2002

I arrived in Uzbekistan to conduct my dissertation fieldwork in July 2002. At that time, the US war in Afghanistan, which had begun on October 21, 2001, was, according to President George W. Bush, successfully over. The president said, "Our Nation . . . rid the world of thousands of terrorists, destroyed Afghanistan's terrorist training camps, saved a people from starvation, and freed a country from brutal oppression" (Bush 2002). If only I had known then what I know now about the length and human costs of this war.

Back in July 2002 in the Ferghana Valley, this "victory" became an important topic of conversation. Some local businessmen, such as my friend Mahmud, envisioned the prospects of participating in the reconstruction of Afghanistan as a lucrative opportunity. He said, "The Afghans will need water, building materials, and manual labor. We can provide all these." Others saw this victory as the sign of impending disaster. According to them, the war was far from over, and the worst—with local people differing on what "the worst" meant—was yet to come. "They [the Americans] should have learned from the Russians [Soviets]," a seventy-year-old Hovliguzar's mullah told me that year.

American troops stationed at a military base in the valley were another topic of conversation among my acquaintances. The American soldiers symbolized a different future, which some locals imagined as prosperous, technologically advanced, militarily powerful, and politically (relatively) stable. As the walking and breathing artifacts of Amerka (a bastardized form of "America")—a name featured so prominently in the giggles of the kids tailing the soldiers—the soldiers occasionally appeared at Hovliguzar's central bazaar. In some private discussions, these soldiers, like the Voice of America, were symbols of freedom; in other discussions, they were signs of American imperialism. In general, they were a topic of conversation rather than a threat or an object of desire.

The Nord Ost siege became another topic of conversation. In late October 2002, I woke up to unfolding news, aired on a satellite television channel, about a hostage crisis at a Moscow theater. The Russian Broadcasting Corporation's channel 1 was reporting that a "death squad" of Chechen *shahid*s had taken more than eight hundred hostages. In the Russian anchor's report, the term *shahid* meant something very negative and different from what it stood for in the spiritual message from Tursun-oi's dead father. The commentators used the term *shahid* (Russified plural *shahidi* for men and *shahidki* for women) interchangeably with another word, *terrorist*, which they coupled with *Islam*: these "Islamic terrorists," *shahidi*—some of them veiled women, *shahidki*—demanded peace in Chechnya.

The resolution of this hostage crisis was tragic. Estimates indicated that more than a hundred hostages died in the Nord Ost siege, but, as things turned out, they were killed by inhaling gas used by the Russian Special Forces (Spetsnaz) sent to rescue them, not by the "Islamic terrorists." But these events happened fast, and the ensuing narrative, known as the official history, emphasized that the hostages died as a result of the theater's seizure by the "Islamic terrorists" and not as a result of the liberating assault by the Spetsnaz. Those who remember this story differently continue to assign responsibility to Russia and not to "Islamic terrorists" (see Dunlop 2006; "Nord-Ost Ten Years On" 2012).

In the United States and other countries, as I learned by email, the media were critical of this liberating assault. Such criticism mattered little to Russia since, despite the deaths, this operation enhanced Russia's image as an uncompromising force in the evolving global "war on terror." The Uzbek government, like Russia, insisted that "Islamic terrorists" should and will be destroyed no matter the costs. In the days following the event, I heard some women discussing it at religious gatherings. Many condemned terrorism, defining it as "not Islamic," others as inhuman. Some denounced the war in Chechnya (which had been ongoing since 1994) and viewed its brutality as the reason the hostage crisis had occurred.

The war in Chechnya was important in my self-formation. I am a Caucasian—a person born and raised in the Caucasus, a region in southern Russia adjacent to the North Caucasus Mountains, which was a part of the former Soviet Union, previously conquered by the Russian Empire during the eighteenth and nineteenth centuries (on the origin of the concept "Caucasian," see Hunter and Blumenbach 2011). While growing up in the Soviet Union, I cared little about religion. After the union disintegrated, in Russia, which was unwilling to give up any part of the Caucasus, the mass media portrayed religion as a catalyst for the war that broke out between Chechnya and Russia. I dated a Chechen from Grozny, Chechnya's capital. We read Friedrich Nietzsche and listened to Pink Floyd together, and so, despite the Russian mass media's focus on emerging nationalist histories, our ethnic self-identification and the lack of a religious one made no difference in our relationship. Yet we observed how increasingly antagonistic representations of regional ethnic and religious identities formed a nationalist discourse on the opposition between "Muslims" (the "Chechens" and others) and "Christians" (the "Russians" and others) that was used to explain violence and strife in the region. I developed an interest in religion in order to make sense of the emerging discursive and extradiscursive (e.g., checkpoints on the roads leading to the region, the military, weapons, and death) differentiation fracturing our lives (cf. Foucault 1960).

After moving to the United States in 1995, I continued working on several projects connected to Chechnya sponsored by the Andrei Sakharov Foundation in Moscow and New York City. In 1999, while working on my doctorate in sociocultural anthropology, I planned to carry out my dissertation research in Chechnya focusing on local paramilitary groups fighting Russia's military during 1994–96. I wanted to learn to what extent Islam was or had become important in the lives of the individuals within these groups. But, while I was preparing for the fieldwork in 1999, the war between Russia and Chechnya was reignited; it was no longer safe or feasible to conduct research there because my contacts in the existing government in Chechnya became "terrorists" overnight. Chechnya was one geographic area I was familiar with; Central Asia's Ferghana Valley was another. My research interest in Islam brought me to the valley the first time in 2001, and I returned to the valley in July 2002 to conduct my dissertation research.

Islam and National Security

Since the late 1990s in Uzbekistan, individual religiosity has been inextricably linked to the country's national security. The government described the February 1999 bombings in Tashkent as an attempt on President Islam Karimov's life by political and religious opposition with networks extending to Turkey, Pakistan, and Afghanistan. The individuals allegedly involved in the bombings were severely punished, and the president "called on *mahalla* leaderships to monitor the populations and mosques . . . for indications of what the government considers 'extremist' tendencies" (Rasanayagam 2010, 113; see also McGlinchey 2007). Since that time, consistent religious observance by Muslims has become suspect, and the struggle against "Islamic extremism" has become a common justification of the state's violence in the valley and beyond. The two stories that local women, Nodiraopa and Marifat, shared with me in the late fall of

2002 exemplify the link between individual religiosity and national security and the government's use of violence in the name of public safety and order.

Article 159 of the Criminal Code

In 2002, after the annual celebration of the *Mustakilliq*, President Karimov signed an amnesty for prisoners—except religious and political ones. Several local women gathered in front of Hovliguzar's city hall to find out why the president's recent amnesty did not apply to their husbands, sons, and brothers. Nodiraopa was among them. Her husband was convicted in 2000 under Article 159 of the Criminal Code of the Republic of Uzbekistan for offenses against its constitution, including distribution of materials that threaten public safety and public order and participation in prohibited religious organizations.

Nodiraopa described her husband as a humble man who never harmed anyone. He taught his children and wife to "love God" and in his free time trained young people at a local mosque how to pray and how to recite the Qur'an. "He never punished his own children; he was very loving and respectful and caring," she said and wiped the tears running down her face with the ends of the scarf tied under her chin. "It all started with him going to the *masjid* [mosque]."

In 1993, people in their *mahalla* had built a new mosque. The *mahalla* committee asked Nodiraopa's husband to serve as an imam. He responded by saying that they should "bring a knowledgeable person as he was not properly educated [had not gone to a madrasa, a religious school]." Even though he responded this way, he really wanted to be an imam. "Other people" who also wanted that position, however, used his admission that he was not "properly educated" against him.

First, Nodiraopa's husband received threats from a former student. Then one night in 2000 police officers came to their house and arrested him. She did not see him until the court hearing months later.

"After we got married, he did not want me to leave the house and brought everything in the house," said Nodiraopa. He even took her passport picture. Traditional Muslim women, according to her, stayed at home and "did not go on the streets." But the night he was arrested, after the officers handcuffed him and took him outside the gates, she ran after them. There she saw a car full of soldiers wearing balaclavas that covered their faces. Nodiraopa was shocked. She remembered her husband turning around and saying, "I will come back; please, go inside the house." But he did not come back. And the next morning she went "out on the streets to look for him."

When Nodiraopa got back home, several police officers were already searching her house. Her youngest daughter was crying; the house was a mess. "Even the Qur'an was on the floor." "The Qur'an is a holy book and is not supposed to be kept below one's waist," she explained. One of the officers came out of the barn where they kept chickens and cotton she planned to use to make blankets. He was wiping his hands on his pants. Nodiraopa told her younger daughter to quickly fetch some water in order for this officer to wash his hands.

In a little while, two other officers searched the barn again and returned with a pack of leaflets, which, they said, her husband was hiding inside the packs of dry cotton. "God will judge [everyone] one day. I do not want to complain. He [the officer] put the leaflets in the barn, and my daughter offered him water to wash his hands!" She chocked up. "They kept on saying '*varaka*' [leaflets], '*varaka*'! They took all his pictures," continued Nodiraopa. Her son asked the police officers to show him the leaflets, but she did not allow him or the other kids to touch them. She said, "We did not have these before and would not want our fingerprints to be on them!" These leaflets became the main evidence used to convict her husband.

During the hearing, Nodiraopa found out that someone from the *mahalla* had written a letter about her husband to a local office of the Ministry of Internal Affairs, stating that he had plotted against the government. Several people signed that letter. Charged with anti-government activities and convicted four months after his arrest, he received an eight-year sentence, to be served at a correction facility. He was fifty-two years old at the time. "[You] have to thank God for everything. One day we will be happy, *Insha'Allah.* God gives us this life to test us, to go through all kinds of difficulties," she concluded.

After her husband's arrest, Nodiraopa became the head of the family. She had to provide for her children and grandchildren and so made a living by stitching traditional skullcaps, *do'ppi.* Her son sold these handmade embroidered *do'ppi* at a local bazaar for about ten thousand soms each and the "simple" ones for about five thousand soms apiece (ten and five dollars, respectively).

"Life is hard," Nodiraopa complained. The government's help was given rarely and only for her underage children. But they managed. "Let Allah give justice to those people who set up my husband. I pray every day, all the time, that he return soon. . . . It is a trial from God. God will judge and reward those punished unjustly," she stated.

The husband of Nodiraopa's oldest daughter, Marifat, was arrested a year after her father, in the summer of 2001. She was then four weeks pregnant with her third child. Her husband's arrest meant that her family, too, lost its breadwinner; it was "incredibly difficult to make both ends meet without him." As a single parent of now three children, Marifat was supposed to receive the government's help, about thirteen thousand soms a month (around thirteen dollars). This money was not enough to raise three children and was never paid on time and never in full.

Marifat described her husband as a hardworking man who built homes. He was very close to her family; her parents treated him like a son. After her father's arrest, Marifat's husband became the head of the extended family, but not for long.

Immediately after the marriage, Marifat had moved in with her husband and his parents. His parents' health was rapidly deteriorating; they died in a year and a half. After her husband's arrest, she could no longer afford to pay for utilities and so moved back in with her mother. Now, in order to survive, they pulled their meager resources together.

Marifat believed that her husband was arrested the first time because of the explosions in Tashkent in 1999. "He was suspected because he prayed every day," she said. He was also not very social and "kept to himself." He needed money to take care of his ill parents and worked long hours. As a result, he rarely participated in social events in the *mahalla*; he had no money to contribute and no free time.

Members of the suspected Hizb-ut-Tahrir (Party of Liberation, also locally referred to as "the Hizb") were said to stay away from social events that included music and alcohol consumption, so Marifat thought that some neighbors might have misunderstood and interpreted her husband's lack of socializing as a sign that he was engaged in a secretive organization such as Hizb-ut-Tahrir. "Maybe they [the police] thought he had something to hide," she concluded.

But the real reason why he was arrested in 1999 was his failure to pay back the money he had borrowed from "some people" for his sister's wedding. The lender bribed the police to "teach him a lesson." The police officers came by the house and "took him away." He returned home after a week of detention. According to Marifat, his body was bruised all over. He could not sit down or stand up. "His sister could not hug him. He was badly hurt." Marifat's friends recommended writing a complaint to a regional office of the Ministry of Internal Affairs. But he refused; he said that Marifat did not know what would happen to their family if he were to complain.

When his body healed, Marifat's husband continued working hard to pay off the debt. Yet after that first arrest, whenever anything happened in the *mahalla*, he was picked up by the police and beaten even though there was never any evidence against him. The last time, although he never smoked, her husband was arrested for marijuana possession. At first, this was a minor charge. Later, after the police officers searched the house and found leaflets and a rifle, which, Marifat insisted, they themselves planted, "they said he was a Wahhabist, a Hizbut."

With this arrest, Marifat took her children to her mother's house. When she returned to her own house to pick up some clothes, neighborhood kids playing on the street told her that a police officer had gotten inside the house when no one was at home. "The door was locked, so he had to climb the wall, the children said," added Marifat. At the moment, she was too worried about the current charges of marijuana possession against her husband and did not think much about the children's story.

The next day, although Marifat was afraid, thinking, "If they were to arrest me, what would happen to my children?" she decided to go and "tell the authorities" that her husband never smoked. As soon as she arrived at the police station, an old BMW drove up to her and "*esenbeshniki* [SNB agents]" pushed her inside the car. They said they had to search her house. As soon as they got to her house, neighbors and the elders of the *mahalla* gathered around them. The elders insisted that the three policemen conducting the search "show [what was] inside their pockets"; this community did not trust the police.

The two officers seemed to have nothing with them, and the third one had a video camera. Then another man in civilian clothes came into her courtyard. This man said that he was an "investigator" and would not allow anyone to search him or inspect a thick folder he carried with him. He, the "investigator," brought this folder into the house. First, he looked at two rooms and then went into the kitchen and sat at the table as if he were about to write something. And then while Marifat was in another room with the officers, the "investigator" yelled that he had found leaflets on shelves in the kitchen. "Here they are! Here are *varaka*!"

The officers continued searching the house. Inside her husband's copy of the Qur'an, they found Qur'anic verses written on pieces of paper, which her husband used to carry with him for good luck and to learn by heart during a break at work. The police officers said that they too were evidence against him. "'He is an extremist,' they said," Marifat continued. Then three more officers came in. They surrounded Marifat and took her into the kitchen, where she could not see what was going on in the rest of the house. This is when the officers found a rifle in the attic, which, Marifat said, had been planted in the house by a police officer the day before, when she took the kids to her mother's house. The elders asked the officers to bring her husband home to explain where the leaflets and the rifle came from, but the officers refused.

Marifat was not allowed to see her husband until the hearing organized soon after his arrest. During the hearing, she asked the judge how the officers could find marijuana in her husband's pocket if he never smoked. She also asked if the prosecution could prove that the rifle belonged to her husband: she did not see the officers taking fingerprints off the rifle or the leaflets. "If the rifle and the leaflets belonged to my husband, where are his fingerprints?" she asked the judge. The judge replied, "Maybe you are a part of Hizb-ut-Tahrir as well!" Marifat got scared and asked no more questions.

Her husband's lawyer told Marifat that the case made no sense; if her husband indeed were a member of the Hizb, he would not be smoking marijuana, and he would not have weapons. According to this lawyer, the Hizb was against violence and drugs, but no one listened to the lawyer.

Marifat's husband was sentenced to nine years of hard labor. He and his lawyer appealed the court decision, arguing that the police had planted the evidence against him. During the appeal hearing, the judge stated that the court needed no additional proof of his guilt, such as fingerprints, because the rifle and leaflets were found in *his* house: "The case is closed." In his last statement, Marifat's husband said that he "worked hard for bread and water," that there was no justice, and that if he were to come out alive, he would be a different person. She did not understand fully what he meant, "but this is what he said."

When Marifat saw her husband before the appeal hearing, he told her that when he was arrested that last time, the officers had asked him to plead guilty. He had responded by saying that he had nothing to feel guilty about because he had done nothing wrong. He could not plead guilty to crimes that he did not commit. They beat him every day for seven days, but he did not sign the confession.

Marifat's husband was sent to a labor camp, where, she said, "he is starving and has to break stones with his hands and then carry them on his back." She was afraid that he would die there, that he would never come back. She did not cry while telling her story. Since her husband had been arrested, she had "hit the very bottom of this life" but had to find "a way to go on," to feed her kids. She finished her story by saying, "If they give me money that I can use to feed my kids, I will do anything, even distribute the leaflets [there were rumors in Hovliguzar that Hizb members were paid one dollar per distributed leaflet]. . . . Use my name in any article, any book, anywhere. Tell them. There is no justice here. I am ready to do anything. . . . I have nothing to lose."

Personified, 2003

Although relatively uneventful in the valley, the New Year celebration of 2003 was a critical time for me. I was pregnant. While I was agonizing about my personal life and struggling with accompanying health issues, history happened. The anticipation of the US-led invasion of Iraq and numerous antiwar demonstrations in Europe and the States were aired on satellite television. In Hovliguzar, people did not protest the approaching war. In public, many avoided the subject altogether. The discussions about the impending war took place mainly in the private space of individual homes.

At the very end of March 2003, during one *ehson*, a ceremonial gathering to express gratitude to God, when I was asked, "Why does the United States want to occupy Iraq?" one of the women preempted my answer by saying, "America is helping us [referring to the US aid provided in exchange for military bases in Uzbekistan], and so we cannot criticize it too much." She turned to me and whispered, "This is the official position. How can we approve of killing other humans, other Muslims? This is *our* position." Such discussions could be dangerous. By that time, I knew this lesson intimately: several days before that meeting, my interest in the war had resulted in my detention by local police.

The first time I felt that my research was about to unravel was on March 13, 2003. A feeling of acute connection between the personal and the political that I had that day became a self-fulfilling prophecy. That day Nainahon and Tahsir came to the apartment I rented in Hovliguzar so that we could take part in a religious ceremony together. Nainahon, an aspiring *otincha*, was a successful businesswoman and a diligent student of Islam. Tahsir was a healer who claimed to be in the thirty-fourth generation of the Prophet Muhammad's extended family. During the Soviet era, he did not want to attend "the unbelievers' schools" and so had received only eight years of education. As a result, he had worked as a taxi driver until Uzbekistan's independence from the Soviet Union in 1991. Now, in a "democratic independent Uzbekistan," he could live as "a true Muslim" and be a healer.

Nainahon was wearing on her head two scarves embellished with glass pearl beads. The top white scarf's untied ends rested on her chest. The pinkish-colored scarf under the white one was tied at the back of her neck. A dark magenta dress covered her ankles, and a small amount of cleavage exposed a thick shiny golden chain around her neck. Her smile, too, was shiny because of the many golden crowns that filled her teeth.

Tahsir was wide shouldered, clean shaven, and head and shoulders above Nainahon and me. He was wearing black slacks, handmade leather boots, and a long white shirt with a *chopan*—a padded robe—over it. A black-and-white embroidered *do'ppi* covered his bald head. I wore a loose suit made of thin local silk. I had had no time to warm the water to wash and style my hair that morning and so wore a silk scarf tied loosely at the back of my neck.

Tahsir, Nainahon, and I planned to petition Allah for a successful first trimester of my pregnancy and the successful immigration of my Lebanese Canadian fiancé to the States. The ceremony included Qur'anic recitation, cooking and eating dishes appropriate for the occasion, and chanting a phrase in Arabic, "*La ilaha illa Allah*" (There is no other God but God), as a part of *zikr*, which my guests explained as a process of getting closer to Allah through the repetition of this phrase.

Prior to this meeting, Nainahon had told me it was an honor and a blessing to eat food prepared by Tahsir. I understood why while watching him cook. He made a delicious Uzbek *osh*, a rice and meat dish, while reciting the Qur'an over the ingredients. I could see his lips moving but heard nothing except "*Bismillah ir-Rahman ir-Rahim* [In the name of God, the Caring, and Compassionate]" occasionally. Particular types of cooked food, Tahsir told me, carried healing powers for the human body, while particular words perfected the human spirit. He was mixing these words into the *osh*, making it special.

That year the rap performer Eminem was very popular in Hovliguzar; local venders and street peddlers sold numerous cassettes and compact discs with his music. Among other foreign artists' performances, his songs, played again and again, replaced the Russian commercials usually aired along with retransmitted programs from the Russian Federation's TV channels. While we were getting seated around the coffee table, Eminem vehemently insisted from the TV screen that everybody had something to say; yet "when they move[d] their lips," it was just "a buncha gibberish" that came out of their mouths (Dr. Dre 1999). I asked Tahsir and Nainahon if I should turn down the sound. Nainahon looked at Tahsir, smiled, and said, "Leave it on." Eminem's rapping did not seem to bother them, but I continued to be distracted by the lyrics of another song: "My name is . . . (who?) [scratches] Slim Shady" (Eminem 1999). Eminem's American English street slang continued to mix in with the Qur'anic recitation. "*La ilaha illa Allah*," Tahsir and Nainahon chanted. "My name is . . . ," Eminem interjected several times as if in response to "*La ilaha illa Allah*." In order to focus on the recitation of the Qur'an, I turned the TV sound a bit down.

Tursun-oi taught me that the divine light—*nur*—dwells wherever the Qur'an is recited. If this is true, then the living room of my rented Hovliguzar apartment, my private space, became a public place, unlike the street but nonetheless public, where the divine and human worlds converged through the medium of the word; then we, including Eminem, were in the presence of the *nur* germinating in and radiating from the recited words of the Qur'an. While thinking about this relationship, for a moment I felt that I lost track of both Eminem's voice and the chanting. But "Guess who's back?"— he was back (Eminem 2000).

Eminem's return reminded me of my fiancé, whose image was silently gazing at us as the wallpaper of my Sony VAIO laptop's screen. Tahsir occasionally hit the space bar in order to refresh the image to assure my fiancé's virtual presence at the ceremony. Like Eminem, my fiancé was not *really* there, but this did not bother Tahsir, whose powers, he claimed, extended over borders, seas, mountains, and oceans.

In addition to the Qur'anic recitation, Tahsir evoked jinn, invisible beings created by God from smoke and fire. He said he had "his own" jinn who worked for him. They were expected to work on my fiancé's behalf and alleviate his problems with immigration. Tahsir added that the Qur'anic recitation combined with animal sacrifices, which I had to arrange to be performed on my behalf during the next month, would continue ensuring my own, the child's, and my other immediate relatives' well-being.

My guests took a break from chanting to eat and discuss religious and family matters as well as global politics. The TV provided ample material for political discussions by featuring public demonstrations in Europe and America against Bush's insistence on the necessity of war on Iraq. When the commercial break came, it replayed the song featuring Eminem: "This is the millennium of Aftermath. / Ain't gonna be nothin' after that" (Dr. Dre 1999). To Tahsir and Nainahon, these particular lyrics were, as the lyrics themselves said, "a buncha gibberish." But I thought that in the context of an imminent war, the message communicated by these two particular sentences was very profound.

Nainahon compared Eminem's popularity in America to that of Yuldus Usmanova, a very famous Uzbek female singer, in Uzbekistan.

Usmanova, who was born in the valley, was the local celebrity. I heard her love stories dramatized and retold with empathy or judgment at least twenty times and on one occasion was introduced to her mother. This, I was told by the women who introduced us, was a "big honor." Nainahon continued her comparison with a smile, "Eminem is cursing in his songs. He often says, 'Fuck,'" but "Yuldus [Usmanova] does not curse." Nainahon's knowledge of English was very limited, but the truly global word *fuck* was not unheard of in Hovliguzar. Tahsir smiled too and said that in spite of such language, "Our local youth love him and listen to him. His songs must get into their hearts. *Alhamdulillah* [Thank God]."

I mentioned that some of Eminem's songs were about social issues. Nainahon replied that in Uzbekistan songs were mainly about love. "Our singers cannot sing any political songs. They sing only about their love for mothers, women, our people, and our motherland." "True," agreed Tahsir.

While foreigners were fleeing Iraq and the world was praying for peace while preparing for war, we ate *osh* and drank Coca-Cola in the Ferghana Valley city Hovliguzar, discussing my health, God's unknowable ways, the relationship between a wife and a husband, jinn, economic instability in the world, troubles with water, electricity, and gas in the region, and the social meanings of Eminem's songs. Tahsir nodded, "It is all from Allah. But we have to do our part," and continued chanting, "*La ilaha illa Allah, la ilaha illa Allah.*" In order to do her part, Nainahon joined him. Feeling anxious about what was going to happen to my child, me, my fiancé, the war, I too joined the chanting.

Personal and Political

History happened beyond protests against the US invasion of Iraq, including severe cold in Siberia and northern parts of Russia, an opening of the Dublin Spire monument, and civil war in the Ivory Coast. The available non-Uzbek satellite stations briefly mentioned these events but focused on the imminent war, violence, and politics.

The local Uzbek channels featured the government and citizens' various achievements; national, Russian, Turkish, and Korean soap operas and movies; and artistic performances. My daily life in the valley continued in this historical context. By the end of March, however, it came to include a fear of the Uzbek government.

At the beginning of February 2003, Tahsir, after sizing me up from head to toe, had announced that I was pregnant and predicted that I would have a healthy boy. He had recommended praying and performing occasional sacrifices. An Uzbek obstetrician had ordered me to stay in bed and take various vitamins and iron pills so that my anemia would not affect my pregnancy. I followed the instruction given by both Tahsir and the obstetrician.

Jahon and Tursun-oi offered prayers on my behalf. Nainahon made special food that would make my son healthy and my childbirth easy. Following Tahsir's advice, she made sure to sacrifice roosters on my behalf regularly. Rashida, my friend and Uzbek language teacher, told me to wear red and to eat red food, such as tomatoes, if I wanted to be sure to have a boy. She also taught me how to cook not just "traditional" or "Uzbek" or "Russian," but "healthy" food. She said that now, at thirty, preparing to be a mother, I had to learn how to be a "real woman." Cooking was part of being a "real woman." It is not that local men did not cook. They did, as I had observed on various festive occasions and as Tahsir demonstrated. But as an everyday responsibility, as in other parts of the world and at other times, cooking for the family was, as Rashida said, "women's duty."

My pregnancy opened up new learning opportunities in my research. Now I could address the subjects that were either avoided or barely discussed earlier, such as intimacy between husband and wife and childbirth. Jahon, using her family as an example, reminded me that sexual relationships were an important part of women's lives and that being "truly" Muslim was about more than knowledge of religious texts and ritual prayers. According to her, being a good Muslim woman also meant being able to sexually satisfy your spouse. This required education and occasional self-reinvention, such as learning new sexual practices and abandoning feelings of shame in the bedroom.

Expecting a child also affected my relationships with some of my local male acquaintances; two of them became my friends. Pregnant and soon to be married, I was no longer available. This fact allowed us develop what I call "spiritual" intimacy, including sharing stories and caring about each other in a familiar familial way—as if we were members of one extended family. Instead of inviting me out to local restaurants, they brought nurses to my apartment if and when I needed immediate medical attention. Some of my male friends came to "sit with me" and talk about politics and their daily lives. One of them was Mahmud. This tall, strong, and wide man had a disarming smile. In his late thirties, still unmarried, he was involved in some type of shady but profitable business.

Mahmud used to come by just about every day and stay for hours at a time sharing his personal love stories of women, some as young as eighteen years old, and stories about his family and childhood, and bringing me up to speed on local gossip. He fed me chocolate and delicious local sweets and made us tea. Through his visits, I learned an important lesson about the value of children and gender dynamics in Hovliguzar. "A home with children is like a market [*bazar* or bazaar], but without children it is like a graveyard [*mazar*]," says an Uzbek proverb (Nalivkin and Nalivkina 1886, 168). In spite of existing gender ideology, which assigned all responsibility for children to local women, expecting a child was (usually) a joyful experience for all members of a family equally, both male and female. As a result, not only local women but also men provided emotional support to and took care of a future mother. Children brought not only families but also strangers together.

But these nurturing experiences were not the only learning opportunities that opened up for me in 2003. In February, I noticed surveillance. My experience of surveillance was not unique; other researchers shared stories about the SNB agents' interest in their research (e.g., Rasanayagam 2010).

During my research, I occasionally, though perhaps unwisely, engaged topics that could be construed as political, thinking of them as a diagnostic of changing levels of religiosity among local Muslims, which I inferred from a proliferation of academic works discussing the relations between Islam and politics. By filming some social events and occasionally interviewing individuals whose family members had suffered, according to them, unjust persecution by the Uzbek law enforcement agencies, I not surprisingly attracted the SNB's interest in my research.

At the end of February 2003, SNB agents followed me around by foot and in vehicles and photographed and filmed my movements, not unlike an anthropologist would do, except the latter was supposed to have the subject's informed consent. They ordered the driver I often hired to remove his car's window tinting and questioned my friends about my whereabouts.

I initially found the surveillance amusing. I joked in one email to a friend that I would never be mugged as I had plenty of bodyguards around me. The surveillance notwithstanding, I decided to continue my research, reasoning that if I were to end it abruptly, the SNB agents might interpret this sudden change as an admission of guilt, as if I were doing something criminal.

On March 21, 2003, when the news about the US invasion of Iraq (which commenced on March 19) finally reached the valley, I decided to attend a *Jumma namoz* (Friday congregational prayer) at one of the local mosques. This seemed to me to be just the place to demonstrate my intentions as a social scientist researching ritual life. I wanted to find out if and how "Islamic renewal" manifested itself, whether and to what extent local Muslims felt a part of the global Muslim community (umma). I thought I would be able to infer this connection from their responses to the invasion of Iraq. I reasoned that if local Muslim men sympathized with Iraqi Muslims, then their allegiance was more to the global Muslim community than to their government and its condoning of Iraq's invasion. This sounds simplistic, but at the time, it made perfect sense to me.

There was another reason for that mosque visit. By that time, I had gathered enough material about *otinchalar's* role in daily life of local communities. In order to provide a balanced representation of the local "Islamic revival," I had to learn about the role of male leaders. The mosque, attended by men only, was one of the places where this leadership was manifested.

All my previous attempts to visit mosques during the *Jumma namoz* had failed. For instance, in January 2003, in order to observe a Friday prayer at one of the local mosques, I met with a local imam. He insisted that interviews with imams would provide me with all the necessary information about what was going on at the mosques on Fridays. According to him, an imam's main goal was to lead prayers and help people learn the Qur'anic message by reciting the text. At his mosque, for example, the men mainly prayed. When they did not pray, they read the Qur'an. At that time, they had almost finished sura (chapter) al-Baqara, the Cow. The imam also mentioned that, unlike ceremonial gatherings in domestic space, in his experience the Friday prayers at the mosques did not include didactic stories (*masalas*) or hymns (*hikmatlar*).

The imam eventually yielded to my requests to learn more about what was happening during the Friday prayer at the mosque not just from him and promised to allow a local man to document the process for me by audiorecording it. The next day, however, he sent me a message through a friend: "It is not permitted." To be able to document a Friday prayer, even if not in person, I still had to have the local government's permission. In the valley, getting this permission, like any bureaucratic process, took a long time and often money and would only add to the state's interest in my research. I did not give up, though. One way to achieve my objective was to stand on the street outside a local mosque, where the imam used a microphone during the Friday prayer, and try to listen to the process, including his message to the congregation (*khutba*) and their response to it. There was one such mosque in Hovliguzar. Tursunoi's student Jahon accompanied me to the mosque on Friday, March

21. She described the process and summarized parts of the *khutba* for me.

At the end of the message, the imam mentioned the war in Iraq. He said that each war had to have a reason because everything had a reason and that any war was a punishment from God for wrongdoings: "If people are not good, there will be no peace as peace depends on people." Because Islam is a religion of peace, he called on the congregation to be patient. The imam concluded his speech by saying that the Prophet Muhammad disliked war and fought only when he had to defend his people. He highlighted God's power and stressed human agency by turning the news about the war into a moral message, reminding them what and who were good and how a good person should behave in order to avoid war. The audience responded with "*Allahu Akbar* [God is the Greatest]!"

I waited for the imam to leave the mosque and approached him on the way to his car to ask questions about his view of the current events and the logistics of the Friday prayer. He replied that he was in a hurry, got in the car, and drove away. While his car was turning around the corner, a uniformed police officer appeared in front of me as if from nowhere. He asked me to follow him. In response to my questions—"Why? What did I do?"—he accused me of distributing Hizb-ut-Tahrir leaflets. According to this police officer, he had several witnesses.

At the time, the Uzbek state and the United States classified Hizb-ut-Tahrir as a terrorist organization. My acquaintances in the valley told me that distributing Hizb-ut-Tahrir leaflets could result in a lengthy prison term, anywhere from seven to twelve years, served at a remote prison camp (*zona*) in Karakalpakistan, an autonomous republic that occupies the entire western end of Uzbekistan. I also heard about routine use of torture by the representatives of law enforcement agencies to obtain confessions. After a lengthy discussion of who I was, where I came from, what I was doing in Hovliguzar, and which local address I was registered at, the police officer allowed me to make a phone call. Frantically looking for help, I called my friend Mahmud and an acquaintance in

Tashkent, a representative of the European Bank for Reconstruction and Development.

Mahmud and his friend, a relative of a "*vazhni chelovek* [important individual]," a member of the local government, arrived within an hour. After a conversation with Mahmud's friend, the police officer agreed to follow me to my apartment. There I showed him my passport and some supporting documents, including a letter from an American university about my dissertation research. Written in English, the letter was of no interest to the officer. Maybe he already knew the reasons for my staying in the valley, and this detention was only meant to give me a reason to leave the country. He left after informing me that the police would contact me if there were any more questions about my activities and whereabouts in the area. Mahmud's reassurances that I had nothing to worry about did not calm me down. The surveillance was no longer amusing. I realized that "important individuals" might not be able to save me from the Uzbek government and its law enforcement agencies the next time.

After that incident, continuing my research became a real challenge. I was afraid that individuals whom I visited would be questioned by SNB agents or detained—that I would harm "human subjects" whom I, as an anthropologist, had vouched to protect. But the primal worry about myself became primary to other worries. In light of this priority, I came to distrust my acquaintances and friends—at times all of them. Some of the personal stories that I had heard, including horror stories, became parts of my dreams. Before this incident, I had dreamed about walking up a ladder into the sky in Mecca, just like some of my friends in their stories about reorienting their lives toward God. Now I dreamed about a metamorphosis of peach blossoms, homegrown silk worms, and countless cotton fields—parts of the Ferghana Valley's landscape—into deep, dark, and stale water. I was drowning in it. In these dreams, I crashed my car and fell into an abyss. I was blinded by a spotlight in an interrogation room, as in the movie images that often materialized in my head while I was listening to the stories of someone else's detention in the valley. I found these dreams eerie. The fear, permanently planted in my cortex, destabilized my health and the small social universe that I had created in the area over the previous two years. Cold hands and feet, cold sweat, racing thoughts, and an inability to focus on anything other than personal security—these felt maddening. I knew what I had to do.

"It is all from Allah," Tahsir had said earlier that month, at the *ehson* on March 13, 2003. Then he had added, "But we have to do our part." I tried to do my part, but after about three more weeks spent under surveillance, I left the valley for Tashkent. At the end of April, I was in the Caucasus (Russia) with my family. I left some good friends and teachers in Uzbekistan. I did not go back for eight years.

The Next Eight Years, 2003–2011

My life and the lives of people in the valley have changed significantly since 2003. I had a healthy son, *alhamdulillah.* The jinn sent by Tahsir to my fiancé at the time, who in the intervening years became my husband and then my ex-husband, helped him to leave rather than stay in the United States. I am sure my ex-husband came to appreciate this outcome. During the first decade of the twenty-first century's "war on terror," the United States was not a very welcoming place to native Arabic speakers. As Tahsir said in March 2003, "It is all from Allah," but we all have to do our part.

Over the next eight years, through emails and telephone conversations, Nainahon and her son kept me informed about local news and changes in their lives and in the lives of my other acquaintances and friends. For instance, Nainahon's favorite singer, Yuldus Usmanova, had disappeared from national television and from Uzbekistan. According to Nainahon, the singer had moved to Turkey to live with her new husband, "a wealthy Turk," in 2007. According to other sources, Yuldus Usmanova moved to Turkey because of "political persecution in Uzbekistan" (Ashur and Najibullah 2011).

Aside from occasional anecdotes about local celebrities, the government, economy, and our common friends, Nainahon's conversations were centered on her family and her kids' marriages. She arranged her daughters' marriages, two of them for a second time. She also arranged her son's marriages; he did not like his first wife and, as Nainahon told me, "sent her home [to her parents]." Then he married a young Uzbek woman whose family lived in Ukraine. They had a son. The number of Nainahon's grandchildren multiplied; by 2010, it was nine, two of them twins.

Nainahon and I also talked about Tahsir. In the spring of 2003, he had two wives and five children. His first wife and her children lived with Tahsir, while the second wife and her children lived in an apartment complex elsewhere in Hovliguzar. Tahsir's first wife, Onahon, found the second wife for him because, she said in 2003, he was "a strong man [sexually active]"; one wife could not satisfy him. Pleased with her daughter-in-law's decision, Tahsir's mother, Ova, told Onahon, "If a wife finds other wives for her husband, she gets special blessings from God and goes to paradise."

In 2003, Tahsir's mother and grandmother shared his household. They had separate quarters, across from his bedroom. His younger sister lived nearby. All of these women, including Tahsir's first wife, were religious and spiritual teachers and leaders for many local women and some men. Several times a week, they presided over various ceremonial social events and Qur'anic lessons, traveling around Hovliguzar and occasionally outside of Uzbekistan. Nainahon told me that they had "many *murid*s [committed followers]," both women and men. She was one of them.

Tahsir's house was a popular place. In 2003, I visited him twelve times, and every time I saw twenty or more men, women, and children, Uzbek and not, Muslim and not, crowding his courtyard. Some were seeking healing, others blessings from his elderly grandmother and religious knowledge from his mother and wife. According to Tahsir, neither he nor his other family members invited anyone. Rather, Allah had guided all these individuals, including me, to his house.

In 2003, Tahsir held healing ceremonies almost daily in one of the semidilapidated dwellings on his property, which he called the "patients' room." Waiting for their turn to be healed, those who were very sick or had traveled long distances spent the night in that building. All of the structures on Tahsir's property were adjacent to the *mazar*, where his father and grandfather and other relatives were buried. The graves of these people—who, Tahsir claimed, were relatives of the Prophet Muhammad—were sacred (on the significance of sacred descent, see Privratsky 2004). Five visitors told me that by spending a night praying next to the *mazar*, they incurred *barakat* and earned "*katta savob* [great merit]."

Tahsir's patients had various health and social problems, including brain damage and infertility, quarrels in the family, and a lack of money. In order to heal them and fix their problems, he used Qur'anic recitations, help from jinn, and *zikr*. Tahsir claimed that his medicine was so powerful that it could restore the health of Uzbekistan's president, who was reported to be seriously ill at the beginning of 2003.

In an interview in 2003, Tahsir told me that the words in the Qur'an were at the center of his healing process, but jinn were also important. According to him, the Qur'an was the Word of God; every word in and sound of it were powerful. God knew everything and had power over all illnesses. Tahsir insisted, "Only Allah knows the Truth. No one knows Allah; only Allah knows Allah. If Allah wills, the head and the whole body can go through the small eye of a needle."

Just as God created humans, God created jinn but endowed them with special powers to either heal or harm humans; some of them were "good" and "helpful," but others were "bad" and "unhelpful." In order "to make them work for you," the jinn had to be fed the blood of sacrificed animals. "The more you feed them, the better they obey you," said Tahsir (on the role of jinn in healing, see Flueckiger 2006).

Onahon and Tahsir's older daughter had healing powers too. His older son also inherited his powers, but in 2003 this son was still too young to use them. Instead, during my last visit that year he offered to demonstrate his karate skills to me; and while *murid*s were waiting for his mother, the seekers of religious knowledge for his wife, and the sick ones for Tahsir, Tahsir, his mother, oldest daughter, Onahon, Nainahon, and I admired the boy's karate skills. We praised his achievement and predicted his future as a national karate champion.

Coming Back in 2011

It took me eight years to get back to Uzbekistan. In June 2011, despite the US State Department's warning about travel in Central Asia, including Uzbekistan, after American troops killed Osama Bin Laden in Pakistan in May 2011), and my personal doubts about the feasibility of my research, I left the United States with a ticket paid by the Individual Advanced Research Opportunities Fellowship, sponsored by the US Department of State, in order to continue doing my part.

During the eight years between 2003 and 2011, a number of scholarly, political, and newspaper works about the threat of "Islamic extremism" in Central Asia continued to portray the Ferghana Valley as a place of danger (for more on such portrayals, see Heathershow and Megoran 2011). In addition to the term *Wahhabism*, the term *al-Qaedaization* became popular in reference to the region (e.g., Chaudet 2008). The "possibility" of "the spread of Islamic radicalism" and violence also saturated Uzbekistan's national-security discourse and further enabled the Uzbek government's suppression and punishment of real or imagined political opposition, including those Muslims whose self-formation seemed to challenge the existing political regime (Human Rights Watch 2007).

The national-security discourse fostered not only fear of the Uzbek government but also fear of unpredictability. The Osh tragedy in June 2010 in Kyrgyzstan, when hundreds of Uzbek and Kyrgyz inhabitants were killed in intercommunal violence and, as a result, thousands of Uzbek refugees poured into Uzbekistan, became an example of an "insecure state" (Megoran 2010). Daily life there no longer had "a pattern," and one was unable "to render one's desires or personal commitments into an actionable truth" (Greenberg 2011,

93). The Uzbek government claimed that Uzbekistan, unlike Kyrgyzstan, was safe, but daily predictable life had a cost.

Although during my research in the summer of 2011 the Osh tragedy was among the subjects not talked about in Uzbekistan, the stories about and images of violence in which the Kyrgyz were the perpetrators and Uzbeks the victims continued to circulate. My friend Mahmud saw plenty of images of violence that led him to believe that "they [the Kyrgyz] hate us [the Uzbeks]." In his opinion, "[Uzbekistan's president Islam] Karimov was smart. He did not let them [Uzbek refugees from Kyrgyzstan] stay in Uzbekistan long. He helped them. He said that the Uzbeks *would continue* living in Kyrgyzstan. He did not kill the Kyrgyz [wage war against Kyrgyzstan]. He does not want it [intercommunal violence] to happen here." The stories and images of violence, exchanged orally and displayed through still and moving images on mobile phones and the Internet, made any measures of social control seem justified. There were alternative assessments of the Uzbek state's response to the Osh tragedy. Nainahon recalled, "Some [people] said that the [Uzbek] government, by helping the refugees, was trying to make up for Andijon." She was referring to the army's massacre of civilians in Andijon in 2005, another subject not talked about.

While acting on the president's orders, in 2005 the Uzbek army massacred civilians who had gathered in the central square of the city of Andijon in the valley protesting against persecution of several local individuals (Denber and Levine 2005; Khalid 2007; McGlinchey 2011; Rasanayagam 2010; Whitlock 2010). Government representatives argued that these individuals belonged to an extremist political organization named "Akromiya," a derivative of the group's alleged leader's name, and that violence was justified and necessary to protect people from this group (Akiner and Central Asia–Caucasus Institute 2005). According to several scholars and local activists, however, there was no political organization named "Akromiya," only a commune based on adherence to Islamic principles (as understood by these individuals) but not imposing these principles on others; the state's national security, not local individuals, had invented the name and demonized it in order to justify the massacre (see Ilkhamov 2006; Whitlock 2010).

In the summer of 2011, while describing what happened in Andijon in 2005, an acquaintance in Hovliguzar said, "They [some local people] came to ask us to join [the protests], but we said 'no,' and you see, we did the right thing. [A long pause.] What did they want? Did they not have enough? Our state [the Uzbek government] gave them everything. [President] Karimov did the right thing [in giving the order to the army to fire at the protesters]. [Another long pause.] Why did they do it? Why not sit quietly and enjoy life?" Her response demonstrates that in order to enjoy predictable life in a state that worked, citizens' behaviors had to correspond to the state's models of good citizenship; otherwise, the order was restored through violence deemed to be legitimate by the state and accepted as such by some citizens.

Tahsir, 2011

In 2011, as I approached Tahsir's house, I saw a beautiful new arch marking its entrance. I passed the patients' room. It had not changed. In it, in addition to mats on the floor, water, herbs, individual photographs of Tahsir's long-distance patients, a woman was sleeping in one corner, a man praying in another one, and three women were chatting in the space between them. Across from the patients' room, in the middle of the *mazar*, there was a small new memorial. Built above the ground, it marked the burial place of a holy person. This was the resting place of Tahsir's grandmother, who had died in 2009.

In the courtyard, Tahsir's *murid*s were skinning a lamb that had just been sacrificed on someone's behalf. Onahon came out to greet me and said that Tahsir would join us shortly. Meanwhile, she invited me to visit with his mother, who now occupied Tahsir's grandmother's former quarters, across from Onahon and Tahsir's rooms. Like his grandmother, his mother, Ova, spent her days sitting on the string metal bed praying and offering *pataha* (supplications) to God on behalf of others.[1] Those receiving *pataha* gave her money in return, however symbolic the sum might have been.

Ova said she was happy to see me. She told me that her life had changed; now she rarely ventured outside the house to teach or preside over *meropriyatia*. Her sister, however, continued to officiate at social events in Hovliguzar and other towns and villages in the valley. Always driven in a car, Tahsir's maternal aunt still wore *paranji* (a form of modest dress that resembles a long jacket worn on the top of one's head) and a veil—a dark-colored, lightweight, semitransparent scarf—covering her face. Ova reminded me that as distant relatives of the Prophet and thus holy people and as modest women, they were not supposed to show their faces. Her own bright blue velvet *paranji*, its front stitched with intricate designs and Qur'anic verses, hung on the wall next to her bed.

Before I left her room, Ova showed me a "pen Qur'an," an electronic device in the form of a thick plastic pen, which upon touching a particular verse in the copy of the Qur'an that came with the pen played a beautiful prerecorded recitation of the verse. Several women visiting with Tahsir's mother at the time joined me in marveling at this technological invention. After getting a *pataha* from Ova, Nainahon (who had accompanied me that day), Onahon, and I came out into the courtyard to greet and meet with Tahsir.

Tahsir was already waiting for us. I thought he had not changed a bit. He smiled, shook my hand, and invited me to come inside his room. We settled on the floor mats around the low table. He gave me permission to take notes, and I pulled out my Mac Air computer.

Taking me by surprise, Tahsir responded to my first question about the changes in his life by noting that because of the war in Iraq America had lost "the world's respect." He said, "If Saddam Hussein were a dictator, God, not the United States, would punish him." If

1. In a personal communication to me on October 13, 2011, Marianne Kamp suggested that the word *pataha* is probably a derivative of the word *fatiha* (opening), also used for the opening chapter of the Qur'an.

he were against God, he would certainly die because "all who fought against God, such as Stalin and Lenin, died." He continued, "America wants democracy? If one is cornered, he will become a dictator. Each nation has its own religion and traditions. If we respect each other's traditions, we will be friends. There will be peace." Tahsir smiled, while putting his hands together and shaking them, as in a greeting. He continued by saying that the main changes in his life were connected to the changes in the country: "Our Uzbekistan is becoming [economically] better and better. If our country is rich, we will be rich." He smiled again.

In 2003, doing his part had not made Tahsir rich. His bedroom had a cracked clay wall. The rooms had a very modest interior, their furnishings limited to a carpet on the floor, a couple of low tables, and Onahon's trousseau (*sep*), which included a couple of tea sets inside built-in wall shelves, floor mats, and stacks of cotton-filled blankets (*kurpacha*) and pillows stacked on top of a trunk (*sunduk*). The pillows and unrolled blankets became Tahsir and Onahon's bed at night. According to Nainahon, the crowds of people in his yard and his *murid*s were Tahsir's wealth. She had explained in 2003 that as a holy man, a healer, and a man knowledgeable in religious matters, he wanted "spiritual goods." Yet he could not feed the family with spiritual food only. Those seeking healing brought material gifts with them that he accepted.

In 2011, however, the same room was freshly painted, the windows had new curtains, mobile phones crowded the table, a new wall carpet covered the crack in the wall, and a large flat-screen TV sat on a low table. These changes were not surprising. Tahsir said that except Saturday and Sunday his services were not free. "If I give only one thousand soms [the monetary unit in Uzbekistan, equivalent to fifty US cents] to a *taxist* [taxi driver], he will not take me to Moscow." According to Tahsir, healing worked the same way. Some people were very sick, and it took time and energy to heal them: "I charge them so that I can heal them."

The previous eight years had been very eventful for Tahsir. He had married off each of his three daughters. His oldest daughter became an *otincha* and a healer. His "karate kid" finished college and wanted to get a master's degree in physical education. He became a healer working alongside his father. This son was not yet married.

Tahsir himself now had three wives. Onahon had found him the third wife, who was one of Onahon's friends. The third wife was pregnant and lived in the same *mahalla* as Onahon and Tahsir but in a separate residence. Onahon cut in, "*Alhamdulillah* [Thank God] for [multiplying the number of] Tahsir's children." The second wife still lived in an apartment building elsewhere in Hovliguzar. Onahon, as "the head wife," continued doing her part, making important decisions related to the extended family's well-being and trying to be friendly with and helpful to her co-wives.

Tahsir continued doing his part by sharing his knowledge with his *murid*s. Every other week one of his *murid*s "graduated as a healer"; the longer they stayed with him, the more powerful healers they became. Praising them, Tahsir emphasized that he did not teach them Islam. He paused after this statement about teaching and restated that he *did not teach*—something he had to emphasize because unofficial religious instruction was prohibited. Rather, Tahsir said, he taught them how to heal. For instance, he taught them which verses from the Qur'an were supposed to be used to heal certain illnesses.[2]

In the previous eight years, the number of Tahsir's patients had not decreased.[3] They continued coming from different parts of Uzbekistan and from other countries, including Russia and Kyrgyzstan. Some of them had psychological illnesses, whereas others had a physical ailment such as diabetes or cancer; yet others were

2. By 2011 in Uzbekistan, even the word *teaching* had become taboo unless qualified by a statement about what kind of knowledge was shared: scientific, culinary, traditional, medicinal, and so forth.

3. Some sources suggest that in 2011 Uzbekistan's health-care system was in no better shape than in the 1990s. In this context, traditional healers had to cater to an increasing number of patients, who preferred the healers to the country's inadequate health-care system (see "Uzbekistan's Health Care Reality" 2011).

partially paralyzed. Tahsir said that the medical doctors could not help the patients who came to him seeking healing; only God could. And he continued doing his part by healing others with God's and jinn's help. Tahsir worked on "the most difficult cases" on Tuesday, Wednesday, and Thursday. Friday was his "day off." On Saturday and Sunday each week, often overnight, he held free healing sessions in the patients' room on his property. "These days the number of people could be anywhere between twenty and fifty," Onahon interjected.

In order to receive treatment and for the healing to work, Tahsir's patients did not need to be Muslim, but they had to recognize the existence of one God. He said that "the main religions and religious books were from God, the One and only." The Qur'an was "the last book," which contained "the program for a good life" that everyone should try to follow. "When the number of unfaithful [people] increases, God brings about calamities; if more people would believe in God, there would be fewer calamities," he concluded.

Because Tahsir believed that jinn play an important role in the healing process, his sessions were often accompanied by animal sacrifice. The "good" and "helpful" jinn "lived" in the middle of his courtyard, in a "deep hole" covered by a piece of plywood. "You eat bread, they eat blood," said Tahsir. The blood of the animals sacrificed over the hole fed these jinn. Upon Tahsir's advice, I gave one of his *murids* seven thousand soms, equivalent to three dollars at the time, to buy a good sacrificial rooster. In fifteen minutes, the blood gushing from the rooster's slashed neck fed the jinn on my own and my son's behalf.

Thinking about reports on religious persecution I had read over the previous eight years, I gathered enough courage to ask Tahsir whether he felt safe in his country. He replied, "I heal people, I have nothing to fear," and added that in the Soviet Union he had been afraid to heal people: "I was waiting for this time. Now we have democracy. I am not a slave. I am free." Further, this "new democratic Uzbekistan" was "becoming better and better," and he could use his healing powers without fear of reprisal. Tahsir finished his statement with a broad smile. I took that as a signal to put away my computer. The part of the interview where I asked questions and wrote down answers was over.

Pointing to my right shoulder, which was always in pain, Tahsir said that my heart caused this pain. He clarified that it was not heart disease, but stress and fear. With a smile, he offered to let me wait for a free healing session. But now he had to return to another healing session that my arrival had interrupted; he had to continue doing his part.

Definitional Freedom

After meeting with Tahsir and on the way to Nainahon's place, I felt increasingly confused about the interview. Nainahon's observation that Tahsir was "really smart" and that "he is covered from all sides" added to this confusion. To my question "What do you mean?" Nainahon replied, "Democracy and all." If I were to take Tahsir's responses to my questions at face value, then Uzbekistan was a democracy where freedom of expression defined the dynamics of people's daily lives, and my preexisting fear and political views precluded me from observing and experiencing this freedom. Or was Tahsir simply disingenuous? In any case, my experiences and biases and his responses required more analysis.

My presence certainly had affected Tahsir's public persona, which, in turn, affected his responses but did not determine them. *He* spoke to me not as a friend or a healer, but as an individual standing for a country, a religious leader representing Uzbekistan. He spoke to *me* not as his friend or a patient or a student, but as a researcher who taught at an American university, informing him of a possible future publication of his responses, potentially making them available to a large international audience. While telling me about his life, Tahsir skillfully authored himself in the context of other narratives about Uzbekistan's foreign and domestic policies, economic development, normative statements about history, and politically correct religious sensibilities. He articulated *his* history as meaningful—as the history of an individual who was not afraid to heal (or to teach others *how to heal*) in a country with a stabilizing economic system, where he was able to make money by healing others and freely practice his religion, Islam, which offered "the program for a good life." He was also able to openly criticize foreign governments for not respecting the "religion and traditions" of others and as a result losing "the world's respect."

In this narrative, Tahsir fashioned Uzbekistan as a democracy protecting individual freedoms, including those of religion, expression, and association. But these freedoms were "definitional" (Rouse 2004, 209); they had limits. Tahsir's account and possibly his experiences were located *within* these limits. He was free to practice Islam and promote it in the ways that did not challenge the existing political regime. He did so by healing in "traditional ways" and by not teaching informally about Islam. He was free to criticize other states, such as the United States, Uzbekistan's former patron, which fell from grace with that government in 2005 after criticizing human rights abuses in Uzbekistan. But Tahsir's criticism of the US invasion of Iraq was also within the established limits. He did not decry the lost lives of other Muslims or innocent civilians. Rather, he was critical of the ways in which the United States disrespected other nations' traditions and these nations' leaders, such as Saddam Hussein, who, according to Tahsir, initially was not a dictator but had become one under US pressure.

Tahsir also had and exercised freedom of association by meeting with *me*, a researcher from an American university who was not a politician, military representative, or subversive reporter. I was an acceptable audience. He talked to me without fear of being disciplined or punished as long as he stayed within the limits, the definitional parameters of these freedoms available to individuals, himself included, in a "democratic" Uzbekistan (for a discussion of controllable democracy in Uzbekistan, see Ilkhamov 2002). He learned about these parameters by interacting with his environment, including Uzbekistan's national television programs, and by listening to existing stories about local political persecution and global stories about "Islamic terrorists."

My own and Tahsir's assessments of democracy in Uzbekistan reflected our definitional understandings of freedom, which differed in the size we assigned to expressive territory. Because my expectations of this territory exceeded his, I traveled into places that were off limits in his definition. As a consequence, our experiences and understanding of democracy in Uzbekistan were different. He may not have experienced the restrictive consequences of criticizing the government of this post-Soviet state. To him, this criticism was unnecessary, but to me it was unavoidable, as were the consequences.

While describing his life to me, Tahsir did not just reiterate the government's views of and models for politically correct citizenship. Not determined but informed by his social environment, his statements about democracy and individual well-being were personal, purposeful, and creative. On the one hand, his "smart" story provided an insight into existing political and historical discourses in contemporary Uzbekistan. On the other hand, his ability to cover—to narrate himself as important and his life as meaningful in a safe and protective way and to choose our conversation's focal points—was a "practice of individuality" (Rapport 2003, 29) exemplified by his creative storytelling and its social effects in the form of this book. His "smart" but covered "from all sides" responses not only reflected history with its existing normative macronarratives and political discourses but also co-created this history.

3

Nonliberatory Discourses on Women's Rights

Proposition: Individuals create liberatory and nonliberatory discourses on rights and duties that lead to social change.

Hovliguzar, Uzbekistan, August 2011

Tursun-oi meets us at the gate. It has been more than a week since her husband passed away. The compound's gate continues to stay open so that people can drop in without prior notice to express their condolences, to help, cry, and empathize with her and the rest of the extended family. This evening Tursun-oi plans to have a special iftor *for her husband's friends.*

When she finishes reminiscing about her husband and how kind he was to her, I, trying to hold back the tears, say, "I am so sorry." I feel like a small child lost in a huge city: I feel it is my fault, but I did not do it on purpose; I did not get lost on purpose. I fail to control my tears. "I am so sorry for everything, please forgive me for the scarf, for your loss, for my short visit, and for not staying to help you to prepare for the iftor*—for everything." Jahon interjects and says that I am also upset because* esenbeshniki *are following me. Tursun-oi responds, "Svetlana, please do not cry. This is Allah's will." Gently touching my shoulders, she tells me that the scarf and I have nothing to do with her husband's death; God does. And she has plenty of help, so there is nothing for me to feel sorry for. But I already do. I already feel sorry for everything, including the first day I decided to do research in the valley.*

I say good-bye. Tursun-oi offers a blessing and a prayer for my son, my parents, and me and for a safe trip back to Russia and to the United States. We hug each other. She hugs me tight, as if I am a part of her family, and I reciprocate.

*Jahon asks Tursun-oi if we can leave through the back gate. Tursun-oi answers, "*Mayla *[very well]." "I will call," I say. "Please do," she replies, wiping her eyes with a corner of her head scarf.*

Jahon and I go through the back gate, but the same white car and the same three men are already waiting for us. Back gate or front gate, we cannot win. We cannot run away. There is nowhere to hide. Why am I so scared? What is the worst thing that can happen to me? I feel stupid, exposed, and guilty. I mention it to Jahon. She tells me not to worry, not to give them the pleasure. She says I need to smile, to stay happy, to show them that I am not afraid. She is not afraid, she says, and smiles.

I wave down a cab to drive me to Rashida's. Standing next to me, after hugging me good-bye, still holding my hand until I get inside the cab, Jahon says, "Women's solidarity! It is going to be all right [vse budet horosho]*!" She smiles again, "Do not worry." The cab driver takes off. The white car follows us.*

I get to Rashida's at about four in the evening. I walk inside the courtyard, close the gate, wait a moment, and peek through the crack in the wooden fence. The white car is parked across the street. I walk into the apartment. A quick hello to Rashida, and I run upstairs.

After a short, cold shower, I put on headphones and play Joby Talbot, String Quartet No. 1, an mp3 file saved on my mobile phone. High-frequency, piercing violin sounds, determined and at times abrasive—the string quartet sounds how I feel. I type up all I remember about meeting my friend at the café and about saying good-bye to Jahon and Tursun-oi. I write about the surveillance and my feelings. I have no time for the details—just words such as guilty, *pregnant with meaning. I send these notes to my online email box. Then I erase the remaining interviews, leaving only my personal audio notes. I can always erase them later. The modem is crappy. But I manage to get two-minutes-at-a-time access to the Internet.*

I know they will come for me. I feel it, yet I still hope that I will be able to leave for Tashkent before they do. I make three phone calls. I call my mother, my friend in the United States, and one of my friends in Tashkent. I tell my mother and my friend in the States that if they do not hear from me in the next day or so, they should get worried and contact both the Russian and the US consulates. Without explaining my reasons, I ask my friend in Tashkent if I can come at night. She responds that at night it is dangerous to drive through the mountain pass separating Tashkent and the valley. She says I should wait until the morning. "Okay, I will wait," I respond. But they do not wait until the next day. They come today.

Nainahon, 2003

In January 2003, I visited Nainahon's unfinished lavish compound. She claimed she spent about one hundred thousand US dollars building it. The compound had separate living quarters for her son's future family, her daughters, her mother-in-law, guests, and herself and her husband; a small swimming pool; internal and external kitchens; and other unfinished amenities that not many people in the valley could afford. One of her daughters met me at the gate and led me inside the house. Nainahon, standing in the middle of a long corridor that doubled as a living room, was talking to someone on her mobile phone. Her son was sitting on a sofa with packs of Uzbek banknotes next to him, amounting to about one hundred dollars. He told me that this was a day's profit from one of their *kalbasa* (sausage) stores.

After going through the greeting niceties, asking each other about each other's health and families, Nainahon and I sat down next to her son, who, she insisted, had to get married. She complained that he spent hours in a local Internet café. "He is shy. Maybe he is looking for a wife on the Internet."

"This is how I live," Nainahon continued, changing the subject and pointing around the house. "*Zor* [great and beautiful]?" she asked. I pointed to the six-foot-tall Ka'ba (the sacred cube-shaped building located in Mecca, Saudi Arabia) painted on one of the walls of the corridor and answered, "This is really *zor*!" She then smiled and said, "Go ahead! Ask me questions." I started with questions about her personal history.

A Businesswoman

From the late 1980s to the early twenty-first century, economic liberalization, coupled with a growing social austerity, necessitated and enabled local women's participation in various small-scale business ventures. Nainahon's life during this period was rocky. Now, in 2003, she was a successful and financially stable businesswoman. But her path to success was a long one.

In 1974, Nainahon entered a polytechnic institute, where she met her future husband. He was her classmate. They fell in love and were married during her third year of studies. For many young adults in the valley, parents selected spouses through their personal networks. Among Soviet educated elite, however, it was not unusual to allow children to choose spouses. Nainahon's parents, Soviet teachers who later became school principals, must have accepted an ideological appreciation of individual decision making and rejected class and status differences, considering that Nainahon's husband came from a "poor family."

In Soviet Central Asia, motherhood was still glorified as the most important manifestation of local women's humanhood. Ten months after the wedding, Nainahon gave birth to a son. Becoming a mother, Nainahon said, made her feel "very happy." A year later the family welcomed a daughter.

During the 1980s, the Soviet Union went through a rapid economic decline. The expanding informal economy developed in response to the weakening of the formal economy (see Sahadeo 2011). At that time, Nainahon's new family, with two young children, "was poor." She, a recent university graduate, started teaching at a professional technical college. But the teaching job did not pay well, and she "had to do something else." She turned to her mother-in-law, a seamstress, who in the 1980s had started a small-scale coat-making business.

Since making coats was more profitable than teaching, Nainahon joined her mother-in-law's enterprise.

Traveling abroad became easier after the Soviet Union's disintegration. In the early 1990s, after Nainahon gave birth to her fourth child, she expanded her mother-in-law's business by traveling abroad and acquiring "fancy" fabrics for coats. While Nainahon was traveling, her mother-in-law cared for her children.

Nainahon went to Turkey first and then to Poland. The coats made out of the "fancy" fabrics she acquired in these places sold really well at local bazaars in the valley. Nainahon's husband accompanied her on these trips for physical and moral support, while she did "all the business."

Nainahon and her husband eventually became informal "tourist agents." Being familiar with the process of and potential problems with traveling abroad, they took groups of local traders to Poland to buy goods to resell at local bazaars in the valley. Nainahon claimed that the traders made more than 500 percent of their state-paid monthly salaries. Soon she and her husband led separate groups of traders. In this capacity, she traveled to China and then to India, Egypt, and Cyprus.

In the early 1990s, an unstable economic climate in post-Soviet Uzbekistan sustained women's participation in the labor market. In this context, despite the gendered social expectations, reinforced by a national ideology, that men not women should be the main, if not the sole, providers for their families, local women continued looking for income not only in Uzbekistan, but also abroad. In 1994, Nainahon and her husband went to Moscow, where they made and sold baked goods. They invested the money made in Moscow in coat-production operations in both Hovliguzar and Moscow. This investment proved to be profitable. They made one hundred thousand dollars in one year and used this money to build a large new house in Hovliguzar.

Nainahon had to "start from zero" several times. Growing corruption at Tashkent's Customs Office and the new customs laws caused her to "lose money." In the early 1990s, in order to avoid paying high import taxes, she bribed customs officers or paid small fines when returning from her trips with fabrics and other goods. In 1997, however, she was fined about thirty thousand dollars, and all of her goods were confiscated at a Customs Office in Tashkent. After this devastating fine, Nainahon did everything and anything, including selling dresses and cows. But she did not give up. Three years later she started a profitable new business selling sausage produced in Moscow and Tashkent.

Nainahon used to travel twice a week to Moscow to assure that the sausage was delivered on time. She was her own accountant and made sure that the business was profitable. The sausage business slowly took off, but Nainahon was not satisfied. In 2003, despite making "good money," she still wanted to be "up there with those who have a lot of money." Despite "the barriers" created by others, she said, she "could not sit still."

A Sacred Dream

Business was one area where Nainahon excelled; religion was another. Although she came from "a Communist family," she had had a desire to learn about Islam since childhood. She remembered her mother saying, "There is God." One day Nainahon's mother gave her a piece of paper with *ayat*s (verses) from the Qur'an written on it. She instructed Nainahon to learn them by heart, warned her not to show the paper to anyone, and told her to use these verses to "talk to God" and to pray to God in her mind, "not out loud." Nainahon began praying regularly several years into her marriage after she had a dream that increased her faith in God and interest in Islam. After that point, she worked on reorienting her life toward Islam, on becoming "truly" Muslim.

In 1981, Nainahon had a special "sacred dream." In this dream, she was walking the streets of Mecca in Saudi Arabia when she saw a tall ladder piercing the sky. "Each step of the ladder had *ayat*s written on it." Despite wanting to climb the ladder, she did not want to step on the sacred *ayat*s. Then angels appeared. Pleased with her reverence for the holy words, they gave Nainahon a book. The book was the Qur'an.

Dreams "are borderlands between the manifest and the hidden dimensions of reality . . . between the here and now and the various imaginary horizons toward which people orient themselves" (Louw 2010, 280, citation omitted). They have potential emotive motivational impacts on individual decision making (Lyon 2010, 265). Nainahon's sacred dream motivated her "to learn more about Islam"; she "had to find a knowledgeable *otincha*." These teachers were not easy to find because in the Soviet Union "the KGB was hunting them down."

A Devout Muslim

While still teaching at a local college, Nainahon noticed a woman who "was reading a book." She told Nainahon that the book was the Qur'an and that she was an *otincha*. This *otincha* asked Nainahon not to tell anyone. In return, she agreed to teach Nainahon Qur'anic Arabic, a letter a day, and proper corporal movements to perform ritual prayers. Although busy with her many responsibilities, Nainahon studied the Arabic alphabet just before going to bed, "taking small steps." She also started praying daily.

Although meeting the *otincha* was significant for Nainahon, she did not describe herself as someone who was a sinner before but saved now. Hers was not a story of conversion, but of transformation—a gradual self-formation into a better, more Muslim human (on Muslims' conversion stories, see Hafez 2011). Nainahon continued making mistakes, mainly unintentionally. Her increased knowledge of Islam helped her to "recognize these mistakes" and to be able to correct and "not repeat them."

According to Nainahon, God's love is in direct correlation to human love: "the more you believe and love God—God loves you more." In 2003, she was certain that God's love toward her was expressed through her children's health, the family's new house, her still-living mother, a good mother-in-law—in short, in "everything."

God even gave her "big dollars." She thanked God for all these gifts and attributed her fortune to regular prayers and religious education.

Although God was the one who gave her everything, Nainahon had to "stand up and make at least one step toward [her] goals." "If you do nothing, you will not get anything." By actively moving toward achieving her financial and spiritual goals, Nainahon did her part in getting her "everything" from God.

Religious Sensibilities and Pragmatic Choices

On her path to becoming a better Muslim, Nainahon decided to perform the hajj. She wanted "to see that holy place [Mecca]," and her mother-in-law had been "dreaming about it all her life." Nainahon did not discuss with me her husband's reasons for going on pilgrimage. Whatever they were, he had to accompany them on the journey because, according to Nainahon, women could not "travel there by themselves."

After Uzbekistan's independence from the Soviet Union in 1991, apolitical and spiritually oriented "national Islam" became the most important among the country's national traditions. The government, as a "de facto theologian," authorized selected stories about history and certain Islamic sensibilities and behaviors (Mahmood 2006, 327). The country's "Golden Heritage" now included famous Muslim theologians, philosophers, and spiritual leaders, such as Imam al-Bukhari, Ahmed Yassawi, Baha al-Din Naqshband, as well as such religious practices as the hajj (for this recovery of national heritage, see Adams 2010; Louw 2007; Rasanayagam 2010, 245). The pilgrimage animated and encouraged individual piety and communal solidarity among Uzbekistan's Muslims as well as between them and other Muslims throughout the world. Therefore, the government's support and promotion of the hajj, Nainahon's growing knowledge about Islam, and a desire to become a better Muslim contributed to her decision to perform the pilgrimage.

In the 1990s, the easing of restrictions on international travel allowed more citizens of Uzbekistan to travel to Saudi Arabia. Yet the increased cross-border mobility did not decrease the state's control over the traveling that its citizens did do. Administrative institutions monitored by the state, such as local *mahalla* committees, closely controlled the pilgrimage. To get permission to travel to Mecca, individuals were required to join long waiting lists. The pilgrimage trip itself required at least one thousand dollars per person. On five occasions, I was told that bribery was not unusual in securing space in an annual group of pilgrims; long waiting lists facilitated economic corruption. In this context, most individuals who could afford to perform the hajj were relatively wealthy.

Nainahon knew that theologically an individual should perform the pilgrimage with *halal* (pure) money and intentions; doing otherwise would invalidate the hajj. The money she used for the trip to Mecca, she said, might not have been "pure" because she had bribed government officials to get her goods through customs. This doubt, however, did not prevent her from going on the pilgrimage. She said that God was well aware that she didn't have much choice in the context of systemic corruption, where making "pure money" was very difficult. In 1997, Nainahon, her husband, and her mother-in-law avoided the waiting list and traveled to Mecca by going through Kyrgyzstan; this option was also less expensive.

The pilgrimage "purified [her] soul" and desires and endowed her with "holiness." Upon her return from the hajj, she began wearing a *hijab*, a large scarf covering her hair, shoulders, and neck, leaving only her face exposed. She also wore long ankle-covering monocolor dresses and, when appropriate, a robe on top of the dress. Through her modest dress, she wanted to show others her "ever-growing love and respect toward God" and her status as a *hoja* (a person who had performed the hajj).

The changes in Nainahon's appearance were not only symbolic, but also relational, made with the recognition that she had to consider other people's desires and feelings. For instance, her husband did not approve of her wearing the *hijab* after the hajj and told her not to dress so conservatively. By that time, sartorial practices were already politicized in Uzbekistan. Some of them, understood as nontraditional expressions of piety, were defined as appropriate only for official religious leaders and prohibited for the general public by state law in 1998. It is possible that Nainahon's husband was concerned that her *hijab* would be perceived as a marker of political identity in opposition to the state's traditionalizing discourse on Islam. According to Nainahon, he "simply" wanted her "to look modern." In response to his request, she decided to "loosen up a bit," to look modest yet "fashionable and modern," and so started wearing smaller scarves and dresses that would show a small amount of cleavage.

Nainahon felt conflicted. As a *hoja*, she was expected to abandon self-interest and transcend attachment to material possessions. Yet she still wanted to be "up there with those who have a lot of money," if not for herself, then for her children. She also wanted to devote all her time to prayers and religious education but was unwilling to give up her career as a businesswoman. Further, she felt ambivalent about performing the "man's job" of providing for the family. Yet her husband, she said unequivocally, "could not do it [alone]."

Islam is not "a grand scheme" that explains all choices and actions made by individual Muslims (see Metcalf 2009; Schielke 2010, 1). "The existential and pragmatic sensibilities of living a life in a complex and often troubling world" often trample on other individual needs and wants (Schielke 2010, 1). Nainahon's attempts to reorient her life toward becoming a better Muslim had to be reconciled with the compromises she had to make in moving through her daily life. She used not only exegesis but also and more importantly common sense and pragmatism to resolve her ambivalence about her role as a provider and her occasional unethical behavior (for more on these approaches, see Rouse 2004). Since she and her children needed money, and her husband, as she said, could not provide for them to the extent that she could, and since she had to make a living in a context of existing bureaucracy and corruption, her doing the "man's job" and occasional unethical behavior were justified, if not necessitated. Theologically, in her view, a merciful and omniscient God created and was aware of daily constraints in her surrounding environment. As a fallible human, she was able to overcome some of them, but not others. While transporting sausage to Hovliguzar, she continued bribing customs and traffic police officers. Although bribery was a sin, she said she sinned *because of* living in a morally corrupt society and not just *in order to* further her personal and professional goals (on "in order to" motives, see Rapport 2003, 52).

After completing the hajj, Nainahon continued her religious education with "a new teacher." In the late 1990s, her friend Zulfia introduced her to a local woman who belonged to a "*turamlar*" family, whose members claimed to be descendants of the Prophet Muhammad. This new teacher, Ova, was "so good"; she made Nainahon "feel the *nur* inside," which "cleansed [her] soul." Onahon, a daughter-in-law of Nainahon's teacher, became Nainahon's best friend, and the teacher's son, Tahsir, instructed Nainahon how to heal human maladies.

Nainahon heard that this teacher's "great-grandfather, a very powerful *domla* [male religious practitioner or mullah]," helped to build the "foundations of Islam in Hovliguzar."[1] He was also a *pir* (spiritual leader) and could perform *karamat* (miracles). His male and female descendants allegedly possessed *barakat*. They were also very knowledgeable, "like the university professors," except they held weekly lessons about Islam not at official educational centers such as universities, but at local individuals' homes.

There were "all kinds of Muslims in Uzbekistan," said Nainahon. Some claimed to be related to the Prophet Muhammad but had no religious knowledge; others were "liars, crooks," unable to recite the Qur'an, yet others "stole from people," thinking "only about how to fill their pockets." The problem, in Nainahon's view, was twofold. First, they lacked a proper Islamic education, and, second, economic corruption prevented them from living Islamically. Like her, in order to have a fulfilling life beyond survival, they occasionally sinned.

1. In terms of kinship, this individual was probably further removed from the family I am referring to than this word implies.

In Uzbekistan, growing conspicuous consumption and sorting between authentic and inauthentic religious expressions made religious knowledge—as much as veils, *tasbih* (prayer beads), computer programs offering Qur'anic studies and recitation, and copies of the Qur'an (skillfully engraved, leather bound, or lettered in gold)—a commodity. In this context, in Nainahon's view some *otinchalar* were "*bisnesmenshi* [businesswomen]"; they "traded Islam [like other goods]." Nainahon, however, chose to focus on getting into paradise in the next life, not on other people's sins in this one. While tolerating the sins of others, she tried to curtail her own when possible.

An Otincha for Her Family

Nainahon defined "a real *otincha*" as a "pure woman" who has religious knowledge and is "exceptionally kind to and respectful of" her family and everyone else. An *otincha* is a role model who remains a student of Islam all of her life: "Islam is *nauka* [science], and no one can ever master it all. No one can say, 'I have finished [learning Islam].' Islam is infinite because knowledge is infinite." Nainahon did not want to be the kind of *otincha* who led religious ceremonies, recited the Qur'an, and received gratuities for doing so. She made enough money through her business. She did not want to teach others, either, as Tursun-oi did. She wanted to know more about Islam in order to live and teach her family how to live Islamically.

First, Nainahon acquired what she considered to be sufficient knowledge about Islam. This knowledge, she believed, enabled her to behave as a "true Muslim"—to be kind, caring, ritually observant, respectful, and modest. Second, she started teaching her children about Islam: "If you are a good Muslim but do not teach your children Islam, when you die, your children will be running after you and asking, 'Why do you want to go to heaven by yourself? Why do you not take us with you? Why did you not teach us [Islam]?' [They will not be able to enter paradise.]"

Nainahon taught her children how to distinguish between "bad and good," between "black and white." She eliminated "drinking [inside her house] and *discoteki* [dance parties organized outside the house]." By 2003, two of her four daughters were regularly performing ritual prayers. He son "beautifully" recited some parts of the Qur'an but did not attend the mosque or pray regularly. She knew that "he will, in his time." Her grandchildren, too, were learning ritual prayers while observing others performing these in the house. To demonstrate this, Nainahon called on one of her granddaughters. The two-year-old girl ran up to us, got on her grandmother's lap, and said, "*La ilaha illa Allah.*"

Third, Nainahon wanted to change her husband. Although he was a *hoja*, he was still drinking outside the house on occasion. Nainahon said that he did not know much about Islam and had difficulty differentiating between "good and bad." She shared with him stories about the Prophet and his Companions and about the Prophet's behavior toward his family, and she reminded him about the Islamic prohibition on alcohol consumption. As a result, according to Nainahon, "his eyes" were "slowly opening." He had quit drinking in 2002, six months before our first meeting.

Nainahon noticed that since she was learning more about Islam, particularly between 1999 and 2003, her neighbors showed her more respect. The women attending *meropriyatiya*, such as a *toy* (wedding) that she was a part of, "respected" and "loved" her because she "loved God" and "knew more about Islam than they did." Even after Nainahon moved to her new home in a "new *mahalla*" in 2002, neighbors from her "old *mahalla*" came to visit and invited her to various social events.

I asked Nainahon if individual religious devotion was a post-Soviet phenomenon. She responded that there had been plenty of Muslims who prayed regularly in the Soviet Union. "Simple people," she said, "never judged or persecuted these Muslims." Only "the KGB and the Communists in high places" criticized religion. These Communists gave orders "to destroy some of the sacred places" and "punish those who loved Islam." But even some of these Communists "in high places," Nainahon believed, used to pray in private, "secretly." After Uzbekistan's independence, "the same Communists" who derided religion became "very religious."

According to Nainahon, after the *Mustakilliq*, everyone was free to pray, to study Islam, and to teach others. However, you had to learn and teach the "correct" not "Wahhabist" Islam. She added that in order to "get rid of bad Muslims" and stop the spread of "Wahhabist teachings," the government closed some of the religious centers and mosques and authorized "*chistki* [purges]" among local Muslims. But the "correct" Islam continued to "spread." In 2003, Nainahon was hoping that "terrorism wouldn't mess up Islam" in Uzbekistan and the world.

"Women Are Women"

Nainahon said that she was curious to hear the Friday sermons (*khutba*) in person during *Jumma* congregational prayers, but in Hovliguzar only men went to the mosques. "This is our tradition." According to Nainahon, this tradition made sense. In Uzbekistan, unlike "other countries" such as Russia, mosques did not have a separate space for women. In her experience, it was only during the hajj in Mecca that women and men prayed together in the same space. Although while there in Mecca, "at the most important Mosque," she prayed along with both women and men, in the valley she followed "our tradition"; she prayed with other women "during *meropriyatiya*" officiated by *otinchalar* and during weekly lessons with Tahsir's mother or his sister, but "never" at the mosque.

During one ceremony exclusively for women in 2002, I asked the participants if they wanted to attend congregational prayers at local mosques. Among thirty-eight women, ten said that if their mosques had separate places for women, they would like to attend the *Jumma* prayers. Three women argued that the Hanafi *mashab*, the theological interpretation of Islamic principles predominant in Uzbekistan, prohibited women from going to the mosque. (The Hanafi *mashab* is among four interpretive positions or schools of jurisprudence that historically characterize Sunni Islam, following the Prophet Muhammad's tradition; the other three are the Maliki, Shafi'i, and Hanbali. Carrying the names of their founders, these interpretive positions differ in understanding Islamic principles inferred from the primary texts of the Qur'an and sunna, or the Prophet's tradition.) An *otincha* officiating at that ceremony and one of her friends corrected the women regarding the Hanafi *mashab*; according to them, the Hanafi *mashab* did not prohibit but "released women" from attending mosques on Fridays.

Whether theologically justified or not, the fact that local women did not attend mosques made sense to Nainahon because "women are women"; they have different thoughts, feelings, and desires from men. According to her, God made a woman from Adam's rib (on this belief, see Stowasser 1994). Although a woman was part of a man, she was also very different from him. She had a different "nature." As a result, for women, it is difficult to focus on God during the *Jumma* prayer but "natural" to focus on the material world, thinking about "the price of this dress or this set of gold earrings."

Nainahon asked me if I could imagine "six or seven women going to the mosque on Friday." She answered this rhetorical question by saying, "They would be chatting all the way to the mosque and not focusing on God." Inside the mosque, she added, "women's eyes would be always looking where they are not supposed to look," and their minds "would be distracted from [focusing on] Allah." If a "true Muslim" decided to go to the mosque, she had to "prepare" herself for it, to act against her "nature," which was not easy. God made women to "love things," such as clothes or jewelry, and prohibited men from wanting such things. Men were "made to focus on God." This was not their choice, but "God's will."

During her travels, Nainahon also observed that in the countries where women are allowed to attend mosques, they often wear colorless or black dresses and overcoats and cover their heads and sometimes faces; "there is nothing for other women and men to see" and they will not be "distracted" from focusing on God. In Uzbekistan, according to her, women "traditionally" dressed in bright clothes and showed off their shiny jewelry. She noticed that during *meropriyatiya* and the lessons she attended, while some women were reading the Qur'an and praying, others were gossiping about other attendees and discussing the latest fashions. They were distracted because "women are women." The same thing would happen at the mosque. This was the reason why, in her opinion, women were advised to pray to God at home, focusing on God and on no one and nothing else.

"Ehson *Is Like a Mosque*"

Although recognizing that women are better off praying individually, similar to Tursun-oi, Nainahon considered *ehson*s to be equivalent to the Friday prayers at the mosques for two reasons (see chapter 1). First, these ceremonial gatherings and feasts, held to express one's gratitude to God and make special requests, were, like the men's gatherings at the mosques on Fridays, meritorious acts. By holding an *ehson* and providing food and goods for others, the hostess honored God. In return, God could financially reward the hostess or grant her wishes.

Second, these feasts included processual components similar to those in the Friday prayers at the mosques. During these ceremonial events, *otinchalar* recited the Qur'an or the stories about *ashir* (commemoration of the Battle of Karbala, in which the Prophet's grandson Hussein was killed) or *mavlud* (the Prophet Muhammad's birthday celebration). Then these women "told *masala*s and sang *hikmatlar* praising God or the Prophet or local saints." These stories and hymns "touched women's souls" and "opened their hearts to receive God." In Nainahon's view, women were emotional beings. They, unlike men, became more open to God "not through the mind," but "through the heart, through feelings." Because *masala*s and *hikmatlar* were not a part of the ritual at the mosques, women's "hearts would be closed to God" there.

Finally, like the men's congregational prayers at the mosques, women's voices united in praying and reciting the sacred words of the

Qur'an generated the divine light, which carried a promise of personal and social change and turned their homes into sacred places. In such places, Nainahon noted, anything could happen. As a result, women could ask God to grant their wishes either directly or indirectly through a mediator, such as an *otincha*. Therefore, Nainahon concluded, if the goal of going to the mosque is "to remind you of God's presence in your life and to communicate with God," then, "*ehson* is like a mosque," meaning that *meropriyatiya* such as *ehson* led by *otinchalar* are equivalent to mosque attendance.

In order to qualify as a meritorious act, according to Nainahon, each *ehson* has to be carried out with proper intentions and according to individual means. Instead of focusing on celebrating God, some women, by spending "more money on God than others" and, as a result, offering more food of better quality and variety, use such ceremonial feasts to show off their wealth. This is a sin. It is also "a sin" to hold an *ehson* expecting God to multiply the money spent on its preparation.

Although Nainahon never visited local mosques for *Jumma* prayers, after the *Mustakilliq* she, "like many other women," often attended and hosted various social events such as *ehson* or *gap* (rotating meetings in one's social network) (for more on such networks and ceremonies, see Kandiyoti 1998; Kandiyoti and Azimova 2004).[2] She heard that official religious leaders in Tashkent and locally were critical of women's frequent social gatherings. She also heard that during one *Jumma* prayer in Hovliguzar, the imam advised local men to limit their wives' attendance at such social events; "he said that women should stay at home and pray." Despite this stricture, in Nainahon's view and experiences "the women more often than the men go to and hold *meropriyatiya* because our life has changed." Because "almost all" local women were engaged in some form of business or trade and were making "their own money," in some cases even more

2. A *gap* gathering is a festive occasion where the attendees contribute money to a host's or hostess's project.

than their husbands, "many women" could sponsor social events without their husbands' help. Whether official religious leaders felt unhappy about it or not, "this is how we live now!"

Existential Vulnerability and Allah

Nainahon felt existential vulnerability on many levels. As a businesswoman, she was vulnerable to the state's laws, government officials' corruption, and growing competition (on globalization and growing competition, see Adams 2002). In addition to her friends' changing loyalties and her aging physical body, the possibility of a civil war or a terrorist attack, as in Afghanistan and Tajikistan, she said, contributed to her vulnerability as well (for more on "precarious life," see Butler 2004; Lear 2006). According to her, the only shield against existential vulnerability was her faith in God, who never left her and was always with her. When she needed God's help, she prayed particularly rigorously.

This existential vulnerability extended to Nainahon's personal life. In 2003, she did not feel as happy as she would like; she had "99 [percent] and missed one [percent]." The one percent she missed was her husband's fidelity. As a "proud woman," she offered her husband a divorce, which he rejected. She was "very beautiful, faithful, a true believer, and well educated"; despite his infidelities, he could not cope with losing her. Being worried that he would "commit suicide" if she were to divorce him and meet another man, she decided not to pursue the divorce. Nainahon concluded that as "a true Muslim," she had to be patient: "This is my life. I could be poor and sell sunflowers—but I love my life. We fight because I still love him!" Everything—the law, her friends, her children, her business, her body, and her husband—could fail Nainahon, but not God. As a result, even though she felt vulnerable, she never felt helpless and stayed optimistic about the future (on vulnerability and helplessness, see Cavarero 2007, 30–32).

Nainahon's story about her life revolved around two topics—business ventures and faith in God. This story was built on the compromises and pragmatic choices she made in relation to her immediate environment in order to achieve her goals. In the future, she saw herself becoming a very successful businesswoman, having lavish marriage ceremonies for her son and daughters, buying "a good foreign car," and traveling with her husband "all over the world." Because sons were traditionally expected to care for their elderly parents, she also expected her son to take over the sausage business and eventually to support her and her husband financially. Finally, she wanted to go to Mecca "six more times" and "die there when she was one hundred years old." "If you are buried there, the angels will take you to face God's judgment the same day." Then she could be in paradise or face hell fire. Nainahon did not want to go to hell. She said that she had sinned more in the past and was trying to live like "a true Muslim" now. She believed that God would grant her wishes because God had done so before by helping her to succeed so far. She took a pause long enough for me to finish writing down her words and said, "This is how it is. Now ask me more questions!"

Jahon, 2003

Jahon graduated from a technical institute in the early 1980s and worked for several years as an engineer. After her third child was born, she quit her job and became a stay-at-home mother and later an *otincha*. Unlike some local *otinchalar*, Jahon did not receive religious instruction or the status of an *otincha* from her relatives, but from Tursun-oi, whose knowledge of Islam was not hereditary either (on the importance of descent for becoming a religious teacher, see Fathi 1997). In 2002, Jahon had been studying with Tursun-oi for almost five years, who described Jahon as a "famous *otincha*."

During our first interview, Jahon chuckled and said that because she was mostly unknown, she led "a simple life [financially]." Other "known *otinchalar*" were "wealthy." They were invited to people's homes more often and were paid handsome gratuities. In order to become "known," she was rigorous in her studies of Islam so that in the future she would be "wealthy too." "*Insha'Allah* [God willing],"

I responded. "You will see; if there is a competition among *otinchalar*, I will win!" Jahon made the animated promise by nodding her head, raising her eyebrows, and giving me a coy smile.

Jahon's Dream

Jahon always knew that she was special. One night, like Tursun-oi and Nainahon, she had a special dream. She dreamed about talking to Imam al-Bukhari. Anxious to find out why this famous theologian and holy man had appeared in her dream, she consulted with Ruhshonoz, the same seer who, through the interpretation of Tursun-oi's special dream, established Tursun-oi's connection to Sheikh Naqshband.

Ruhshonoz told Jahon that it was a sign from the imam; he chose Jahon as his disciple. She and al-Bukhari were now "connected with a special thread." Since that time, in order to help her make Islamic knowledge relevant to daily life and comprehensible to others through didactic storytelling, "the imam's spirit" put her "words together" while she told *masala*s. For instance, the imam's spirit helped her to explain why truly Muslim people have a special light emanating from their faces, "just like the halos you see on Christian icons of Mary and Jesus." According to Jahon, because these people have lived like "true" Muslims and have "pure" souls, they have received the *nur* as a gift from God. "This [divine] light came from Allah into their pure souls" and "like a blood stream" spread across their whole bodies, affecting their faces, postures, voices, and actions; this light makes them glow.

"The Lady Solver of Difficulties"

Although Jahon referred to herself as an "unknown *otincha*," I attended at least ten different ceremonies that she facilitated, and I missed many more. One chilly January morning in 2003, Jahon and I walked up the stairs of a panel block apartment building in Hovliguzar. We entered an apartment on the third floor. In its tiny hallway, several women greeted us and offered us water for a hand-washing ceremony, in which water is poured over your hands three times, and then you dry them with a towel. We took off our shoes and walked into the living room. A lavish *dasturkhon* (meal) was set on the table in the middle of the room. The room was small and could barely fit twelve women sitting on the chairs around the table. Awkwardly, after accidentally knocking down a bottle of Coca-Cola, I greeted each one of them by touching their arms above the elbows.

These women gathered on Tuesday to participate in a propitiatory ritual Bibi Mushkil Kusho, the Lady Solver of Difficulties, named after a popular female saint, a mediator between human and divine worlds who solves problems and bestows blessings on her devotees.[3] This ritual was expected to assure the hostess's husband's and her friends' successful trips to Russia—"to open up" their "road."

First, the hostesses asked Jahon to lead another propitiatory ritual aimed at receiving blessings from another female mediator, Bibi Seshambe, the Lady Tuesday, among the older women occupying an adjacent room. The legend about this saint, similar to Cinderella's story, features an older woman who helps to assure a young woman's happiness.[4] Because young and pregnant women were not supposed to be present during that ceremony, I could not join Jahon.

The women who remained and I exchanged stories about our daily lives in the valley and in the United States, respectively. These women, except for the two women leaving to trade goods in Russia, worked at local kindergartens. They complained about small salaries and a lack of electricity. The women who worked in Russia recounted difficulties traveling and finding affordable lodging. But all of them seemed to be optimistic about the future, when their salaries would be comparable to the ones in Russia and the United States, and when local women and men would no longer have to leave their

3. In one of the versions of the legend's narrative, as an example of her power, Bibi Mushkil Kusho helps an old poor man, Chol, to deal with his daily troubles.

4. For one version of the story about this saint, see Fitz Gibbon 2005.

families and embark on long-term trips to Russia in search of a sufficient income.

When Jahon came back, she turned the conversation to Islam and children. She said the Qur'an required parents to be active in their children's upbringing. Parents who lead Islamic lives but fail to teach their children Islamic behavior will face hell fire. The women agreed with her. Then Jahon reminded the women that in Uzbekistan the year 2003 was "the Year of the *Mahalla*." The president called on citizens to clean their *mahalla*s, neighborhoods, but Jahon said that all citizens should not only clean the streets in their neighborhoods but also purify their souls. Showing each other support, giving advice, helping financially were some of the ways to do this. "Such actions," Jahon noted, should stem from "pure desires," such as "love of God" and "God's creation."

In order to "prepare the women" for the main part of the *ehson*, Jahon always, not only on this occasion, told several *masala*s. This day, her stories were related to the women's work and their relationships with children at local kindergartens. Because teaching Islam to minors was prohibited, she pointed out subtly, without saying it directly, that our cultivation of good manners is a form of Islamic education through the *masala*, starting with a reference to "the Christian tradition of praying before a meal."

According to Jahon, Muslims need to learn from Christians to pray before every meal and cultivate this practice among their children. She said, "We know that everything is from God; that food is from God." Elevating her hands, palms facing her chest, she continued, "In Islam, unlike Christians, we should raise our hands. But this does not count if we do not fill our hearts with prayer, thanking God for food and a good day. The prayer and words should come from the heart. The hands should be raised by the heart's desire. If we begin our morning by raising our hands and our hearts in prayer, our whole day too would be wonderful." Later, on the way home, Jahon told me that she hoped these women would remember her *masala*: "[I] ask them to please think about what I have said; 'Maybe later, maybe tomorrow, but please think about it.' I am sure it comes back to people."

Jahon commenced the next part of the *ehson* through the prayer seeking forgiveness from Allah (*astaghfirullah*). Then she recited six fundamental theological principles of Islam (*kalima*s) followed by the verses from the Qur'anic sura al-Fatiha (the Opening) and parts of the sura al-Baqara (the Cow). The next part of the ceremony involved performing the propitiatory ritual Bibi Mushkil Kusho. Jahon whispered in my ear that "they," the women, had asked her to lead the "Mushkil Kusho" ritual; otherwise she would have read and explained more from the Qur'an.

For this final part of the ceremony, the hostess brought in *issiriq* (a bitter herb), honey, salt, bread, water, candles, raisins, rough cotton, flat bread, and a special sweet dish prepared for this occasion. These objects and the food on the table would be blessed during the ceremony. Jahon burned the *issiriq*; its smoke purified the place, and she read from her notebook the story of Bibi Mushkil Kusho. Meanwhile, each woman tore off the stems of the dried grapes and rolled them into cotton balls, as the saint has instructed in the story. To solicit Bibi Mushkil Kusho's favor, after the ceremony the women would throw these cotton balls into the *ariq*, a stream at the side of the road. These were appropriate actions demonstrating the women's remembrance of and respect for this female saint. Jahon finished the ceremony by reciting the Qur'anic sura Ya'seen (titled for the two Arabic letters *ya* and *seen*).

After the recitation, the hostess's husband came into the room and asked Jahon for a blessing. She read a *duo* (supplication) for him and then for everyone present at the ceremony; she also read a longer *duo* for the two women traveling to Russia. Each woman gave Jahon some money. Later she explained that however small the amount someone gives, something should be given because "in Islam we should not be in debt to any person. I prayed for them. They thanked me for it. Thus, we are even. They do not owe me anything in the eyes of God and in their hearts."

Before we left, I asked the women about relationships between female and male religious teachers and leaders. Mahisha, one of the women, replied, "Sometimes a *domla* [male religious practitioner, a mullah] gives advice to an *otincha*. Other times an *otincha* knows more than a *domla*. We go to an *otincha* if there are issues between a husband and wife, such as *talaq* [divorce], or if somebody is sick in the family. A *domla* usually has no time for [these things]. *Otinchalar* have time. An imam [here used synonymously with *domla*] usually decides big problems, an *otincha* small problems."

Jahon added to Mahisha's statement, "We are women, and we are lower than men; we can give advice to our men, not make decisions." This statement reminded me of another conversation Jahon and I had at the end of 2002. While discussing local generational and gendered hierarchy, she recalled watching "a Christian film about Genesis," which explained how and why God created humans and why Oto ("Father," here Adam) and Havo (Eve) fell from grace.

"According to Christians," Jahon said, "Genesis explains the first sin." In her view, it explained "why we [women and men] are unequal"; although God punished Havo for sinning and leading Oto into sin, this story was not just about disobedience and punishment but explained ontological differences between men and women. When the first humans were in paradise and a snake brought "the apple of *illim* [knowledge]," by eating the forbidden fruit of knowledge both the woman and the man sinned. "But," Jahon added, "she [Havo] took the *illim* first; then she gave it to Adam." Tasting this apple, according to Jahon, "cleared Havo's mind." As a result, Havo, "before Adam," realized that "she was naked and covered up." The knowledge of the difference between right and wrong helped Havo to make the first moral decision ever—to cover up her nakedness. This film demonstrated, reasoned Jahon, that every human had both Havo and Oto: "Oto is the flesh, and Havo is the soul and mind." They are not equal, but different and equally important. Havo is "cleaner [more morally pure] than Adam" and smarter, but he is stronger than her. Hence, "men should respect women, and," Jahon added, "women should stay women and respect their husbands." "But," she concluded, "in this world, women have no respect."

Nainahon's Solutions to Women's Problems, 2003

Nainahon went to the kitchen to perform a *magreb* (sunset) prayer. Her younger daughter and the daughter's college friend, Saluba, had already finished their prayers and retired to the daughter's room. According to Nainahon, Saluba was a "true Muslim girl"; she wore *hijab*, but her daughter was "not ready" for it. I heard music playing in Nainahon's younger daughter's room and went into the room uninvited. Soon they and I were dancing, waving our hands in the air.

After her prayer, Nainahon joined us. She took off her scarf, shook her short thick red hair, and said, "Girls, put on an English song!" I stepped aside, making space for Nainahon. First, her hands went up in the air, while her feet half-stepped left to right and right to left. But then she moved her feet apart, shoulder width, squatted, and positioned her arms at her sides, bending them slightly at the elbows, as if rotating them at the joint. Lifting her right leg for styling in sync with the music, she twisted at the waist from right to left like a pro. She pulled in her daughter, then Saluba. They formed a circle and, one by one, danced inside it, waving their hands and moving their palms in a fanlike fashion while twisting at the waist. Laughing and clapping, trying to be louder than "the English song," Nainahon yelled, "We know modern movements too, not only our Uzbek national dance!" She pulled me in, pushed me in the middle of the circle and commanded, "Teach us some traditional movements from the Caucasus!" I did, making them up as I went along.

When the song ended, Nainahon bowed down to the girls and then to me and said, "*Rahmat* [thank you]." She raised her hands, palms facing her chest, and said a *duo*, in which she wished her daughter, Saluba, and me good husbands, many children, success in our studies, and good jobs. Nainahon's wishes for our future were pragmatic and commonsensical. In her view, marriage and children are biologically natural and decreed by God. Ideally, she would like us to marry men who would provide for the family without our help, so we could focus on educating our children and taking care of the family's daily needs. From her experiences, though, she knew that the global economic context could turn ideals on their head. In order to be safe, we had to be prepared to join the labor market. This required education, which was not only necessary to be a good mother, but critical for getting a job. In Nainahon's contemporary society, education mattered more than in the Soviet Union because finding a (good) job was no longer easy in Uzbekistan, and daily life was exponentially more expensive.

After the *duo*, Nainahon volunteered to share her opinion about the problems facing Uzbek women and to offer solutions to these challenges. The first problem was a false opposition between piety and fashion, where some women were "ignorant" about religion and fashion, others about fashion, yet others about religion. Some women were too conservative in dress and overly religious, and others were too modern and did not "really" believe in God. In her view, women had to be "modern and have faith in God, live their lives Islamically, and be well-dressed—necessarily both!" A balance between religion and fashion was very important and "natural," but extremes were unacceptable and "unnatural."

The second problem was wage labor. According to Nainahon, the family's material provisioning and financial stability were men's natural and Islamic responsibilities. "In Uzbekistan," she said, "too many children are on the streets without proper upbringing and childhood, while their mothers are at the bazaars, [selling goods and] trying to make money." This was "wrong." Instead of focusing on making money, women should care for their children, husbands, in-laws, and parents, do the cooking, and keep the house clean. In order to perform these natural and Islamic duties, women have a right *not* to work outside the house and so to be "liberated" from wage labor (for more on Muslim women and the burden of wage labor, see Rouse 2004).

"First of all," Nainahon said, participation in wage labor prevents women from getting educated. In order to properly raise children, one of their main Islamic duties, women have to get an education: "to study both science and Islam and not to trade at the bazaars." The other important Islamic duty for women, she continued, is to "take care of their husbands." In order to do this, women have to look beautiful, be fashionable, meet their husbands "with kind words, be tender, and cook good food." Having a job outside the house "rob[s]" women of the time they might spend on beauty care and styling. Feelings of inner beauty, ability to converse on various subjects, and awareness of the latest fashions are stimulated through socializing. Therefore, women have to have time to attend social events. This would be very difficult if they have full-time jobs in addition to extensive family-related duties and responsibilities.

"In short, women have to pray and dance," said Nainahon. "This" is the "women's world," which is not just homosocial (consisting of women only), but qualitatively different from the men's world. She "personally" felt tired of doing men's work in her family, of being a part of the "men's world," and could not comprehend why some women would "fight" for a right to work. "The Communists and feminists thought that having a job outside the house is women's liberation." "Instead," she said, it is "exploitation," an aberration in the natural order created by God. "Women's husbands should work, not the wives, like now," she concluded.

"Women's full liberation," according to Nainahon, can be achieved only in a clearly gendered hierarchical society, where women and men follow their "natural" and "God-decreed" duties. In such a society, husbands are superior over wives; mothers, "the second sacred beings after God," superior over sons; and God superior over all. This gendered and generational hierarchy is, according to Nainahon, "Islamic" and "natural" but has to be founded on respect and love, not on fear. If women must be "one knee below men" because "we are not made equal," men "should respect and love women." As far as she knew, "the Prophet Muhammad never cursed or beat his wives." Therefore, the men too "should know their place" and follow the example of the Prophet Muhammad, "be like him," while the women should model the Prophet's wives.

Logical and informed by her sociohistorical context and her unique experiences, Nainahon's view of women's rights was nonliberatory, but not uncritical or apolitical. She argued that women have a right to be free from wage labor, from having to provide financially for their families' needs, and a right to adhere to and enjoy their different duties and responsibilities and their "women's world." To achieve such gender dynamics, according to Nainahon, requires social change, which both women and men have to be a part of. This view of women's rights was not unique in Uzbekistan; it was shared by Jahon and other individuals I met in the valley and elsewhere (for more on this topic, see Mahmood 2005; Rouse 2004).

Nonliberatory Discourses on Rights

Socialist ideals, including gender equality, although widely promoted were never completed in the Soviet Union (see McBrien 2009). Some scholars (e.g., Tabishalieva 2000) note that after the Soviet Union's disintegration, the intellectual elites and many citizens of newly independent Central Asian states embraced various "pre-Soviet" traditions, including a patriarchal family structure. Other scholars (e.g., Akiner 1997; Alimova and Azimova 2000; Fathi 1997) explain this increasing popularity of patriarchal views and behaviors among local women in terms of their post-Soviet split personalities—a result of a conflict between the ideals of Soviet "equality" and the reality of post-Soviet patriarchy and nationalism, which weakened local women's ability to think critically about their rights.

Such analyses reflect an assumption of the oppositional difference between tradition and modernity conflated with corresponding pre- and Soviet historical periods. They also assume that sociopolitical activism and a struggle for rights should be expressed in terms of resistance to and subversion of normative (patriarchal) culture(s). If we accept these assumptions, then local women's nonliberatory views on their rights, such as the ones expressed by Nainahon and Jahon, demonstrate these women's passivity or negative agency; they did not create but were constituted by and reflected or reacted to their sociopolitical and economic context.

Taking a lead from Saba Mahmood (2001, 2005, 2008) and Lila Abu-Lughod (2010), however, I argue that an analytical approach based on the tradition/modernity dichotomy and on a reduction of political activism to resistance limits our understanding of nonliberatory discourses and views on women's rights expressed by women such as Jahon and Nainahon. Such a limited approach obscures both existing gender dynamics and the dynamics of social change in Uzbekistan. Jahon's and Nainahon's narratives and stories about their lives demonstrate their ability to evaluate and articulate their rights in terms of gendered and generational hierarchy, to criticize the existing state of these (nonliberatory) rights, and to offer solutions to their problems. In order to understand why some local women continue to use these nonliberatory terms to define their rights, I propose that we look beyond the "split-personality" and "pre-Soviet traditionalism" explanations of their discourses and examine what Talal Asad (1999) calls a "historical genealogy" of religion and secularism in the region. This genealogy did not determine but certainly informed the local women's individual experiences and understandings of their rights.

In this section, I scrutinize twentieth-century debates about gendered rights and duties and illustrate the mutual constitution of religion and secularism in Central Asia in producing flows of discourses about rights, social change, traditions, natural capacities, and family values. These discourses provided local women with terms they used to articulate their views on their liberation. By learning about and from nonliberatory discourses on women's rights, we might better understand liberal views on the subject of women's and human rights.

Pre-Soviet Criticism

In the secular Soviet Union, religion (e.g., Islam) was a necessary condition for the nation-building process in that the Soviet secular discourse defined itself in *contrast* to the religious ones (Asad 1999). In Central Asia, the Soviet secularization campaign continued a trend of blaming Islam for local women's social oppression, a trend started by what I call "Russia's imperial gendered Orientalism" (for more on Orientalism, see Said 1988). This criticism did not question male dominance per se but disapproved of the terms in which it was expressed because the region's economic and political viability was more important to imperial Russia than gender equality. Aiming to undermine the status of existing religious leadership, this critical discourse blamed Islam and existing religious leadership for women's oppression, animated by the seclusion of women and polygyny. In short, in this discourse the image of the oppressed Muslim woman came hand in hand with an image of the uncivilized, ignorant Muslim man unable to dominate correctly (on a very different description of gender relations in pre-Soviet Turkistan, see Nalivkin and Nalivkina 1886).

Through the Slavic migrants, the colonial period added to an existing awareness of feminist and liberal ideas among a (small) portion of the native population. The colonial administration also established imperial courts prohibiting underage marriages, abolishing the death penalty for adultery, and legalizing prostitution (Khalid 1998; Nalivkin and Nalivkina 1886). Although it is unclear to what extent and in what ways these feminist and liberal ideas and de jure reforms affected local women's daily lives and social position, this critical discourse certainly politicized women's rights. Further, Russia's imperial gendered Orientalist discourse derided some local traditions and valorized others, such as cuisine and (Eastern) women's beauty; in the colonial Turkistan, this combination "likely . . . led to an increase in the seclusion of women" and "made polygyny into a form of conspicuous consumption" among emerging economic elites (Khalid 1998, 223).

The native reformist movement, jadidism, which emerged in Turkistan at the end of the nineteenth century, was one response to the Russian colonial critique of Islam (Khalid 1998; Muminov, Gafarov, and Shigabdinov 2010). These mainly male reformers, *jadid*s, admired

Russia's technological achievements and new forms of social control. They imagined a future Turkistan as an independent, deeply religious, and unified "enchanted modern" and gendered society technologically compatible with other countries (Deeb 2006). To create such a society required educational reforms, among other things.

The reformers criticized women's excessive seclusion, promoted women's rights to education and divorce, and the right to refuse polygynous and child marriages (for a similar emphasis on women's education in Iran, see Najmabadi 1998). This criticism resonated with advocacy for women's rights to choose a spouse and their rights to financial maintenance and with a view of marriage as companionship, articulated at the same time by some Turkistani women writers (Kamp 2006). While emphasizing women's role in collective nation building, the *jadids*' discourse on women's rights was not based on the concept of broad gender equality and (individual) freedom. In this discourse, women's rights were still biologically and ontologically determined. Responding to the *jadids*' criticism, existing religious leadership in Turkistan insisted that women's rights were not equal to men's; men and women had "rights according to one's station as adjudged by the shariat [*sic*]" (Khalid 1998, 268). As a result, women's rights became a political token in the anticolonial discourse and ideological struggle between conservative religious leaders and the reformers.

Soviet Criticism

After the Great October Revolution in Russia in 1917, the Bolshevik Party's (and later the Communist Party's) leadership, in an effort to incorporate Turkistan into a new union of the Soviet Socialist Republics, co-opted the *jadids*' discourse on the "enchanted modern." While adopting the reformers' rhetoric about education, women's rights, and progress, the leadership was very clear that the new Turkistan would not be unified by the reformed religious sensibilities but unionized by an ideology of communism; the region could and would be "modern" but not "enchanted."

The party's modernizing project aimed at secularizing the regional population was gendered (Kamp 2006; Northrop 2004). Gender relations were the center of social change; they had to be modified in order to reform the existing social structure in Turkistan. In the late 1920s, the party's famous campaign focusing on women's emancipation from the patriarchal family included women's unveiling. This ritual symbolized women's liberation from patriarchal families and their entrance into what organizers understood to be a new public space liberated from religious superstitions (Massell 1974). The Bolsheviks' strategic placement of women's emancipation at the center of the secularizing discourse further politicized women's rights, even while male primacy associated with in-family leadership remained largely unchallenged (Ashwin 2000).

The Bolsheviks' secular discourse on women's liberation stressed women's employment and married Russian (and European) feminists' understandings of women's participation in wage labor. Symbolizing liberation through wage labor was in synch with the party's need for participation of both women and men in the production necessary to satisfy the needs of the growing Soviet Union (Kamp 2006). Yet the Soviet public's participation in wage labor was gendered; women and men were often employed in fields of production intact with women's and men's "distinct characteristics and qualities" (Ashwin 2000, 11; see also Kon 1995).

In this secular discourse, women were still featured as dependents; previously dependent on their families, they now were (and expected to be) dependant on the state. This dependence, relocated through appropriation of their productive labor, was intended to transform "women's consciousness and render them more amendable to the state's control" (Ashwin 2000, 10). As primary caregivers, the women could extend the state's control to their offspring and into the private domain of their homes. Therefore, the Bolsheviks' discourse on women's liberation simply continued to naturalize gender roles and did not confront the principles of gendered (men over women) and generational (older over younger) hierarchy.

"National Traditions"

Facing ongoing resistance from local populations, by the late 1930s the Communist Party ideologically endorsed what I call a "traditional subjectivity" maintained by discourses on "differences in gender roles," the importance of sexual honor and family values, and "views of marriage . . . [as] companionship more than equality" (Kamp 2006, 230; see also Tabishalieva 2000). Defined as not secular and hence lacking equality, Islam came to be associated with the private domain as being among the "national traditions." These traditions, including certain foods, holidays, modest dress, arts and crafts, and gender roles were preserved through the writings of the Soviet ethnographers, who criticized some beliefs and practices as backward but normalized gender and generational hierarchies and some local beliefs and practices as national and traditional characteristics passed from generation to generation. These characteristics included a model of the "Eastern woman," who was submissive, modest, domestic, and hardworking (see, e.g., S. Abramson 1962; Snesarev 1974; Zhilina and Tomina 1993).

The discourse on "national traditions" was gendered and emphasized biological differences between men and women. "Traditional" men were expected to "engage in the rough and tumble of the world," and "traditional" women were to birth and care for children and "guard the chastity of the home and of the community" by embodying its "inner values" (Khalid 2007, 103; see also Kandiyoti and Azimova 2004). As a result, Soviet secularism and its "traditional subjectivity" normalized the association of domestic space with women and religion and of public space with men and a lack of religion.

This gendered divide was concomitant with solidification of a particular model of parental and spousal responsibilities. In order to diminish the importance of the patriarchal family, motherhood was promoted as the main social institution, and fatherhood was undermined. For instance, it was often mothers who were awarded custody in the case of divorce. By limiting the men's family role to "traditional" breadwinner who performed not solely but mainly in public space, the secular discourse further removed them from parental responsibilities toward the children and sharing some household chores with their wives (Issoupova 2000).

Discursive secularism and emancipation came hand in hand with extradiscursive practices, such as social reforms, policies, and infrastructure (e.g., schools and kindergartens) (Hardy 2010, 73). These reforms included emancipator-obligatory secular education for men and women, ensured women's participation in the labor force, and promoted internationalism and gender equality rhetorically and juridically (e.g., women's right to divorce). In light of these reforms, Soviet citizens, both women and men, were expected to perform equally in the secular public domain, but only in the areas corresponding with their "natural" qualities and "traditional" characteristics. Soviet women's social and traditional responsibilities, based on their perceived-as-natural abilities, were supported by the state through a range of benefits, such as monthly subsidies, childcare, "health services and . . . [lengthy paid] maternity leave" (Kandiyoti 2007, 608). Soviet men's social responsibilities to the state were expressed through wage labor and sociopolitical activism. In their families, however, men were still idealized as and expected to be traditional breadwinners and decision makers.

A view of biology as destiny continued to permeate everyday life in the Soviet Union. Women's participation in wage labor did not assure their independence and continued to sustain gender hierarchy; men were still considered to be the families' leaders and, in Central Asia in some cases, the sole providers. Even if women were able to achieve their professional career plans, their families always came first. Jahon, for example, was an engineer who left her professional career to care for her growing family, and Tursun-oi had to create a family first and then continue her education and professional career.

In Soviet Central Asia, existing gendered discourses established a direct link between wage labor and emancipation, politicized women's rights as markers of nationhood, naturalized women and men's duties and rights vis-à-vis each other and the state, both valorized and criticized national traditions and characteristics, emphasized a gendered and generational hierarchy, and normalized a gendered division of public and private domains (if not rhetorically, then experientially). Nainahon and Jahon lived in the sociohistorical context informed by these gendered discourses. As a result, their feelings about women's rights and their visions of social change were not inimical to male dominance. They, like some Turkistani women writers in the late 1890s and early 1900s, advocated women's rights to choose a spouse, their rights to financial maintenance, and a view of marriage as companionship. Similar to the *jadid*s, Nainahon and Jahon promoted individual rights to education, divorce, and ability to refuse polygynous marriages. These women's views on their rights cohered in a context where motherhood was glorified, individual independence and equality did not clash with social gendered hierarchy, and family values were paramount in spite of or because of existing divorces.

Post-Soviet Criticism

The post-Soviet Uzbek state embraced Islam not as a political force, a legal paradigm, or a societal structure, but as a traditionalized and apolitical national characteristic. This understanding of Islam became central to the discourse on national identity, which selectively criticized Soviet (defined as colonial) gendered secularism—which, in turn, was understood as forcing women to abandon their natural and traditional roles to wage labor. This discourse blamed the corruption of interpersonal relationships on Soviet (understood as Russian) behaviors and ideology, portrayed the state as a "protective patriarch," stressed Uzbek traditional values "explicitly target[ing] the family and gender relations," and excluded a broad liberal understanding of equality among men and women (Kandiyoti 2007, 610, 614).

Post-Soviet discourse on national identity (not unlike the Soviet secular discourse) emphasized women's natural and traditional duties as mothers and homemakers and encouraged men's intrafamily superiority as income earners and leaders. Yet as Uzbekistan joined the global market economy, these gendered expectations became increasingly difficult to fulfill. The economic reforms left many men jobless and necessitated and enabled women's participation in the formal and informal labor market, including employment in the service economy overseas. Nainahon's experiences with work-related travel and trade took place in this economic context. The discourse on national identity also praised values of collective obligation, paternalism, and nationalism and harshly criticized the values of liberalism, individualism, and materialism perceived to be Western. The economic realities, however, undermined the value of collective obligation by increasing conspicuous consumption among the state and local elites and individual citizens and by emphasizing "exteriority, fashion, and youth" (McBrien 2009, S140; see also Kamp 2005).

The Uzbek discourse on national identity and its ideas about biological, social, behavioral, moral, and political differences between women and men informed Jahon's and Nainahon's views on women's rights. Nainahon criticized Soviet gendered secularism for authorizing a woman's dual burden of wage labor (in public) and traditional values (in private). According to her, the ideological association of wage labor with emancipation as a matter of practice took women away from their natural and traditional duties and challenged men's claims to being the sole providers for the families, in many ways undermining their manhood. In order to restore a natural, traditional, and divinely decreed family structure, in her view women's and men's worlds had to be refashioned and realigned in such a way that wage labor and participation in the labor market and homosocial events belonged to "the men's world," but the household, children's upbringing, fashion, and homosocial events were a part of "the women's" world.

Islam, as "a *map* of discourses on how to feel" (Marranci 2008, 8, italics in original) and be Muslim, was a resource and provided terms for both the post-Soviet secular Uzbek state and its political opposition. In the 1990s, new discourses emphasizing a particular relationship between human and divine worlds emerged alongside the Uzbek state's discourse on national identity. Although these new discourses criticized the existing state's secular nature and the secular rhetoric of gender equality promoted by some scholars and politicians, they, just like the state's discourse, condemned Soviet efforts to foster women's emancipation through wage labor and Soviet atheism and capitalized on natural, biologically grounded gender roles. Yet in these new discourses gender roles were not couched in terms of the moral values of a socialist (or secular) state or an Uzbek nation; gender roles were not just "traditions," but divine decrees reflecting ethical standards and ontological differences between men and women created by God to complement each other.

In post-Soviet Central Asia, the historically engendered mutual constitution of religion and secularism produced flows of discourses about freedom, rights, social change, social progress, national traditions, ontological gendered differences, natural capacities and obligations, communalism, and family values. These discourses did not belong to one particular category, such as the secular or the religious, the modern or the traditional, or to a particular ideology, such as jadidism, communism, socialism, nationalism, or Islamism, or to any one perceived epochal period, such as pre-Soviet, Soviet, or post-Soviet. Rather, in tandem with extradiscursive elements these discourses as stories, physical artifacts, and embodied practices were a part of the human and nonhuman environment; as such, by raising emotions critical to self-formation, this environment did not determine but rather influenced individuals interacting with it. When articulated as feelings, these emotions would help to develop an individual "self" and the self's historical continuity as a gendered subject with particular views on her liberation (Marranci 2006; see also chapter 1).

Women's Right to Be Loved and Respected

The individuals I am writing about, including Nainahon and Jahon, were born in the Soviet Socialist Republic of Uzbekistan. They grew up in the context of the Soviet gendered secular discourses on naturalized gender roles and on the importance of education, wage labor, national traditions, and dependence on the state. These women received secular education and became wives and mothers in the context of the Soviet glorification of motherhood as a biological destiny, a secular duty to produce Soviet citizens, and a traditional obligation for Uzbek women; this destiny came with such perks as paid maternity leave, financial assistance for expecting mothers, free childcare and health care, preferential treatment when determining children's custody, and state pensions for "mother heroines" and single mothers. While engaging (with) these experiences and discourses that became part and parcel of their autobiographical memories, these women formed their historical and temporal continuity.

The Soviet association of individual advancement with secular education, the state's rhetoric of equality through wage labor, and the reality of economic stagnation in the 1980s contributed to Nainahon's and Jahon's decisions to join the labor force. One of them became a teacher and the other one an engineer.

Independent Uzbekistan promised but failed to deliver gender equity and to establish an economic system that would release women from wage and productive labor outside their household responsibilities. In this context, Nainahon's unique individual experiences and immediate familial context enhanced her ability to continue trading, and Jahon was able to quit her job, stay at home, and later become an *otincha*. Nainahon had a supportive mother-in-law who took care of the children during her absence and a husband who encouraged and facilitated her business travel. Jahon did not have a mother-in-law to help her with childcare and house chores, but her husband supported her decision to leave her job to look after their children and household.

Growing opposition to the government questioned its discourse on Islam as a national identity, pointing out that this discourse sustained the existing regime headed by former Communist elites. Further, the Uzbek government claimed to be secular, alleging to uphold the values of freedom, human rights, progress, and democracy. Yet the government's punitive responses to the opposition exposed the emptiness of such claims. In this context, Nainahon and Jahon came to further question the state's ability to assure women's rights, but at the same time the state's discourse on "national Islam" informed their desire to learn more about it. Their increased knowledge of Islam led them to believe that these rights could be achieved by following Islam, which, according to them, was natural, traditional, and progressive.

Through religious instruction, these women learned that God affirmed their dignity and ontological difference from men, which informed gender-specific propriety and roles. Similar to the secular discourses already familiar to these women, the Qur'an affirmed biology as human destiny. Contrary to these discourses, Qur'anic gendered equality released women from the social responsibility to participate in the labor market and authorized "equal but different" intrafamily and social gender dynamics. Further, God, the ultimate authority for a believer—not the state, family, society, or men—assured women and men's rights and duties toward each other and adjudicated their correct and incorrect performance.

In light of this knowledge, Nainahon explained behavioral differences between men and women in terms of hierarchical creation, which resulted in different desires, duties, and behaviors. She insisted that local men and women should strive to create intrafamily gender dynamics similar to the Prophet's household. Jahon stressed complementarity as an irreducible part of human ontology. According to her, women and men are ontologically different. Even though every human being has both Havo and Oto, spirit and flesh, mind and body, these elements are not in equal but complementary measures in men and women. Havo, who tasted the apple and realized that human nakedness had to be covered, was ethical before Adam; she was "cleaner" and smarter. Oto was stronger than Havo. He had to protect and provide for her. As a result, in the human world modesty, propriety, ethical behavior, and physical labor were redistributed unequally; women had more responsibility to cultivate and embody the former, whereas men had more responsibility to cultivate and embody the latter.

By saying that women should "stay women and respect their husbands," but also that "in this world women have no respect," Jahon was not criticizing women's inequality in a broad liberal sense. Rather, she was criticizing a lack of recognition of women as *equally important*, not socially equal, members of human society and of God's creation. She condemned a lack of respect for women's natural abilities and their value as God's creatures and ethical beings, loving mothers, and wives. She reasoned that every person is created by God and has both Oto as the flesh and Havo as the soul and mind: flesh is to men like soul and mind are to women. Although these characteristics are still clearly different, both are equally important to make a whole body. Even though she added that women should "stay women and respect their husbands," she believed that their husbands and society also have to respect women for *being women* in return. Also created by God, ontologically different from men, possessing different rights, duties, and desires, women have to be given *equal respect*.

In Nainahon's view, the first step in addressing women's problems is to encourage men and women's natural rights and responsibilities authorized in Islamic as well as traditional and natural terms, emphasizing men's roles as providers and women's roles as caring mothers and wives freed from the necessity of providing for the family. She said that women are meant to be not only caring mothers, but also "Eastern beauties," the image promoted by the Russian imperial Orientalist, traditional Soviet, and contemporary traditionalizing discourses and reinforced by a growing conspicuous consumption focusing on youth and exteriority. Therefore, women, Nainahon argued, have to be "fashionable" as much as they have to be "religious." When it comes to women, the values of education, chastity, love, respect, and patience are both traditional and Islamic and have not only a moral but also an aesthetic dimension.

Jahon's and Nainahon's nonliberatory views on women's rights were not exclusively "traditional" or "modern" and not "pre-Soviet" or "neotraditional." They were neither secular nor religious and neither liberal nor Islamist. Rather, as practices of individuality, these views were particular personal verbalizations of social change informed by the social context at the time and by the stories about history with which they were familiar. Articulated in light of their unique individual experiences and in many ways reflective of these women's active pursuits of their life projects, Nainahon's and Jahon's nonliberatory discourses blended the virtues of conservatism, fashion, education, socialization, motherhood, care, family, respect, chastity, duty, beauty, order, patience, love, devotion to God and to one another, and familial responsibility. These women ideologically rethought, rearticulated, authored, and authorized in new and different ways the knowledge(s), sensibilities, and behaviors formative of various historical and contextual gendered discourses. In the process, they created *in their* terms *their own* but not historically discontinuous views on women's rights.

Not all Central Asian or Uzbek women or all Muslim women in Hovliguzar or Uzbekistan share Nainahon's and Jahon's desire for and understanding of women's rights and social change. Some praise Soviet secularism for giving women equal rights and the post-Soviet state's attempts to preserve these rights. Others argue that the Soviet state failed to give women equal rights and that the post-Soviet Uzbek state should follow the model of liberal equality (see, e.g., Tokhtakhodjaeva 1996). Nonetheless, Nainahon's and Jahon's nonliberatory desires and views are not exceptional. Shared by others locally and globally (for examples of such discourses by Egyptian women, see Mahmood 2005), they require analysis and understanding. Further, these nonliberatory discourses created by local women help to better understand views on gender justice expressed in terms of liberal equality.

I argue that, although articulated in foreign languages, the nonliberatory discourses on women's liberation converge with liberal views in some important ways (on convergence of Islamic and secular feminism in Egypt, see Badran 2009). Expressed in idealist terms (e.g., God), the nonliberatory discourses are paradoxically pragmatic. They reflect existential conditions of some women in Uzbekistan and their daily interactions with a social world where hierarchy is ubiquitous yet dissimilar only to a degree and not in kind from the hierarchy-permeated contemporary life everywhere. Not unlike liberal feminists, these women pragmatically navigate such social space.

These nonliberatory discourses also remind one about different experiences and understandings of oppression and love and about the importance of individual priorities. Nainahon and Jahon desired to be loved not in a horizontal way, but in a vertical way, whereby humans' love is extended toward God, children's love toward parents, and women's love toward men. This vertical love goes both ways, though: God's love is extended toward humans, parents' love toward children, and men's love toward women and children. This reciprocity is not unfamiliar to liberal Muslims and non-Muslims residing inside and outside of Uzbekistan. Although gender theorists such as Luce Irigaray (1993) call for a horizontal love among (different and sexed) equal subjects, daily life is full of examples of nonhorizontal love, such as the love between a child and a parent, which can be as fulfilling as the one Irigaray calls for humans to achieve.

For Nainahon and Jahon, becoming truly Muslim was not about contesting the order of God's creation, where, in their view, men were created first and women second, but about purposefully embodying knowledge of the difference between the creature and the Creator, women and men, and parents and children in ethical—understood as Islamic and universal—ways. Their visions of an ideal society and gender justice were articulated in nonliberatory terms of the universal ethical paradigm and could be achieved only after learning, in-bodying, and embodying it. Also, if they were unhappy about gender discrimination, they (might have) prioritized a desire to become "truly" Muslim over other desires, including a desire to challenge existing gender dynamics, even though this might have left them, as it did Nainahon, feeling ambivalent and vulnerable. The processes of prioritizing needs and desires and feeling ambivalent about that prioritization are not unique to Muslim women in Uzbekistan, and the idea of individual change leading to a social one is always articulated in some terms, be they religious and nonliberatory or liberal (on differences in international feminist thought, see Mohanty 2003; for examples of nonliberatory terms, see Rouse 2004).

The women's rights and by extension the human rights preferred by Nainahon and Jahon—because for them to be a human meant to be a gendered and sexed individual, a woman—were not the rights to wage labor and independence, but the rights to love and respect, to their own important space in God's creation, and to their own women's world, where they could pray and dance, as Nainahon said, "both necessarily!" Desire for love and respect are not unfamiliar to those who articulate gender justice in liberal terms. These desires may not be political priorities for liberal feminists, but without love and respect, even if one satisfies other or different (political) priorities, one will not feel satisfied.

Finally, the rights that these women preferred were ethical and aesthetic, but not *apolitical.* Achieving them, like achieving a liberal equality, requires social change. According to the women I am writing about, achieving gender justice has to start with an individual's learning about how to do the right thing through religious instruction.

4

Pedagogy and Storytelling

Proposition: Individuals develop knowledge about a relationship between human and divine worlds by increasing self-knowledge through a practice of thinking, feeling, and acting, which results in a cognitive opening that leads to individual moral change.

Hovliguzar, August 11

I am at Rashida's house upstairs in a bedroom finishing packing for my trip to Tashkent tomorrow. They come for me around 9:00 p.m. From the second floor bedroom, I can only hear and not see them. I discover in a bit that there are two officers; one is dressed in a police uniform, the other as a civilian.

THE UNIFORM [greeting and then asking Rashida, in Russian, not in Uzbek]: *Hello. Do you have a guest from Russia?*

RASHIDA: *Yes, I do. Why?*

THE UNIFORM: *We need to see her passport.*

RASHIDA: *Why?*

THE UNIFORM: *The holiday [celebration of Uzbekistan's independence from the Soviet Union] is coming up. We are checking registration. It's routine. Show us your passport too. Who else lives here?*

RASHIDA: *My father.*

THE UNIFORM: *And show your father's passport.*

THE CIVILIAN [a different voice]: *Where is your guest?*

RASHIDA: *Upstairs, sleeping.*

They are on the way upstairs. I hear them coming, stomping on the old wooden staircase.

RASHIDA: *Why are you going there? She is asleep. [I take this as a cue. I need to get ready, to compose myself, to think ahead.]*
ME: *Give me a moment to get dressed. I will come downstairs.*
THE UNIFORM [I HEAR HIS VOICE]: *Come downstairs and bring your passport. We need to see it.*

I take my passport and walk downstairs, through the hall, and into the yard. There I see two men in their late twenties, early thirties.

ME: *Why do you need my passport? [It is dark. I shiver. Not sure if it is an evening breeze outside or the fear inside.]*
THE UNIFORM: *We need to check your registration [as a foreign citizen in Uzbekistan].*
ME: *Can I see your badges first?*

The Uniform shows me his, but the Civilian does not. I turn to the Uniform. From now on, I decide, I will communicate with and listen to him only, although I have a feeling that the Civilian is his superior.

ME: *Very well. [I give the Uniform my passport.]*
THE UNIFORM: *What are you doing here? When did you get here?*
ME: *I am visiting my friends. Where here—in Uzbekistan or in the valley?*
THE UNIFORM: *When did you get to Hovliguzar?*
ME: *August 9. I am leaving tomorrow for Tashkent.*
THE UNIFORM [flipping through the passport's pages]: *Where is your registration?*
ME: *On the last page. I have a valid registration for three months in Tashkent.*
THE UNIFORM: *Today is the eleventh of August. Who can confirm that you got here on the ninth?*

RASHIDA: *I can.*
HER FATHER: *I can.*
A NEIGHBOR [who by now has joined us]: *I can.*

Meanwhile, I am calling a friend on my mobile phone.

THE CIVILIAN [the second time I have heard him speak]: *We need other witnesses. [Turns toward me.] Who are you calling?*

I look at him for a moment, deciding if I should answer him at all.

ME: *Other witnesses.*
THE CIVILIAN: *Hang up the phone. Now!*

I manage to make a brief call: "Come here as soon as possible, I need your help!"

THE UNIFORM: *We will have to take your passport.*
ME: *Why? I have a valid registration.*
THE UNIFORM: *We will call Tashkent and check if your registration is not a fraud. If it is valid, you will get your passport back. The other day we arrested two women from Azerbaijan. They could be terrorists. Their registrations were fraudulent.*

The neighbors, Rashida, and her father suddenly quiet down. Incredible, how much cache the word terrorism *has here, there, everywhere!*

ME: *No. I will not give you my passport. This is absurd. Do you not see the stamp and the signature? Do you take every visitor's passport with you to check the authenticity of their registration or only those who come from Russia? I will come to your office tomorrow in the morning, if you want, and we can call Tashkent together. Give me back my passport, please.*

RASHIDA'S FATHER [who is almost ninety and drinks heavily]: *I am a veteran of the Great Patriotic War [World War II]. I know my rights. You cannot take her passport away unless she is accused of a crime.*

THE CIVILIAN: *No. We can. It is routine [and continues in Uzbek, so I do not know what he says].*

RASHIDA'S FATHER [retorting in Uzbek and then in Russian]: *I will complain. You will see.*

THE UNIFORM [ignoring Rashida's father]: *We are going to write a protocol. We are confiscating your passport, and you can come with us now and spend a night* v kamere *[in jail] next to your passport, or you can come tomorrow morning and pick up your passport.*

ME: *No, you cannot detain me without probable cause.*

THE UNIFORM [smiles]: *Your registration might be a fraud. How is that for probable cause? Why do you argue? You are a woman. Just because you are a woman, we will let you spend the night here. We can detain you for forty-eight hours to establish your identity. Do you not know that? We will let you stay here, but your passport stays with us. Do you understand? At nine in the morning tomorrow, I give you my word, you will get it back.*

THE CIVILIAN [pointing at Rashida]: *Take her passport too . . . [speaks in Uzbek to the Uniform and Rashida].*

Rashida's father, while cursing in Russian, raises his arms and shakes his fists in the air.

ME [asking the Civilian]: *What are you saying? What are you talking about? I do not understand. I need an interpreter. What is going on? Give me back my passport.*

THE UNIFORM [ignoring me]: *We need two witnesses.*

By now there are five neighbors around us.

ME [pointing around]: *Here are five witnesses.*

THE CIVILIAN [still ignoring me]: *I will get them. There are two on the street.*

The officers came well prepared; they even have brought witnesses with them. At this point, the friend I called comes into the yard.

THE CIVILIAN [turning toward him]: *Who are you?*

ME: *Another witness.*

FRIEND: *I am a friend. What is going on?*

THE CIVILIAN: *What is your name? Do you know her? When did she get here?*

FRIEND: *My name is [omitted]. . . . Get where?*

THE CIVILIAN: *To Hovliguzar?*

FRIEND: *On the ninth, I think. Why? Is there a problem?*

The neighbors, Rashida, and her father passionately discuss something in Uzbek.

THE CIVILIAN: *We have to check her registration. Do you understand, and . . . [speaks to my friend in Uzbek]?*

FRIEND: *Sveta [leading me away from others], tell them [looking at my hostess and the neighbors congregating in the yard] not to make any fuss. I will fix it. I will get your passport back. He told me that he would give it to me tonight. Do not worry.*

Despite my arguments and begging, I get not my passport but a piece of paper, just as Rashida and her father do, stating that my passport has been confiscated by So-and-So. Signed by So-and-So. When the Civilian, the Uniform, and my friend leave, Rashida comes toward me. I tell her what my friend told me. She is skeptical of his ability to end this. Yet in order to make me feel better, she says, "If he said he can do it, he will do it." She continues, "He is a man; they will listen to him—you know how it is here." "I do," I reply.

I do know. Growing up and living the first twenty years of my life in the Caucasus, I learned to delegate speaking with law enforcement agents on my behalf to my father, brother, boyfriend—to a man. Women, I was told, are weak, incapable of handling the police officers' rudeness. Women, I was taught, are vulnerable, in need of protection. Women are women and should stay away from men's business. Dealing with police is men's business. Maybe this is why I called my friend. I left Russia almost twenty years ago, among other reasons, in order not to be a Caucasian woman anymore, in order to learn how to speak on my own behalf, in order to make men's business my business.

But then in Russia I was also told that women are smart. Women, I was taught, can fool the law enforcement officers better than men can. Women are women and should stay this way—cunning, clever, scheming, knowing how to get what they want by the means that they have, aware that they can use their perceived weakness and vulnerability to their advantage. Maybe this is why I called my friend. I know he knows people I don't know. I know the more vulnerable I look, the more harmless I will appear to be. I know that women should stay women and let men speak on their behalf. Maybe this will work. As Rashida said, I know how it is here.

My friend comes back without my passport. He was told that I can pick it up tomorrow at the downtown OVIR, a part of the Bureau of Internal Affairs. He thinks I have nothing to worry about. But I know I have plenty to worry about. The routine checking of registration does not require prior surveillance. I know why they took my passport. They want to be sure that I will not leave the valley tonight, before they can find out exactly what I am doing here, in Hovliguzar and Uzbekistan.

My friend leaves. I go upstairs. Tomorrow is going to be a long day. Maybe women should stay women, but in this case, whether I want it to be or not, men's business is my business. By being here, in the valley, in the first place, I have made it my business. I plug in a mosquito-repellent device, take a sleeping pill, and curl up in a ball on a cotton-filled blanket on the floor and pull a cotton sheet over my body and my head.

The next morning, at nine, after four hours of sleep and several hours of packing, unpacking, repacking, and agonizing over today's meeting, I go with the same friend to the local branch of the OVIR. He was told yesterday that I would be able get back my passport there.

The building that houses OVIR is next to the one that houses a local branch of the SNB. This is not surprising. The OVIR is an extension not only of the Bureau of Internal Affairs, but also of the SNB.

We wait. We talk. We walk around. We notice surveillance. But this does not matter anymore. What matters is getting my passport back and leaving the valley. My friend, not me, gets a phone call. He is told to wait. Then in about thirty minutes he gets another phone call. He is told to wait again, and in another thirty minutes we are asked to come inside the building.

We walk up the stairs to the second floor. The Uniform, who gave me his word yesterday that my passport would be returned today, meets us in the hall. We enter his office. He asks me to give my bag, sunglasses, and telephone to my friend and sends him to wait downstairs. He closes and locks the door. I see my passport on the desk.

Coming Back, 2011

After the air-conditioned airport terminal, the dry heat was overwhelming. It made my throat sore. I got in a taxi. We drove through the clean, almost empty city. "Where are all the people?" I asked. The driver answered, "It is too late and too hot, and the *oblastnie* [provincials, referring to people who live in the villages and towns outside of Tashkent] are not here." He got my attention, "What do you mean?" He replied:

> They have to register in Tashkent [as did the foreigners], and our Karimov wants them to stay in their towns and villages. He does

> not want large groups of people, young men in particular [in the city]. This year is the twentieth anniversary of our independence. Many important people will be arriving to the city, representatives of different countries. They say something might happen on August 31. He [President Islam Karimov] wants this city clean and protected. I heard that *oblastnie* will not be allowed to enter Tashkent's universities. The summer break at schools started early this year too. There has to be peace in the city. Our *dedushka* [grandfather, referring to the president] and his daughter [his older daughter, Gulnara Karimova] want us to live in peace. They are fighting corruption too. Our oligarchs had to sell their *krutie* [cool] cars in order to hide their money from them [I assumed "them" is a reference to the state, personified by the president and his daughter]. Now the oligarchs are driving Nexias [a car model made by GM Uzbekistan]. But corruption is even greater than before.

The city of Tashkent, Uzbekistan's capital, was an example for the rest of the country to follow. As a result, its appearance mattered more than reality, and everything appeared to be beautiful and peaceful. The main streets were bright and clean. The large billboards featured the smiling faces of youth and the elderly and colorful advertisements. The gardens and trees were frequently watered. The grass was regularly manicured. The markets were saturated with ripe and shiny fruits. The new upscale apartment complexes were rising up around town. Blue, white, and green national flags marked the official buildings on the main streets. Everyone appeared to be happy, but "things are not always what they seem" (Gilsenan 2012, 51).

My Tashkent acquaintances and friends were mainly the "new Uzbeks"; many of them came from "old money," the families of the former Communist elites (for more on these elites, see Hjellum 2000). They liked "*tusit' i kaifavat'* [to *really* party]"; ate at upscale restaurants such as Djumanji; wore Lacosta, Fendi, Moschino, Gucci, D&G, and Versace; and had iPhones and iPads. They drank French wine and single-malt Scotch, smoked American Marlboros, spent vacations overseas, occasionally skied in the Alps, and listened to

Lady Gaga and Eminem. They could satisfy consumer desires that marked their cosmopolitan—often understood as urban and "European"—kind of belonging (see Greenberg 2011).

Raised in guarded mansions with swimming pools and saunas or in two- or three-level condos located in prestigious parts of the city, the children of these "new Uzbeks" were learning English at prestigious colleges in Uzbekistan and abroad and spoke flawless Russian. The parents celebrated their kids' achievements and made sure to remind them how different they were from "other" children outside of the parents' social circles. These families' versions of "nested Orientalism" were manifested through geographic metaphors that inscribed different levels of "civilization and modernity" in their society (Greenberg 2011, 96). They were not *oblastnie*, *haribi*, and *haribki*, the Uzbek terms for usually unrelated men and women populating villages outside Tashkent, but "*sovremennie* [contemporary]"; they were "Tashkentsie [from the capital]." While emanating the appearance of chic, they downplayed the reality of fear, ignored by some of them, but always present in the topics that they and I did not talk about—such as what happened and how many people died in Andijon in 2005 or what was going to happen if President Karimov, who had ruled the country for the past twenty years, should die. And if I were to ask them a question about the president's health, they would answer with a smile, "We cannot answer such political questions!"

From these friends I have learned that Gulnara Karimova, the president's older daughter, recently became a fashion designer. She chose "Guli," the nickname her father used, for her designer label. Some of my Tashkent acquaintances wanted to take me to "Guli's" fashion show, whose designs, they said, were "haute couture," on par with the most famous European fashion houses, "like Chanel." Other friends told me that it was better to stay away from the fashion show and anything that had to do with Gulnara Karimova; it could be "dangerous" to get "too close" to "*the* daughter." They had heard a horror story about an online poker game with Gulnara Karimova that had landed the other party in jail for six months. I did not make it to the Guli fashion show and in five days left for the valley. (The Guli fashion show came to New York City in September 2011. I did not attend it then either.)

Leaving Tashkent in the afternoon heat, I returned to the valley in a car driven by one such acquaintance who was going to Hovliguzar to visit his extended family. Comfortable in a Lacetti, a car made by Chevrolet and codeveloped with the South Korean automaker GM Daewoo, air-conditioned in the city and open windowed in the mountains, we were driving 120 kilometers per hour on the serpentine road of the Kimchik mountain pass (*pereval*).

Although Yuldus Usmanova was not as popular as she had been in 2003, Eminem had not lost his popularity. "I need a doctor, call me a doctor . . . to bring me back to life"—Dr. Dre's song featuring Eminem (Dr. Dre 2011), a big hit at the 2011 Grammy Awards in the United States—was blasting from the speakers and out the car's windows. If only I could capture the sound of Eminem roving through the picturesque landscape. But the traffic signs with messages prohibiting photography and my previous experiences in Uzbekistan kept in check my desire to document reality through images and sound. I did not dare video record or take pictures.

We drove through two checkpoints marked by the green color of police uniforms, one when we were leaving Tashkent and another one when we were entering Ferghana Province, with peddlers of *non* (flat bread) at the side of the road next to both checkpoints, scarves wrapped around their faces to protect them from the heat and the exhaust fumes. We drove through two tunnels marked by signs prohibiting video recording and photography and guarded by armed and masked soldiers.

We passed a beautiful semiarid landscape, mountains, the blue water of a large reservoir, and multiple eateries. We passed cotton fields covered with blooming flowers and dilapidated multistory apartment complexes. The latter were the remaining spatial markers of the simple and functional "Soviet modernist" architectural style, glossed over by arabesque-like designs meant to highlight the national traditions of the Soviet Socialist Republic of Uzbekistan. These architectural specimens emplaced the national and the international, the Soviet ideology of friendship and communal living of different national entities. Now lacking uniformity in color and structure, these giants' appearance was corrupted by built-out balconies and abandoned apartments—their emptiness made obvious by the broken windows. Right next to them were brick, cement, clay, and straw houses, other-styled new apartment complexes, and, of course, occasional private mansions—the mélange of the old and the new, of what was not yet gone and what was coming. Green canopies of grape vines and fruit trees covered the courtyards of the individual houses along the road. I recalled my first trip to Hovliguzar by car ten years earlier, in 2001. It was striking to see vast and dense islands of green vegetation amid patches of dry land.

We drove through Kokand, Namangan, and other cities, all of them full of new commercial buildings and businesses. Some of them had their own aqua parks, swimming pools, and lyceums, one built in the place of a planned madrasa. Navigating among cars excreting almost palpable exhaust that saturated the air and was mixed with pollen from the sycamore trees, we drove by another madrasa turned into a medical facility until we eventually arrived at Hovliguzar.

Visibly expanded through multiple constructions sites, Hovliguzar had changed since 2003. The downtown hub had a big new market, multiple *chaixonas* (local eateries) and Internet cafés, and plenty of other new structures, new foreigners, new cars, and some "new Uzbeks." The main street was peopled by couples strolling to and from the park accompanied by music blasting from their mobile phones. Cell phone reception was available everywhere, and some restaurants featured "free Wi-Fi." On a corner we bought warm flat bread and some tasty locally grown, barely ripe figs. Avoiding local hotels, which routinely reported their visitors to the SNB office, I spent the night at another friend's house. An old air conditioner in the room saved me from the heat, but not from the mosquitoes. In the morning, I went to see Tursun-oi.

Easy to Understand

During our first interview in 2011, Tursun-oi repeatedly highlighted the importance of *masala*, didactic storytelling, which "connected Islamic knowledge to real life." She said she continued to remind her students that these stories were very important; they helped "to connect it [religious knowledge] to real life." "Use everyday words [as opposed to theological or religious vocabulary]. You need to make Islam easy for people to understand," she said she exhorted her students. The women teaching "correct" Islam, in her view, were in a better position to connect religious knowledge "to real life" than were some local imams. These women had space and time and could, unlike imams at the mosques, "say it all," making Islamic knowledge "easy for people to understand."

Tursun-oi's emphasis on the intelligibility of Islamic knowledge was not unique and not recent. In 2002, she had told me that chaos within local families, the economy, the country, and the world made teaching about the "correct" Islamic way of life urgent: "Now especially, correct [Islamic] knowledge and behaviors are very important. If you ask me, there are signs of the end of the world. The Qur'an says that the stupid will rule, there will be *zina* [fornication], peoples and countries will fight, relatives will fight, and those who love the Qur'an will be persecuted. It is taking place right now. It is happening!"

The first decade of the twenty-first century offered many challenges. The most important one, in Tursun-oi's view, was a lack of an ethical paradigm; this was a sign of the end of the world. How can humans act ethically if their present is increasingly unstable and the future is ever more unpredictable? In this context, it is often impossible to anticipate the chain of consequences of individual actions. You can feel patriotic and act as a good citizen but still be unjustly punished by the government's agents. You can become relatively wealthy and lose it all in a matter of days if you are not well connected in the corrupt economic-legal-criminal sector. You can buy a university degree (and pretty much anything and anyone) for the right amount of money but find no employment (for more on this outlook, see, e.g., McBrien 2009, S137). You can lead a pious life and be persecuted for it in a country where Islam is the most important national tradition.

These challenges did not paralyze Tursun-oi. She did not aim to achieve political stability or economic predictability but struggled to rekindle human memory of *knowing and doing the right thing*. According to her, this knowledge is not pre-Soviet, Soviet, Socialist, or post-Soviet, not Uzbek traditional or Islamist, not modern or oppositional or individualistic. It is a universal ethical paradigm, established by God for humanity, applicable at all times and places. The ethical paradigm that can save her society from chaos, Tursun-oi said, does not have to be invented, made anew; it is *always already there*, from the beginning of time, with the final judgment of individual knowledge and effort of leading an ethical life not allocated to fallible humans, but to the infallible God.

Tursun-oi claimed that God has created every human to manifest God's mercy and forgiveness and that every human has a soul knowing its own creation and the capacity to develop her goodness. Learning "correct" Islam by *remembering* the universal ethical paradigm, which is always already there, helps to develop an individual's ability to recognize and realize in action her capacity to be good. This process of remembering was facilitated by women such as Tursun-oi and Jahon, who felt that they had cultivated their morality and mastered knowledge about Islam to an extent where they were entitled to guide others toward moral transformation. By teaching "correct" Islam, women like Tursun-oi helped others develop a capacity into an ability to become "truly" Muslim, better human beings.

Whereas in the Soviet Union only "a tiny handful of students" had access to "formal theological education," in post-Soviet Uzbekistan, partially in response to the state elites' elevation of Islam to a symbol of national identity, the number of people interested in Islam greatly multiplied (Rasanayagam 2010, 84). Although in general the availability of pedagogical resources for and centers of religious education increased, their numbers were still insufficient to satisfy the needs of those interested in learning how to be "truly" Muslim (Barrett 2008).

Several factors contributed to the scarcity of educational resources for and centers of religious education. Among them were the physical destruction of the scholarly theological and classical literary heritage in a zealous fight against religion during the 1920s and 1930s, the Soviet state's atheism, and seventy years of the region's relative isolation from other countries, including those with a statistical Muslim majority population (Khalid 2003).

Further, the initial support that Islamic education received from the government in the early 1990s withered away by the late 1990s, when an alleged attempt on President Karimov's life by members of a political and religious opposition group resulted in the state's repression of religious groups and a greater control of public education (Kandiyoti and Azimova 2004, 342).[1] Many mosques and madrasas that had been reopened or built in the early 1990s were now closed. Some religious teachers and leaders were arrested, while others were exiled. Religious literature published in the country was closely monitored. Therefore, in the early 2000s, eager to help others, Tursun-oi and some of her (former) students, such as Jahon, lacked access to the range of printed pedagogical resources available in other countries (on the availability of such resources in Egypt, see Mahmood 2005).

In the summer of 2011, Tursun-oi showed me a book titled *al-Adab al-Mufrat* (Etiquette and conduct) by al-Bukhari, the second volume, edited by Sheikh Mohammad Sodiq Mohammad Yusuf and published in Tashkent in 2009. The first page of the book was stamped as reviewed and permitted by the government. In this book, *hadislar* are thematically organized under particular topics, such as how to behave toward parents, kin, and neighbors; how to bring

1. Article 14 of the Law of Freedom of Conscience and Religious Organizations (1998) prohibits private (unofficial) religious instruction.

up children; how to express generosity; and so forth. Tursun-oi said that she regularly used this book in her teaching, but it was a relatively recent acquisition. Her knowledge about "correct" Islamic etiquette and conduct, which she shared with her students during religious lessons, previously came from elsewhere. During 2002–2003, responding to a growing popular interest in Islamic etiquette, she and women like her were using readily available materials, including their individual experiences turned into examples, other preexisting knowledge(s) received through secular education, such as knowledge of classical Central Asian literature (for more on Islamic education see Peshkova 2014), in addition to some state-reviewed and approved books about Islam and Qur'anic exegesis (*tafsir*) and *hadislar*.[2]

"Correct" and "Incorrect" Islam

The Muslim Board of Uzbekistan, the official organization financially supported by the Uzbek government, promotes the Hanafi *mashab* as the historically authentic interpretive position. Although the board works toward establishing doctrinal coherence among local populations, local religious leaders' and the general public's assessments and understandings of Hanafi-proper socioreligious practices and theological views sometimes differ (Babadzhanov 2004). Some difference is tolerated, but because the board authorizes only the Hanafi interpretive position, other positions—the Maliki, Shafi'i, and Hanbali—are considered to be alien to the region, nontraditional and dangerous, with the potential of inciting political activism and violence (Babadzhanov 2004; Karagiannis 2006). Therefore, learning and teaching about these "other" positions are prohibited.

In the late 1980s, several religious groups promoted political ethics based on interpretive positions other than the Hanafi. Many

2. In 2003, Tursun-oi used two existing exegeses, one by Mohammad Sodiq Mohammad Yusuf and the other by Abdulaziz Mansur.

members of these groups were eventually arrested, given lengthy prison sentences, or forced into exile (see Naumkin 2005; Rasanayagam 2010, 127). The views they advocated were labeled "Wahhabist," "extremist," or "Hizb," and individuals allegedly promoting these views continued to be persecuted. In time, these labels came to be used in reference to any unsanctioned expression of religiosity; even some members of Protestant groups were labeled as "Wahhabist" (Rasanayagam 2010, 148).

These labels were also used to discredit an individual's religious knowledge or performance of rituals. For instance, in 2003 at an *ehson* I witnessed an argument about how "high" women should raise their hands during ritual prayer or *duo* (supplication), which was triggered by one of the officiating *otincha*'s lifting her hands higher than other women during the *duo*. According to the other two *otinchalar* present at the ceremony, only men could elevate their hands to this level; for women, it was "wrong" and "Wahhabist" to do so. To my knowledge, the criticized *otincha* was not a member of Hizb-ut-Tahrir, the followers of which were often labeled as "Wahhabist," and was unfamiliar with the theological position and practices advocated by Muhammad Abdul al-Wahhab. This eighteenth-century reformer argued that Islam's message had to be cleansed of what he believed to be human corruption widespread in the centuries following the Prophet Muhammad's death. According to al-Wahhab, only the unadulterated Qur'an contained the pure message of Islam and therefore should be understood literally. Because the term *Wahhabist* was divorced from its original meaning and used so loosely in the region, the "Wahhabist" *otincha*'s lack of knowledge of Abdul al-Wahhab's teachings mattered little to the women who disagreed with her understanding of the form and performance of prayers and supplications. They used this label to discredit her actions as wrong and unsanctioned by Hanafi Islam as they understood it.

Muhammad Abdul al-Wahhab's teachings were not completely unfamiliar in the area, however. In 2002, a seventy-year-old mullah in Hovliguzar, well known for his religious knowledge and piety, told me that several copies of *al-Kitaab al-Tawheed* (The book of oneness), attributed to al-Wahhab, had been available in Hovliguzar since the 1970s. According to him, someone smuggled *al-Kitaab al-Tawheed* into the country from overseas. He, too, read this book, which endorsed the "long hair and beard like Muhammad," individual participation "in jihad [in this case armed struggle] all over the world," "creation of the *khalifat* [a state founded on and guided by Islamic principles]," establishment of Islam "as the only religion," recognition of "only the Qur'an and nothing else, no *hadislar*, no *odat* [customs]" as a source of knowledge, and individual belief that "suicide is honorable." Such statements, the mullah said, were "against Islamic understandings."

Although this mullah admitted offering informal religious instruction to other individuals, he immediately extricated himself and his students from association with the teachings articulated in the book. He said, "My students are not Wahhabists. . . . Some [of them] were first questioned [by SNB officers] and then were set free." Therefore, even if the information about multiple interpretive positions was available in the valley, sharing this information was prohibited. In this context, the women I am writing about condemned interpretive positions other than the Hanafi and presented their positions, claimed to be Hanafi, as correct interpretations and understandings of Islam, even though they did not explain why they did so.

For instance, Tursun-oi might know about differences among the four interpretive positions, but in my experience she did not explicitly identify or explain them. Instead, she repeatedly highlighted her support and promotion of "the correct Hanafi Islam." In 2002, she said, "I tell my students that there are seventy-three *oqim* [teachings]. There used to be six, later seventy-two, and then seventy-three *oqim*. Those who profess the seventy-third *oqim*, the Hanafi *mashab*, will go to heaven." In 2003, she stated again, "There are many different interpretations of Islam. They are wrong, some are very wrong. Ours, Hanafi, is the correct [one]." In 2011, she reiterated her support of Hanafi Islam: "How many people will go to *jannat* [paradise]? Muhammad said that out of one thousand only one [will go] because 'a big camel always has a small mole.' His followers were upset. The [followers of the] seventy-two [other] *fiqh* [positions of Islamic jurisprudence] will go to hell. Only [followers of] the one *fiqh* [will] go to *jannat*. It is Imom Azam, Hanafi *mashab ahlus sunnah* [the people of the tradition, of the Hanafi Islam]. [It is] the best *mashab*. We follow Muhammad in *ibodat* [worship] and life."

In line with her understanding of Hanafi Islam, the "correct" knowledge that *otinchalar* ought to share with others should include not only the Qur'anic normative principles and their "correct" comprehension, but also some customary practices (*odat*) that do not contradict the Hanafi *mashab*'s understanding of Islam. In 2003, Nainahon also noted the importance of customary practices: "Those *otinchalar* who teach the Hizb [the religious principles promoted by this party] are closing the doors and hearts of the local people to such traditional *meropriyatiya* as *toy*. They speak against receptions and music. Traditionally people have always done those things. Traditional *otinchalar* . . . think that people should celebrate these occasions [with music]. This is our *odat*."

At the same time, reflecting their increasing knowledge of Islamic normative principles and global circulation of Islamic knowledge, some of these women condemned customary practices that, according to them, contradicted Hanafi Islam. Some of these "wrong" practices, Tursun-oi and her student Jahon argued, were either adopted from Russians or Jews or other peoples historically populating the region or reflected people's ignorance about Islamic ethical behavior. For instance, these women persistently criticized (even though Jahon occasionally officiated at) propitiatory rituals fairly popular among local women at the time—the Bibi Seshambe and Bibi Mushkil Kusho (for more on these rituals, see Kandiyoti and Azimova 2004 and chapter 3).

In 2002, while discussing these ceremonies, Tursun-oi said, "This tradition, Mushkil Kusho, is carried out one day a week, on Tuesdays. Now, our religious authorities prohibit this tradition. Recently [the news came] from Arabiston [a general term used to refer to Saudi Arabia or the Arabian Peninsula] said that this practice is not allowed. It is not Islamic. It is about an old mother, an old woman. When she was alive, she prayed on our behalf. Now she is dead, and we should not ask her to pray to Allah instead of [doing it ourselves]. Although it is not allowed, some people still read *Mushkil Kusho kitob* [the story about the Lady Solver of Difficulties in the form of a book]. Now we should not read this *kitob* but read the Qur'an."

Women such as Tursun-oi and Jahon imparted Islam, whether understood as customarily correct or correctly Islamic, to their audiences during religious lessons or while officiating at religious ceremonies or both. Yet individual possession of correct knowledge did not assure the person's moral transformation. I argue that the final goal of religious instruction offered by these women during religious lessons and ceremonial gatherings, was not to just learn "correct" (in the case of Tursun-oi and Jahon, Hanafi) Islam, but to encourage individual *mastery* of this knowledge, to make abstract knowledge work in changing situations (for more on such mastery, see Thomson 2007). This mastery was expected to enhance the individual's ability to use Islamic knowledge situationally and creatively, thus helping one to purposefully cultivate moral behaviors toward others and oneself (for more on this view, see Mahmood 2001). The pedagogical methodology and techniques these women used were aimed at developing this mastery.

Questions, Answers, and Stories

Answering pragmatic questions that their communities' members raised inside and outside ceremonial contexts was one of the pedagogical techniques that women such as Tursun-oi and Jahon used to introduce religious knowledge and encourage individual mastery of it. According to Tursun-oi, giving advice was also a form of teaching: "God says, 'Whoever comes to you, you need to teach.'" Women and sometimes men approached her and Jahon for help in evaluating their actions as Islamic or non-Islamic or to get advice on how to resolve an issue in an Islamic way. One such issue was corporal punishment of minors.

On multiple occasions during my visits to Hovliguzar, I witnessed how patiently and lovingly parents and grandparents treated their offspring. Nevertheless, adults occasionally used physical punishment as a disciplining technique. In 2003 at one *ehson*, women in the audience asked Jahon if they could or should physically punish their children. She thought for a minute and then replied, "If a child offended you, you should not punish the child. Your child is not guilty. It is you who are guilty. You did something wrong: you did not pray, did not keep *tahorat* [ritual ablutions], or there were simply other religious duties that you have neglected. Your children are a reminder of your own misbehavior. Instead you should thank God for reminding you about your duties through your children. Do not offend God so that you can give a proper example to your children of how to live their lives Islamically and not to offend you. Change your behavior if you want to change your children."

Local women were aware that children were influenced by their parents' behaviors and that they learned about being in the world while interacting with their environment always *in relation to* someone, including their parents. If their parents continued making mistakes or neglecting their religious duties, then the children would act in a similar fashion. In this case, corporal punishment of a minor would not alter an existing social (familial) environment and would not change the child's behavior. In order to resolve this problem, the parents had first to change their behavior.

Yet the pedagogical value of Jahon's answer was not limited to disapproving corporal punishment of minors. When explaining this answer to me, she noted that even though local women recognized the importance of social context in children's upbringing, they also believed in an innate individual potential for making wrong choices and misbehaving. According to her, "many parents believed" that delinquent children were "born bad." Although acknowledging that biology certainly affects human behavior, Jahon's answer moved beyond the sociogenetic explanation of individual behavior; it aimed at stimulating individual evaluation of the correspondence between one's thinking and one's acting.

From Jahon's standpoint, to consider a child to be an independent agent (whether socially or biologically determined) is incompatible with a claim of being Muslim. A "truly" Muslim human has to have faith in the all-knowing and all-powerful God, the creator and the judge of everyone and everything, and to recognize God's power through the signs sent by God. In the case of a child's misbehavior, a "true" Muslim should not physically punish her child but take the child's misbehavior as a sign, a message from God, granting her a chance to reflect on her own behavior and an opportunity to change it accordingly. At the same time, being dependent on God does not cancel the importance of independent choice of actions; a child's misbehavior is a learning experience for both children and parents, who, as role models, are supposed to teach their children how to make right choices and acquire correct actions.

Jahon reported that local women often asked her about the correct (Islamic) response to minors' misbehavior. Her answers were phrased differently on various occasions but always made the same point. For instance, on another occasion the same year she used the situation of verbal abuse toward children to demonstrate a correct response applicable beyond this pragmatic situation's narrative. She said, "Before you go to work, you ask your daughter or son to help you around the house. When you come home, your children did not do what you had asked them to do. This is where you failed as a mother; you should have taught your children better by your example. It is you who must have sinned, and now [it is you who] are getting a payback through your children's behavior. You should not yell at them. Thank God. You should think about what you did wrong, where you [have] failed. Change [your mistakes] first. Your children will change when they see your example."

As before, Jahon emphasized God's power and knowledge and condemned yelling as an undesirable choice of action. But more importantly she pointed out the utmost importance of the individual's work on her own self; self-formation, through a critical reflection on her thoughts and actions, has to precede and enhance her ability to judge, punish, or educate others.

The most important pedagogical technique used by Tursun-oi and Jahon was *masala*. In our exchanges, both of them insisted that *otinchalar* should share their knowledge of Islam through teaching about religious texts, telling didactic stories, and answering individual questions—all the while setting personal examples of ethical, Islamic living that can be emulated by others. Didactic storytelling was a part of every class Tursun-oi taught and every ceremonial occasion she and I attended during my visits in 2001, 2002, and 2003. In 2011, both Tursun-oi and Jahon continued to highlight the importance of *masala*s. Tursun-oi said,

> *Masala*s are very important. They put Islam in simple words, connect it to our life, make it easy. Muhammad left us an example of a *masala*—a *sluchai*, *raskaz*, *skazanie* [an occasion, story, legend]. Muhammad's uncle [Abu Talib, who became the Prophet's patron] died, and Khadija [the Prophet Muhammad's first wife, the first convert to Islam] died. There were people who were against the Prophet. No one could protect him. The Prophet was on the street talking to one man. He finished [the conversation] and was leaving when he overheard a conversation between this man and another one. This other man asked, "Who were you talking to on the street?" The man who talked to the Prophet answered, "No one. The man I talked to was *ozg'in*, *bisplodnij* ["impotent" in Uzbek and Russian, one who has no male heirs]!" The Prophet became very upset. One of Muhammad's followers wanted to protect him and kill the people who offended the Prophet. The Prophet said, "Please, do not do it." And Allah sent an *ayat* stating, "They are *ozg'in*, not you. Muslims are going to be your descendents."

This *masala* provided a wealth of information, including the choice to abstain from violence, the value of not only biological but also spiritual descent, and the necessity of learning about how to correctly follow the universal ethical paradigm set up by God and encapsulated in the Qur'anic *ayat*s, the "signs." But imparting this information, I argue, was not the main pedagogical purpose of didactic storytelling. In the following paragraphs, I explore why

Tursun-oi and others told these stories and attributed such significance to them. I demonstrate the ways these stories affected individual self-formation and explore the forms of knowledge that emerged through didactic storytelling.

Mind and Body Distinction

Scholars often deploy "the mind–body distinction" as an analytical tool to understand individual self-formation or morality (e.g., Mahmood 2005, 157 n. 3; see also Rasanayagam 2010, 91). Women such as Tursun-oi and Jahon recognized the existing distinction and incongruence between individual mind (thoughts, feelings, and interior beliefs) and body (utterances and exterior actions) and considered that distinction to be a problem. According to them, Islamic knowledge—the knowledge of how to do the right thing—is essential to a life well led and should be manifested through both mind and body in tandem; a declaration of faith has to correspond to a state of mind or a feeling and to have concomitant actions.

Didactic storytelling was the most important method that Tursun-oi, Jahon, and women like them used in order to (re)establish correspondence between mind and body, between thinking, feeling, and acting). Created and re-created by storytellers, the pragmatic daily situations narrated in the didactic stories became teachable moments. By introducing thinking situations, they offered to an individual a deeper insight into her own self and helped to undo an assumed or existing separation between thinking, feeling, and acting. This mediation allowed *being Muslim* to become an individual's "whole way of life" (Rabinow 2003, 9) in the sense that what she thought about, felt, and believed in was integral to how she acted in the world. As such, didactic stories became sites for individual self-formation.

In an interview in 2003, Jahon argued that the process of (re)establishing correspondence between thinking, feeling, and acting might not be immediate but is desirable and certainly possible.

> Sometimes I tell a *masala*, and I know that it is hard for people to accept it. They may not agree with me and may not like what I [have to] say, but I ask for their forgiveness and still tell them this *masala*. Then I ask [the audience] to think about it. "Maybe later, maybe tomorrow," I say, "Please think about it." I am sure it comes back to people. Everyone has *imon* [faith]. It is a gift from God. Everyone also has *bondo* [body], which is also a gift from God. *Imon*, *rukh* [soul], and *bondo* are made by God. We should change our lives starting tomorrow and be good because we are made to be good. *Mi sozdani bogom* [We are made by God]. People have to change . . . we, *otinchalar*, have to help people to change. During one battle between the Prophet and the unbelievers, several people were slain and thrown in a *kuduk* [well]. The relatives of one of Muhammad's soldiers were fighting against the Prophet. They were among those thrown into the *kuduk*. Muhammad asked the soldier if he was sad because his father and his relatives were among the dead. The soldier replied that he was. He told the Prophet that all this time he wished for the family to become Muslims, to see the Truth. "But now it does not matter. They do not hear me," said the soldier. Muhammad answered, "Now they see the Truth. They did not hear you then, but they see it now [because] they are near God [aware of one God]." Sometimes people do not want to hear the Truth, but we have to do everything we can to let them get closer to the Truth, [to be able to] to see it.

In this reflection on the importance of teaching and didactic storytelling, Jahon reminded her listeners that getting "closer to the Truth" is a process that can happen now or "later." But this process, entailing struggle and doubt, is inevitable. According to her, the stories about "the Truth" come "back to people" and have an effect on them, if not in this life, then in the next one because the self's nature and destiny are transformative: human soul, body, and faith are gifts from God, who created humans to be good, to have a life well led together with others. Such social life starts with individual self-formation.

Engaging the Disengagement

According to the women I am writing about, in both the Soviet Union and independent Uzbekistan many claimed to be Muslim but did not act accordingly; some individuals claiming to have religious knowledge (*illim*) continued sinning, but uneducated people ignorant about religion (*avom khalq*) could perform meritorious deeds (*savob*) without knowing it. For Jahon and Tursun-oi, didactic storytelling, as a pedagogical technique, provided knowledge about virtues and vices and offered one way of rectifying this incongruity by prompting contemplation as to whether an individual's claims of being Muslim corresponded to his or her thoughts, feelings, and actions.

Any sociohistorical context offers not only multiple constraints but also "multiple responses" to those constraints (Rabinow 2003, 19). Each one of the didactic stories these women told recognized this multiplicity by demonstrating that there are different ways of responding to a particular situation or to a general sociohistorical context. Among all possible responses, a didactic story always points to the correct one. By pointing to a correct choice, didactic stories mark as incorrect non-Islamic way(s) of thinking, feeling, and acting, thus providing knowledge about virtues and vices that an individual should aspire to achieve or to avoid repeating. These stories exemplify how to and how not to act in a given situation and become sites for self-reflection and critique that can, if not immediately then eventually, lead to a self-formation though mediation of an individual's thoughts, feelings, and actions.

Hence, through a *masala* a storyteller does not force an individual to make a right choice, to change, or to disseminate theological knowledge per se, although both making a choice to change and learning about theology are possible outcomes of the storytelling. Rather, didactic stories illustrate that (1) there are incorrect and correct ways of thinking, feeling, and acting; (2) there is always a choice, one correct and others wrong; and (3) the choice to acquire the right choice is individual. I contend that this is the reason why both women found didactic storytelling to be critical to individual self-formation and societal change.

Political or Pragmatic Engagement

Jahon told me the following *masala* about Adam and Eve in early 2003 and repeated it at two ceremonies I attended the same year. She said, "Allah created Oto and Havo. These two later quarreled, and Oto was rude to Havo. Allah became upset. He called on Oto and said that he should respect Havo. Oto replied that she was so beautiful [that] she made him jealous. Allah said, 'I gave you Havo, and I will take her back. She is an *omonat* [someone or something lent for a period of time]. I gave her to you to keep. Respect her and love her because you will give her back to me at the end of life. Do not get upset with your wife.'"

One way to analyze this didactic story is to focus on the story's immediate political messages, such as criticizing the unjust treatment of women. This story shows that women are not exclusive possessions of their husbands (or other humans), contradicting a local ideology that women belong to their husbands and families. Realizing their sacred nature and essential belonging to God might lead some women to resist this ideology. On a political level, this *masala* might be a technique of raising women's activist consciousness while exposing gender oppression and creating dissent among local women against prevalent social mores; it might also provide women with the theological tools to fight this oppression. Yet this *masala* might also be understood as entrenching hierarchical relationships created by God, who gave Havo to the man and not the other way around, thus promoting the existing gender hierarchy (men over women) rather than subverting it.

I propose another way to analyze this *masala*: to examine it as a pragmatic pedagogical technique connecting thought and feeling to action. This technique introduces several choices and points out an Islamically correct one, thus inviting an audience's self-reflection and critique. This particular didactic story introduces the possible actions by men in the pragmatic and familiar human situation of intrafamilial conflict—a quarrel between husband and wife. The man's actions during the quarrel—for instance, being verbally rude—animate individual thoughts about and feelings of frustration and jealousy. By placing a woman in the realm of the sacred—as created by and thus essentially belonging to God—the story demonstrates that jealousy is not the right feeling and that verbal rudeness is not the only possible action, but actually an undesirable response. The other way of acting—the Islamically correct one—would correspond to feelings of and thoughts about respect and love.

If this *masala*'s gendered narrative is not taken as political, but as pragmatic, then this story is meant to help each individual in the audience to think about and evaluate the correspondence between claiming to be Muslim, one who fully entrusts herself to God, and verbal rudeness as an action and jealousy as a feeling. This evaluation can be achieved through self-reflection and critique by contemplating (1) what feelings and thoughts and their concomitant actions are virtuous; (2) how a Muslim should behave toward others; and (3) whether the individual's thoughts and actions correspond to the (Islamic) virtues discussed in this *masala*, such as love, respect, valuation of human life as sacred, and the honoring of an obligation. The behaviors that result from the methods of self-reflection and critique as well as knowledge of virtues and vices can be applied to other situations and places beyond this particular didactic story's narrative.

Creating Teachable Moments

Didactic stories' narratives fashioned by the storyteller's creative imagination can incorporate information from the Qur'an, *hadislar*, and Central Asian classical literature; they can also draw on pragmatic situations and issues and individual experiences. Such stories are never told in exactly the same way but always reflect the context they want to change. Their content and the characters' transformations are not triggered by new knowledge, but by *existing* knowledge. In *masala*s, reminding the audience that each individual is created by God to be good and what being good means, feels like, and how it should be enacted, the characters do not need to look for new ways of being, but for the ways that are always already available to them in this life created by God; in the stories, among the choices available to them, they eventually (have to) choose the right one.

For instance, in an interview in 2003 Jahon reminded me that she chose and changed her *masala*s depending on the audience. "If they are young, I emphasize that they should respect their parents and relatives and thank them for what they have done for them." She told didactic stories in terms that were appropriate but also and more importantly intelligible to the audience and emplaced in a well-known context, reminding them that the option of being truly Muslim is always already there. In these stories, virtues such as respect, love, and patience are not new virtues, but familiar ones. It is up to an individual to choose to in-body (in terms of thoughts and feelings) and embody (in terms of actions) these virtues. Since the didactic stories' narratives, crafted by women such as Jahon and Tursun-oi, reflected the context they wanted to change, in Uzbekistan they addressed individual, societal, and familial issues, including rapid economic change, individual belief in God, and parenthood. As such, they became teachable moments, offering an individual a deeper insight into her own self, and important sites for self-formation.

Economy and Migration

During the first decade of the twenty-first century, some of these stories emplaced issues associated with a massive migration by the local population to Russia and other neighboring countries in search of reliable employment. Just like Nainahon and her husband in the 1990s as well as Nainahon's son and Jahon's husband in the 2000s, more than one-fourth of local individuals migrated outside of Uzbekistan to earn money. They did so in gendered ways.

Some local women, such as Nainahon, engaged in economic trade through travel. Their travel often took the form of short trips abroad, whereas male migrants left their homes for long periods of time. When their husbands left, the women stayed behind to care for their extended families. Tursun-oi said that through didactic storytelling she encouraged women to have faith in God and look for happiness in their homeland despite its current socioeconomic environment.

One of Tursun-oi's didactic stories, which I recorded at the end of 2002, was about "always looking for a better place," alluding to the contemporary labor migration. She said, "Once, the Prophet was traveling from Mecca to Medina on a camel's back. He was invited to stay at many places, but he insisted that he would stay at the place where his camel would stop. He said, 'Where the camel will lie down, this is where I will stay too. Allah sent me here, and I will be happy at any place where Allah wishes me to stay. I leave it to God to choose a place for me.' We too should accept [where we are] and find happiness here [in Hovliguzar]. It is Allah's will for us to be here and now."

This story about the Prophet's traveling, not unlike individual migration in search of a job that will assure economic stability, created a teachable moment offering two possible choices of action. Although the Prophet could have chosen to stay "at many places" to which he was invited, he left "it to God to choose a place." The feeling of unhappiness and financial need led local men and some women to "many places," leaving their families behind. By highlighting the Prophet's decision to rely completely upon God's will in choosing a place rather than accepting other humans' invitations or acting on his own volition, this story demonstrated that leaving for elsewhere is not the only possible or desirable choice of action. The correct choice of action, verified by the Prophet Muhammad's action, is to rely upon God, to stay and be happy at the place God has chosen for you.

The content of this story could have had political implications. It could have been taken as a criticism of migration; by migrating, individuals failed to follow God's will to stay at the place chosen for them by God. This story could also be understood as a call for women staying behind to be patient and to care for the rest of the family because it is God's will. As a pedagogical technique, however, this *masala* introduced the pragmatic context of migration as a site for the audience's thinking about and evaluating the correspondence between claiming to be Muslim and acting as one. The story provided two possible choices of action: to believe that God is omniscient (that "it is Allah's will") and to submit to his will (to stay and work "here") or to act by challenging God's will. By establishing the first choice as Islamic, this *masala* invited individual self-reflection on the correlation between individual belief in divine predestination and acting according to divinely ordained virtues of patience and trust in God—in this case in relation to socioeconomic tribulations.

Some didactic stories I heard reflected Uzbekistan's rapidly entrenching class system. In 2003, Jahon shared with me another *masala.*

> In Islam, it is a good thing to help others, either with money or a good deed or a kind word. Allah says that even one kind word is a great help. The more you give, the more you will get. Even if you share spiritual *bogatstvo* [wealth], such as a kind word or a prayer, you may receive money as a reward from God. If you share money, you may receive spiritual [wealth], find peace and love. Share. God wants you to share. If God gave you money, but you have no *imon* [faith], God will not multiply your wealth. If you do not have *imon*, you will lose your *bogatstvo*. There are, of course, some poor people who don't want to make money. They are lazy. There are people who have no money and are envious of those who do. This is not good either. The envy should not destroy people but make them want to do things. Try changing your [economic] situation. Make it better. God will help you in this effort. If you are envious of those who make money, try to use this envy to make more than they do and share it with others.

This *masala* did not criticize the class system and those who have already amassed substantial financial capital but reminded the audience that wealth has to be redistributed. Although redistribution itself is important, individual intentions that come with the action are similarly significant. Like other *masala*s, this story was not just about economic redistribution, although it might have been understood as such by some in the audience. Its pedagogical purpose extended beyond its immediate content.

During one meeting in 2003, Nainahon noted that some *otinchalar* "[do] not want us to be locked in the house. We dance at *gap* and other *meropriyatiya*. We go to the swimming pool. We read the Qur'an and pray. There are, as they say, two heavens, and one of them is this life, here and now. We should use it and enjoy it. If and when Allah provides us an opportunity, we should enjoy it." She added that individual desire for and experience of financial comfort are also a part of "this life, here and now," the life that humans "should enjoy."

Similarly, Jahon's *masala* neither called for an ascetic life nor moralized against material concerns but recognized the existence of this-worldly human desires. If taken as a pragmatic, not political, pedagogical technique, this *masala* introduced various choices of action in the context of the existing economic instability and growing conspicuous consumption, *a desire to have more* stimulated by a pseudo-free-market economy heavily monitored by the Uzbek government. An individual could choose to make money and keep it for herself (not to share), to make money and redistribute it in the community (to share), or to not make money at all (be poor on purpose). The *masala* reduced these choices of action to one Islamically correct choice, which is to share goods (money) and goodness, such as "to give" a kind word. To be kind to others verbally is also a meritorious act (*savob*) that has spiritual and material consequences (for talk as "a form of social action," see Hensel 1996 and Speer 2005).

While providing a teachable moment by inviting an individual to evaluate the correlation between the internal (thinking and feelings) and the external (actions and talk), this *masala* also examined envy and its corresponding actions. The story identified two kinds of envy: a positive envy and a negative one. The latter results in individual inaction, whereas the former stimulates individual action to "make more money than [others] do" through hard work. But this "making more" than others also has to match up to an individual desire to share more than others.

The audience for this didactic story could have learned that God is the source of economic well-being. Omniscient of human thoughts, God is the judge of all human actions. But, more importantly, this story was meant to generate self-critique, where the self will become an object to be examined carefully because in a life well led individual intentions and actions cannot be disconnected. In order to perform virtuous or meritorious acts, having proper intentions is critical; otherwise, these acts will be nullified. Like other *masala*s, this story created a teachable moment that not only provided information about the universal ethical paradigm but also spawned questions about individual faith in God, virtuous behavior, and the correlation between an individual's claim of being Muslim and her actions.

Individual Belief in God

The sociohistoric context of Uzbekistan informed the Uzbek state's discourse on national identity, which relied heavily on national historic and religious heritage. The state's discourse, in turn, informed the individual desire to live Islamically. This aim generated growing anxiety on the part of those who had previously neglected their religious duties, raising questions about whether it was too late to turn an individual sinful life around and prepare for an afterlife in paradise. In 2002, one of Jahon's *masala*s answered this question: it is never too late.

> It is never [too] late to change your life and live it Islamically. One mother had a son. He was a handsome lad. The mother really loved him. One day she got him drunk and slept with him. Then she had a daughter from her son. When the daughter was born, the mother became ashamed of her and gave this little girl to the traveling Arabs, to the Bedouins. One day when the son grew up, he went to Arabiston and met a girl whom he fell in love with. This girl turned out to be his and his mother's daughter, but he did not know that. They got married. When the mother found out who her son's wife was, she died from shame. Before she died, she told him that his wife was really his daughter. The son was furious

> with his mother. One day he went to his mother's grave. When he got there, he saw light coming out of the grave. He saw his mother in this heavenly light, kneeling as she was praying. She said, "Oh my son, I have sinned, but I read *namoz* [prayed] now, and God forgave my sin." Her *namoz* was a long prayer, for [it was praising] Muhammad. She also said that God wanted her son to read *namoz* so that he would be forgiven as well. You [the audience] should read *namoz* from the heart. If you do it from the heart [having faith in God and proper intentions], God hears it and forgives your previous sins.

This *masala*'s narrative, which emplaced sexual desires and taboos, provided moral support to those who had decided to live Islamically and reminded everyone about the importance of ritual prayer. This support could have decreased individual anxiety about a belated desire to become "truly" Muslim. The story's clearly gendered narrative—where a woman (the mother) was a problem because she initiated sexual behavior toward a man (her son) and was the main cause of sexual behavior considered immoral on the part of the man (her son's marriage to his daughter)—sustained a contested but authoritative gender ideology insisting on control of female (unruly) sexuality.[3]

Aside from moral support, reminders of God's mercy and forgiveness, and a gendered approach, as a pedagogical technique this didactic story offered a range of choices for action. These actions include drinking (or making someone drink), committing a reprehensible act such as incest, abandoning your child, and marrying (unknowingly) one's daughter. These actions can be carried out only by an unbeliever lacking knowledge of a universal ethical paradigm. Alternatively, one can die from shame, admit the wrongdoing, kneel, and pray. These other possible actions correspond to the feelings of and thoughts about shame and repentance that signal individual faith

3. In this story, a female also has the potential for reform; inasmuch as she is part of the problem, she is also part of the solution leading her son to God.

in God. There are several possible choices, but the correct one is to kneel, pray, and call others to do the same, while feeling shame and repentance and having faith in God and God's mercy and forgiveness.

Ali Rouhani notes that "works of fiction, do not simply mimic real world life" but exaggerate it (2008, 45). They let us "play," Marina Krakovsky argues, "with the fire of emotions from a safe remove" (2006, 52). Similarly, this didactic story intensified everyday life and allowed the audience to "play with the fire of emotions" (which, following Gabriele Marranci [2006], I call "feelings") from a safe distance. Narrated as a story about sinning, this *masala* brought to the fore behaviors that are rarely talked about (e.g., incest) or shameful to admit (e.g., abandoning your children), but also very real (e.g., drinking). These behaviors reflect the lack of a universal ethical paradigm. The women who heard the story were able to contemplate these thoughts, feelings, and actions from the safe distance of this *masala*'s narrative.

In this story, an individual's belated faith in God had corresponding feelings and choices of actions that were always already there. An individual does not have to invent them but simply to acquire them. By reminding those listening to it about correct thoughts, feelings, and actions, this *masala* became a space for self-critique, where an individual could examine herself in terms of her ability to discriminate between actions that should generate individual shame and the desire to repent, on the one hand, and actions that manifest individual faith in God, on the other. This story also encouraged its listeners to meditate on self-readiness for being and becoming "truly" Muslim humans, which would mean that choosing incorrect actions, such as drinking, or committing reprehensible acts beyond this didactic story's narrative context would be strictly forbidden.

Parenthood

The relationship between husband and wife, mother-in-law and daughter-in-law, and parents and children within a family was one of the recurrent pragmatic contexts of didactic storytelling in

Uzbekistan. Such stories promoted responsible parenthood, including not only financial and material provisioning for children and the elderly, but also individual responsibility to create and sustain children's moral character through personal example. I heard the following *masala* in 2002 from Tursun-oi and in 2003 from Jahon:

> Once, a pregnant woman walking across the bazaar became thirsty and sucked on a pomegranate that she picked off some merchant's table. Later she gave birth to a son, who was not a good person and was cursed by many people for the things that he was doing, such as making holes in a poor man's sack [making the poor man lose what little he had]. That woman's husband was very upset with their son's behavior and asked his wife if she fed the boy something bad. She remembered the pomegranate, which she had sucked on without permission. He told her to go back [to the bazaar], pay for it, and ask for forgiveness. You should not take anything that belongs to someone else without permission. This is *haram* [forbidden]. You should not steal and then feed your kids with food bought with the money made by stealing. The children will be ill behaved. They will suffer for their parents' actions. The parents should teach their children what is good and what is bad. [They should] be an example to their children.

This *masala* employed no theological vocabulary or symbolism. It was set in the familiar familial context of marriage, pregnancy, childcare, and spousal relationships. It pointed out that taking someone else's property without permission is immoral and that the sins of the parents have an immediate effect on the lives of their children. As a pedagogical technique, this *masala* presented a range of choices. Of course, the primary right choice is not to steal in the first place, but if an individual has stolen something, she can either choose not to understand that this action has consequences or to correct this mistake by paying for the stolen goods. The former choice corresponds to a desire for instant gratification—the woman wanted to quench her thirst, forgetting or being unwilling to recognize that her actions had consequences. The latter animates a desire to rectify the individual's wrongdoing, to repent, to ask for forgiveness, and to correct her mistake: the woman paid for the pomegranate.

As in telling other *masala*s, the storyteller reminded the audience that human potential to have a life well led is always already there. The woman could have bought this pomegranate in the first place. In a causal fashion, her son would then be good, and her husband and neighbors would be happy. The potential is always there. An individual ability to embody this potential can be achieved only through self-reflection by a thinking subject ready to voluntarily commit to leading a "truly" Muslim life by submitting to God's guidance and doing her best to correct her mistakes.

Didactic stories, created and performed by such women as Tursun-oi and Jahon, reminded the audience that every action—whether it is induced by an immediate context and humanly natural desire (such as thirst) or not—has immediate and extended consequences. As sites for thinking critically about the self, these stories invited individual contemplation about the self's readiness to act responsibly and to face inevitable consequences. According to Tursun-oi, learning how to take responsibility is necessary; despite the fact that human existence is contextual and relational, God's judgment is always individual. Further, individual meditation on the correlation between thoughts, feelings, and actions is at the same time the beginning of mediation, a process of undoing an existing or assumed incongruity between individual mind (thoughts, feelings, and interior beliefs) and body (utterances and exterior actions) and of establishing corresponding relations between them.

Stories *Well Told*

In the winter of 2002, at a ceremony Jahon told a *masala* about a dying woman; this story made many women teary. After the ceremony, I asked her why this particular story had such an effect. She answered that *masala*s and *hikmatlar* (hymns) are meant to "touch you and open your soul to God"; this story was an example of such a *masala*.

> One woman was dying. But even at the time of her death, she was thinking about her children: "Are they in the rain? Are they hungry?" She was thinking about her guests and friends: "Are they healthy? Are they well fed?" She was not thinking about herself, but about her children and her people. All her life she lived honestly. She built her family and the community [around her] as a strong and well-grounded building. Nobody has a right to destroy this building. God protects it. Her soul is Islamic [pious]. She raised her children Islamically. She deserves all the respect in the world. She deserves respect, love, and compassion not only on her deathbed, but all her life long. She is [the society's] foundation.

This *masala* was set within the context of family and an individual's life cycle. As a moral story, it focused on selflessness, love, and a desire to care as primary virtues of motherhood, which in the Ferghana Valley, as in other places and at other times, for many women was not simply a modality of but a fully realized ideal humanhood.[4] The story restated an existing gender ideology (broadly defined) of women's primary value as being a mother and a prevailing national ideology emphasizing women's active role in nation building through educating their offspring and taking care of extended families (on crafting educated housewives in Iran, see Najmabadi 1998). While affirming women's social importance, the story pointed out their essential position as the life givers, caretakers, and teachers of future generations and thus the foundation of society. Therefore, as creators of the future moral community, women have to be loved and respected. Beyond the political understanding of its content, as a pedagogical technique this *masala* set up what I call a "*thinking and feeling situation*," a space for personal reflection on one's experiences,

4. I do not mean to say that every woman in the valley had (or had to have) children. Nor do I mean to say that every woman in the valley agreed that individual humanhood has to be actualized as motherhood. This is my *etic* analysis of *emic* storytelling available to me.

including faith and gendered behavior; this space is necessary for inbodying the ethical paradigm created by God for humanity.

To the women in Jahon's audience, the virtues of motherhood and of being "truly" Muslim were participatory in the sense that an individual being in the world is always *in relation to* others. Individual self-evaluation invited by the story was meant to link the virtues of motherhood with matching actions such as thinking about others; sheltering and feeding children, guests, and friends; assuring children's health and education; and building family and community. The virtues of motherhood were inextricably linked to being "truly" Muslim, to living Islamically, and, as a result, to being loved and protected by God and loved and respected by others.

The reference to God and Islam did not drive but "embellished" this story's narrative "made up of [individual] memories [and] reactions to the environment" (Marranci 2009, 85). God and Islam entered the narrative as a reminder that virtuous motherhood is concomitant with being "truly" Muslim, thus connecting and relating everyday behaviors to Islamic virtues. This story pointed out that being "truly" Muslim does not require an extraordinary effort. An ability to be a "true" Muslim is always already there, as expressed in seemingly mundane behaviors. Like the dying woman, many humans are *already* doing the right thing, which is foundational and essential not only to self-formation, but also to the formation of a life well led together as an aggregation of many individuals voluntarily and fully submitting to God. Personal realization of this connection comes through introspection and through self-knowledge, which also has to be nurtured and *affectively* stimulated.

"Sentiment, emotion, passion, and affect" are "core dimensions of moral claims" (Rabinow 2008, 75). In order for a didactic storytelling to have a full effect, it has to have an affect; the story has to be felt. According to Jahon, didactic stories have "to touch you," and, as Nainahon said in the previous chapter, they help "to open" women's souls to God. I refer to the didactic stories that touch a listener as "stories *well told*," not only in terms of the storyteller's performative skills or an intricate storyline, but also in terms of their narrative emplacement.

The *masala* about a dying mother, caretaker, and society maker narrated love, safety (as God's protection), respect, and compassion not as abstract political concepts or demands, but as feelings. This story must have been well told because it touched the women in the audience by making many of them tear up. While covering their eyes with their hands and moving from one side to the other, many of them repeatedly exclaimed, "*Allahumma amen* [Let it be as God wants]," "*Allahu Akbar* [God is the Greatest]," and "*Khudoga shukur* [Thank God]." Later, in response to my question about the reasons behind such behaviors, one woman responded that this story made her "sad," and another woman claimed that the story described her mother.

As I discussed in chapter 1, human emotions, articulated as feelings such as empathy, are ecological "mechanisms through which an individual human being is connected to and learns from their [*sic*] environment [human and nonhuman]"; emotions are shared by other animal species (Marranci 2009, 16–17; for more on human and animal emotions, see Slingerland 2007). If learning includes selecting information from an individual's interaction with her environment, and this interaction is emotion bound, then learning is impossible without "the dynamic of emotions and feelings" (Marranci 2009, 17). As a consequence, in the case described here, individual moral reasoning or learning how to reason morally, essential to self-formation, would be impossible without emotions.

In Uzbekistan, some *masala*s were stories well told. They generated more emotions articulated as feelings, such as happiness or sadness, than did other didactic stories. These emotions enhanced an individual's ability to learn from her environment. In turn, a more effectual display of emotions during didactic storytelling could manifest a better, more successful learning process. Thus, there was a direct correlation between human emotions and learning how to be "truly" Muslim. Some didactic stories "permeated with emotional elements" (Marranci 2009, 81, 86). As pedagogical techniques, these *masala*s, such as the one about the dying mother, facilitated the learning process better than others by generating more emotions on the part of the listeners.

In my experience, each didactic story was never retold in exactly the same way. Like poetry, *masala*s were works of art, lovingly and studiously crafted by the storytellers through revisions, omissions, and substitutions. Each iteration of these stories could be less or more evocative. Nonetheless, the stories well told, depending on their unique reception, were more effective than the stories told otherwise. As sites for self-critique and reflection and hence for self-knowledge, they could stimulate change in individual lives more successfully than the stories lacking passion and affect.

Emerging Forms of Knowledge

Another *masala* told by Jahon in 2003 combined in new ways the characters and the contexts that echoed other didactic stories about God's creation and motherhood. Women's tears and exclamations in the audience animated this story's emotional effectiveness and potential educational value.

> Allah created a woman and told Oto [Adam], "she is so beautiful, respect and love her." A woman is a beautiful creature: she is a mother. She brings another life into this world. Every time she is pregnant and brings a life into the world, it is considered by Allah to be a great *savob*. Each time a woman gives birth, it counts as hajj. The woman suffers through childbirth. [In return] for this suffering, God gives her an additional life, which she can keep for herself, but she chooses to give it to her child. Oh man, respect her. Allah loves her. She deserves to be loved. The most beautiful and strong creature in the world is a woman.

Beautiful, strong, self-sacrificing, and generous women—these images manifested and supported discourses on gender prevalent at the time in Uzbekistan. These discourses created and shared by local women affirmed gender and generational hierarchy, ontological differences between women and men, and motherhood as a divinely ordained female humanhood (see chapter 3). The audience could take this story as a call to action to demand justice, love, and respect. But beyond its political implications, this *masala* helps us to understand the forms of knowledge created by individuals and emerging through didactic storytelling.

This *masala*'s narrative reminded the women in the audience that they were not only God's creatures but also creators of life who choose to give their second God-given lives to their children. Similar to other stories that touched listeners, this was a story well told; by awakening the effectual intensity of images or the listener's memories of relationships with her own body, it generated tears and exclamations on the part of the women in the audience. Later, the women explained their tears and exclamations in phrases used to articulate emotions: "sad," "life is hard," and "beautiful story." This story might have reminded some listeners of experiences of a new life coming into the world through physical suffering and anguish—of the simultaneous magical and ethereal feeling of losing a part of the self while gaining an ability to grant a capacity to be and become to a newborn. For others, it might have brought forth the memories of their own mothers, of life and death, pain and sacrifice, love and respect, and the beauty and strength of their physical bodies. By reminding all of them of the truth that is always already there, this *masala* might have helped them to come into their own goodness (which, according to the storyteller, God has endowed every human with) in their individual ways. This story evoked existing experiential forms of knowledge of the self and of a particular relationship between the human and divine worlds at the threshold of life and death, which is what childbirth is and how it is talked about and often experienced by women.

If humans' relationship with the environment is "essentially emotional," as Marranci (2009, 80) and Kay Milton and Marushka Svasek (2005) argue, and if emotions articulated as feelings are central to thinking, then an intense-feeling situation will also be an intense-thinking one. Following Marranci (2009, 85), I argue that an intense-feeling situation, such as the one created by two of the well-told didactic stories described earlier, results in a "cognitive opening [that] helps facilitate possible receptivity" to new understanding of an already known information (Wiktorowicz 2005, 5). As part of the learning process in the context I focus on here, this cognitive opening facilitated individual learning and self-formation.

Inasmuch as an individual can learn from literary or oral sources or physical artifacts or both, she also learns through and from reactivated personal memories, including memories of her body. These memories, too, form her autobiographical self, while assuring her historical and temporal continuity as a self-conscious or "reflecting" subject (Marranci 2006, 45, and 2009, 94). I propose that didactic storytelling, in particular stories well told, help to create what Michel Maffesoli calls "empathetic 'sociality'" (1996, 15), through which individuals learn from themselves and each other. Marranci contends that emotions generated in relation to human and nonhuman others and the self in different religious and nonreligious contexts are "not ontologically different" from each other (2008, 76). Therefore, even if not all individuals in Jahon's audience shared the experience of giving birth as both painful and rewarding or of losing someone close (such as a mother) or of feeling undervalued and unloved or loved and valued, they still could understand and empathize with each other. While witnessing each other's tears or joy, they could make sense of the emotions experienced by others by associating those emotions with their own emotions, which had already been generated and made sense of in other experiential contexts. By sharing the emotional experience of empathy with others, in this context of empathetic sociality they learned how *to feel the right thing*. As a pragmatic pedagogical technique, the *masala* played a very important role in this learning process.

In Jahon's words, *masala*s, in particular the stories well told, "touched you." In Nainahon's words, they "touched women's souls" and "opened their hearts to receive God" (see chapter 3). These well-told stories narrated divinely ordained virtues of justice, love, respect, and goodness not as abstractions, but as familiar, desired, and remembered feelings (or articulated emotions). The stories' narratives not only pointed out correct choices of action but also made an individual feel that which was right, good, and true. Generating empathy and cognitive opening, the stories well told reminded listeners that these same stories were being felt by and touched others, thereby creating an optimal thinking and feeling situation. In this optimal situation, self-evaluation was emotional and social, not formative of what Victor Turner calls a condition of *communitas*, an unstructured community where social hierarchy is suspended (1969, 132). Rather, such self-evaluation was relational; both thinking and feeling were "oriented from the self outward to others, to things, to events, and then back to the self" (Rabinow 2003, 10–11).[5]

The process of self-formation, including evaluation and self-critique generated by didactic storytelling, took place in these gatherings of women always in relation to the self and others. This process was more effective through feeling empathy both for the self and for others who might have been proximal or distant geographically, historically, or socioeconomically. The forms of knowledge about the self and the world and about a particular relationship between human and divine worlds emerging in this process were in-bodied, embodied, experiential, emotional, expressive, and relational; they were both essentially personal and participatory at the same time.

Affective and Effective

Jahon shared with me the following well-told *masala* in the spring of 2003:

> Oto was made by God from Earth. Havo was made of air. Yet both men and women have Havo. We breathe and have motherly

5. On such occasions in the Ferghana Valley, even though empathy mediated generational and gendered hierarchies, these hierarchies were not suspended.

> beginning in us. And we are Oto because we have body, and it is made of earth. So we are both Oto and Havo. Havo is tender, shiny, and clean. Our souls should be clean, tender, and sweet like honey, shiny like crystal; [souls] should be beautiful like air. If our souls are clean, our lives will be clean. Our bodies should be clean like pure earth, like Oto. We should be proud of our bodies—the body is Allah's house. Both soul and body should be clean and beautiful. You see, God made us beautiful inside and out. It is as if you built a beautiful house for your son, bought a car, and had a wedding. You say, "Here, live and enjoy and thank God." But in a year you see that the house is falling apart, the wife is gone, and the car is broken. This is how God punishes us if we do the same thing with our bodies and our souls. You should be careful and keep everything clean and beautiful. [We] should be afraid of God, for God will punish us if we do not abide by [God's] rules.

Whatever is primary in the process of ethical self-formation—whether thought is formative of action or action is formative of thought or they work in tandem—an individual needs to be made aware of an ethical paradigm according to which she is to be formed. Didactic stories like this one were one of the pedagogical techniques providing knowledge about this ethical paradigm among the women I met in Uzbekistan. These stories, created and performed by *otinchalar*, were in some ways very different and in other ways very similar. Their narrative emplacement was different, and the storytellers' performative skills varied greatly. Yet they all referenced pragmatic situations and presented among all possible choices those that were Islamically correct and clarified ways of thinking, feeling, and acting concomitant to these choices.

The primary pedagogical goal of the *masala* was not only to present what the author or narrator considered to be correct Islamic knowledge, including divinely ordained virtues, but to invite—as Jahon said, "maybe later, maybe tomorrow"—the audience's self-critical meditation on the correspondence between thoughts, feelings, and actions. This meditation would mediate the duality between mind and body, between claiming to be a Muslim and acting as one, and would foster individual mastery of religious knowledge by forming and finessing the skill of creatively using this knowledge in different situations.

Those didactic stories that were well told were more affective and possibly more effective. They literally and physically bridged past and present, memories and reality, thoughts and actions, the self and others, creating a context for learning as *feeling* the knowledge of God's good creation. Such *masala*s animated storytellers' hopes that in the process of feeling these stories, individuals, transformative by nature, would be reminded that their goodness was always already there and that they would be able to remember and realize this goodness at all points during the span of their earthly lives.

Whether didactic stories well told had immediate political applications (or implications), they certainly had an affective and effective pedagogical value (for more on affect, see Forgas 2001). As a part of the *otinchalar*'s pedagogical methodology, these stories had less to do with scriptural sources and everything to do with human emotions and their role in individual self-formation. The Qur'an and *hadislar* offered terms in which didactic stories could but *did not have to be* expressed. These stories and their pedagogical value demonstrated that being "truly" Muslim is not about forming the self into a completely new person or simply about learning the fundamentals of Islam, including scriptural sources. They emphasized that to be "truly" Muslim and to have a life well led together with others, human beings are to become "truly" human, to feel the memory and realize in action the initial and essential goodness with which God endows everyone. This goodness has been always already there.

On some level, to each individual the Uzbek government's control of religious knowledge—its approval of the Hanafi interpretive position and disapproval of other positions—did not really matter. The universal ethical paradigm created by God was not only articulated in the sacred books, which could be censored or promoted, or in the prohibition of certain types of clothing but was also and more importantly located in individual experiences. Didactic storytelling made Islamic knowledge easy to understand and feel because it connected abstract theological knowledge of the universal ethical paradigm to a knowledge that was always already there, present in listeners' memories of human emotions. This connection resulted in a cognitive opening that would lead to individual moral change.

5

Changing Lives and "National Islam"

Proposition: While interacting with and in relation to the human and nonhuman environments, individuals are not constituted by but create discourses on religion.

Hovliguzar, August 2011

Although the window with the view of the SNB building is wide open, it is hot in the room. There is an air-conditioning unit in the window, but it is turned off. I guess it is broken. The room is large. It has plenty of space for a desk, a wooden stool in front of it, a safe, a wardrobe, and several chairs along the wall. At least I do not feel claustrophobic. The Uniform asks me to sit down. I do. The stool breaks underneath me, and I fall on the floor in an awkward position. He apologizes and smiles. Embarrassed, I sit down on the chair next to the wall, after asking if this was done on purpose. He responds, "Of course not!" and smiles again, then walks toward and unlocks the door and asks someone to bring in another stool. An officer brings in the stool. I sit on it.

The Uniform asks me if I have any recording equipment on me. He asks me to show him my watch and my bracelets. "Are you hiding it in your watch?" He chuckles. "Where did you buy this watch anyway?" I reassure him that I have no recording equipment on me and note that it is irrelevant where I got my watch; what is important is to talk about my passport. He smiles again and says he wants to get it over with, too, because he wants to go back home to his wife and that he is hungry and tired. I say that I am tired too and have places to be.

Trying not to antagonize him, I compliment him on his command of Russian and ask him about his family. He is not humble: he says that his wife is beautiful and that he is very smart. He went to a "national" school where Uzbek was the main language of instruction, so he had to learn Russian by himself, and now he is good at it. While looking through my passport, he adds, "I am twenty-six; younger than you are." Feeling veins pulsating in my temples, trying to appear calm and charming, I smile but keep thinking about what will happen after this "small talk."

I ask again when I can have my passport back. He replies that this country has a registration regime that I violated. He reminds me that today is August 12 and that I arrived at Hovliguzar on the ninth. By now, I should have registered in this city because I have to register in every city, wherever I decide to spend a night. I have to register IMMEDIATELY! I ask him to show me the law that states that I have to register immediately; I was told at Tashkent's OVIR that if I register in one place and travel to other places for no more than three days, I do not have to reregister in those places. I continue, "You took my passport with you yesterday; I was supposed to leave today, early in the morning. Therefore, I have not violated this country's registration regime." He says that he IS the law and that today it has been more than three days. "If you want this to end quickly," he says, "you should listen to me because it can take a long time—it can take days."

He suggests that in order to end this matter quickly, I should write a note admitting that I have violated the Uzbek state's registration regime, and stating that I will never do it again. In return, he promises to give me a preduprezhdenie, *a warning, and send me on my way to Tashkent. All this time, he studies my visas and assesses my appearance in the photographs on the passport's front page and on the foreign visas. "This one looks better," he points at the picture with my hair tied in a ponytail. "Not like this," he points to my loose hair now.*

His offer does not make any sense. I am supposed to admit that I have violated a law that, as far as I am concerned, I did not violate.

Maybe he is simply trying to pass time until something else happens. Nonetheless, I do want to end it quickly. If I will get only a warning, I have nothing to lose. "I will do what you want me to do as long as I get my passport back and will be able to leave the valley today." He nods and says, "I understand."

The Uniform gives me a piece of paper and a pen and tells me to write that I admit violating the law, "Write, 'I arrived at Hovliguzar on the seventh of August and failed to register.'" "But," I interrupt, "I arrived on the ninth and was supposed to be in Tashkent by now." "Just write what I tell you to write," he says in a stern voice, now, without a smile. He adds that I should write about my reasons for being in Uzbekistan and in the valley, detailing who I stayed with, where I live in Russia, whether I have children, how many, if I'm married, what is my occupation, whose address I am registered at in Tashkent, and so forth. He does not need that much information for this particular note. But it is a small price to pay for being able to leave the valley and get back to my son.

"Continue, 'In the future, whenever I visit Uzbekistan, I will follow the country's registration law.' Done?" he asks. I nod. "Now, write, 'I have no pritenzij *[complaints] about the way I was treated by the* predstavitilyami pravoohranitel'nikh organov *[representatives of law enforcement].'"*

He reads through the note and says I have to rewrite it. According to him, it is hard to read my handwriting. His "boss" will not be able to understand what it says. I copy the note and sign it. I tear the first version and leave it on the table. He picks up another document, a form in Uzbek, and tells me to sign it. "What is it?" I ask. He replies, "This is a warning [a form]." "Is this all it is?" I ask. He answers, "Just a warning." I hesitate because I really do not know what it says. "I need an interpreter," I reply. "This is just an official form for a report," he retorts. I sign this untranslated form impulsively. He takes the new copy of my note, this document, and my passport, says that he will return soon, and leaves the room. The door is shut behind him. I pick up the torn version of my contrived and dictated confession of breaking the law and put it the back pocket of my jeans.

I wait a couple of minutes and knock on the door. A guard opens it. I ask to go to the bathroom. He says that it is not permitted. "But I am not detained or arrested, why can I not leave this room?" I ask. He says I need to wait inside and shuts the door in my face. It is about noon now. I walk around the room. I feel an excruciating pain in my right shoulder. Why? Because, if Tahsir was right, I am stressed out, I am scared. Something tells me that I will not get out of this office with a warning only.

An hour passes. The door opens. The guard brings in another chair, takes away the wooden stool, and tells me to sit down. It is very hot. I ask for water. He says that I will be given some soon and leaves. Another forty minutes passes. I knock on the door. No response. The door is locked. I walk around. I make an airplane from another clean piece of paper I find on the table. Not sure why, I write on one wing of my paper plane, YOU CAN DO IT, *and on the other one* I FORGIVE YOU. *I send this plane flying across the room.*

*As soon as the plane lands, the door opens. The Uniform comes in, complaining about the heat. He looks at the airplane on the floor and tells me to pick it up. Feeling as if I did something wrong, as if he is my parent telling me to pick up my toys, I follow his directive. He takes the plane away from me and reads the English words, "*YOU CAN DO IT. I FORGIVE YOU.*" He puts the plane on the desk, looks at me, smiles, picks up his hat, and says, "I forgot it." I want to yell, "Give me my passport! Let me go! You have no right to keep me here against my will!" but trying to not irritate him, I ask, "Please leave the door open. It is impossible to breathe." He nods and leaves the room. The door stays open but guarded. I grab the paper plane and tear it apart. This is not the end. I am not flying or driving anywhere today. Now I have a feeling of knowing: I know that I am not leaving the valley today. Can I do it? I think I can.*

I ask again to go to the bathroom and to have some water. The guard at the door tells me to wait. Restless, I walk back and forth from the window to the door. The guard tells me to sit down. I come to the door again and yell my friend's name. The guard shuts the door in my face. Now I feel angry. I am counting from one to fifteen. My stepfather taught me that this helps you to calm down.

By now, it is about two in the afternoon. The door opens. The Civilian comes in. He smiles. I try to smile back and ask when I can get my passport back and leave the valley. He says that I have nothing to worry about. This is just a general procedure. He has a thick notebook and a bunch of documents, including my passport, in his hand. His shirt is not tucked into his pants and is bulky around the waist. Maybe he has a gun or a voice recorder there.

The Civilian asks me if I have a telephone or a voice recorder. I reply that I do not. He asks me to stand up and turn around. "Why?" I reply. "I do not even know who you are. You did not show me your badge," I add. He pulls out his badge from his pants' back pocket. Holding it in his hands, he lets me read it. He is an SNB officer. I ask if I have been charged with anything and whether they have probable cause for keeping me here. He says, "We have a cause. In order to let you go, I need to ask you some questions, so please stand up and turn around," he repeats. I stand up and turn around. Gently, he pats me from my hips down. It's pretty obvious that I'm not concealing anything because I have on a pair of tight pants and a tight T-shirt. A copy of my confession stays in the back pocket of my jeans unnoticed. According to him, this search is just a formality; he needs to be sure I have no weapons or recording equipment. Then he asks if I have any complaints. I tell him that it has been about five hours since my last bathroom visit or drink of water. He apologizes, goes to the door, and tells something to the guard, turns toward me, and looks through his notebook.

I try not to look at him. I notice how shabby the chairs are. The metal safe needs painting. The nonworking air-conditioning unit looks worn out. The table is old but clean. I stare at it, trying to find any marks, any notes or scratches, maybe "Peter was here." There is nothing on it. The Civilian comes back to the table. From his pants' pocket he pulls out his mobile phone and puts it on the table. The sound of it hitting the table interrupts an awkward silence.

In a couple of minutes, a female officer comes in. She accompanies me to the bathroom downstairs and then allows me to wash my face and drink some water from the water fountain in the office courtyard. She asks me why they (the officers) are so interested in me and if I did something wrong. I thank her and tell her that I have no idea what is going on. I do not trust her.

When I return to the room, the Civilian asks me if I am thirsty and hungry. I tell him that I had some water in the yard. He says that he is going to ask my friend to buy us something to drink and eat. We can eat while we talk. He says that he knows my preference for Coca-Cola. Wondering why he knows this, I realize that yesterday at the downtown café I ordered a Coke. He could have learned this from the other agents. From the back pocket of his pants he pulls out a pack of cigarettes and a lighter and puts them on the table in front of me. The situation feels unreal, as if every interrogation in the world is scripted. The interrogation always starts with cigarettes and "Do you smoke?" "Smoke?" the Civilian offers. I take one. I quit smoking five years ago. Whether prompted by the behavioral script of being interrogated, a suppressed addiction, or my fear, I feel I need one now.

He offers to have a discussion, to talk honestly about my reasons for visiting Uzbekistan and the valley. He says, "If you tell me honestly what you are doing here, I will let you go." I ask again if he has any charges against me, and if he does, I would like to make a phone call, to find a lawyer, and to call the Russian consulate in Tashkent. "I know my rights," I add. He regrets it, but he cannot let me do that. According to him, this is not an interrogation, but a talk. There is no need for a lawyer unless I did something unlawful. With a smile, he asks me if I did something unlawful. I answer, "No."

He begins, "So Svetlana Alexeevna, who are you working for?"

"I teach at a university."

"Which university? Where?"

"A university in America."

"You see, Svetlana Alexeevna, now we know about America. [Smiles.] Why did you tell us that you were Russian?"

"I am a Russian citizen."

"All right," he agrees, "You are. You are a Russian citizen who teaches in America. I understand. But WHO are you REALLY working for? For an American university and who else?"

"I told you. I teach at a university. This is my only job," I respond, while thinking, "Oh my god, he thinks I am a spy. My research is partially funded by the US Department of State. What happens when he finds this out? What if he decides this is true: that I am a spy?"

He nods and continues, "Let us be friends. Just tell me who you are working for and what you are doing here in Hovliguzar. I need the truth. We can help each other. You can help me, and I can help you. You want to go home, do you not? You have a son to go back to, right?"

We can help each other. What does he mean? What happens if we cannot help each other? My brain answers these questions by activating horror stories I have heard before. These horror stories create and sustain fear. Suddenly in this heat I feel cold. There is no need for air-conditioning; all it takes is a little bit of fear. Feeding on horror stories—the ones that I have heard and the ones that I have imagined—fear spreads thoughout my body. The fight-or-flight syndrome redirects blood from the extremities to your major organs, making you feel cold. Once fully in-bodied, fear becomes embodied; a portable prison, it circumscribes your movements, breathing, speech, and thinking; staying inside this prison can drive you mad.

Among the horror stories you have probably heard is the story of torture, which makes you afraid of yourself, of your vulnerable body, of your mind. It starts with detention. At first, you are verbally interrogated and offered the option of signing a confession. You decline. They insist. You decline again. Then the first blow. You can take it. You bounce back. At first, you feel scared but also angry; you wish you could hit back, defend yourself. But you cannot. Your hands are cuffed. Then more blows follow. And more. And harder. Till blood spills. And more. Till your dignity is shattered. And more. Pitiful, you cry out, you beg them to stop. They say they will. Just sign this confession. You refuse. Another blow, again and again. More blood. You taste it. The pain is inside and out. Madness of helplessness. The sound of a fist moving through the air feels like a razor blade cutting through your eardrum into your brain. Memories flash and melt away. Disorderly. Random. Delirious. You feel your head. It is both empty and full of racing, excruciatingly unclear thoughts. You feel your body. It is a bundle of pain. It aches. Some of it is swollen. Some of it is worn out. Your skin cannot enclose your whole body anymore. It ruptures in some places in order to enclose other ones. Overused. Overabused. Tired. This body needs rest. But the blows continue. Like in a dream, in a nightmare, you are not asleep, but you cannot wake up. These blows . . .

Then something else. You leave the body and float above a semi-arid land dotted with occasional half-dry ponds, cut through with a rare road. Sunburned and washed out. Blurring edges. The mountains are like ripples in the water. The water is muddy. And then this turns into sand, into dunes. The sea of sand. Desolate. Rainless. Windy. A sandstorm hurts your eyes. It makes you blind. And then an oasis. Water. More water. Lakes and ponds and rivers. Here and there. Then everywhere. Tears. They are your tears. You can see. You see the light that blinds. It is all light. The light through tears. You drown in this overwhelming light . . .

Then you return to your almost lifeless body. You come back to life. You wish you did not. And this goes on: leaving and coming back until they are done.

When they are done, your body is no longer your temple. It has been conquered and destroyed. It has no more to give. And this is when you sign. You sign as long as you have some body left. They tell you what. They tell you where. You do. They let you be. You are. You live through this pain, this experience. It becomes you. And it becomes a story. Both uttered and neutered. Both exaggerated and untold. This horror story lives on. It outlives you. Others hear it. They listen and remember. The story becomes embedded. Then it becomes embodied. It achieves its purpose. It horrifies and occupies by taking root in your memory. It's like fog, both palpable and impalpable. It obscures. You never know what is behind—behind the fog, behind the story. There can be sun or storm or yet another blow.

Horror stories. They are short but last as long as we are. By editing our lives accordingly, we live. These stories live with us, sometimes helping to avoid creating our own horror stories because all it takes is just a little bit of fear. . . .

"Sveta-opa, I am talking to you!" says the Civilian. I look at him and light another cigarette.

No Longer 2003

Much has changed since 2003. For about five years, between 2005 and 2010, the United States had fallen out of grace with the Uzbek government (Olcott 2007). The reasons included US criticisms of human rights abuses by the Uzbek government and law enforcement agencies, in particular the state-sponsored massacre of protestors in Andijon in 2005 (McGlinchey 2011). Uzbekistan ignored human rights groups' and European governments' calls for an international independent investigation of this tragedy. In order to persuade the Uzbek government to improve its human rights record, the United States and the European Union imposed sanctions on Uzbekistan, including an arms embargo and a visa ban on the officials thought to be responsible for the massacre. The Uzbek government responded by (1) insisting that the protest was led by violent religious extremists, who *had to be* stopped by the government forces; (2) closing the US air base in Karshi-Khanabad; (3) expelling the majority of nongovernmental organizations with US or European connections; and (4) nurturing and strengthening existing relationships with Russia and China, Uzbekistan's closer allies.

In October 2006, the president of Uzbekistan spoke at the Andijon Council of People's Deputies, noting that limited opportunities for self-fulfillment and self-realization made the valley's youth vulnerable to propaganda by such religious organizations as Hizb-ut-Tahrir. In the president's view, this propaganda led to religious extremism, which led to protests, and protests led to violence. In order to prevent such scenarios, he urged local governments, with the help of and under the control of the national government, to create more opportunities for young people, including new infrastructural projects (e.g., schools) funded by the government and more employment opportunities. (Some scholars note that this rhetoric of change went largely unfulfilled [see, e.g., Khamidov 2008].)

In order to curtail "untraditional" or "alien" forms of Islam, such as Hizb-ut-Tahrir, the new governor in Andijon Province, Ahmadjan Usmanov, appointed in 2006, advocated for and enforced new restrictions on religious practices.[1] For example, performing daily ritual prayers at work was prohibited. Violators faced steep fines. SNB officers—their number also increased in the area after the Andijon massacre—continued holding "preventive talks" about the ills of radicalization among some Muslims. Muslims whom the SNB officers considered to be acting overly devout were accused of affiliation with Hizb-ut-Tahrir and detained.

The administrative changes that followed the Andijon massacre also affected religious officials in Tashkent. Some, such as the deputy mufti Nematulla Jeenbekov, were accused of corruption and dismissed. Several imams in Tashkent were accused of Wahhabism. The new religious leadership was adamant about fighting "Islamic radicals" and about restricting the activities of Protestant missionaries.

It was claimed that, like "untraditional" forms of Islam, Protestant missionaries and their local followers were undermining national unity, made up of, according to the government, Hanafi Muslims and Orthodox Christians. The Russian Orthodox Church's leadership fully supported curbing "sectarian" and "foreign" missionary

1. For President Karimov's warning about "alien forms of Islam," see Rasanayagam 2010, 108.

activities. In the process, among other organizations, the US Peace Corps was accused of funding Protestant missionaries and promoting their religious ideologies and so had to suspend its program in Uzbekistan.

Earlier, in 2003, in order to achieve "a cherished goal" of building "a new state, a new life, based on the harmony of national ideas," President Karimov called on all media sources in Uzbekistan not to "limit themselves to mere coverage and reflection of reality," but to engage actively in the nation-building project (quoted in Kendzior 2010, 42). In order to assure "correct" media coverage and engagement, the government aggressively pursued control of all online and offline media sources through registration and other means. Falling in line, several television programs targeted the missionary activities of Protestant religious groups. One of these programs, *Hypocrisy*, aired at the end of 2006, accused Protestant missionary groups of operating illegally and paying locals to join their ranks. In order to prevent discord in families and society, *Hypocrisy* urged the general public to stay with their traditional religion—Islam.

By 2010, the relationships between Uzbekistan and Russia as well as between Uzbekistan and China continued to be strong. In addition to shared economic interests, the shared geopolitical interests among Uzbekistan, Russia, and China continued to include national security. In order to prevent public unrest "after NATO leaves Afghanistan in 2014," Russian and Uzbek armies conducted joint military training in 2011 "aimed at defeating negative developments shown from the examples of Libya and Syria and the export of destabilization" (Nikolski 2011).[2]

By this time, though, the relationship between the United States and Uzbekistan had improved. Uzbekistan could provide a more convenient supply route for the American troops still stationed in Afghanistan. This led to the rapprochement between the two

2. The Nikolski article may be impossible to find; as an alternative, see Felgenhauer 2011.

countries, which came at the expense of US official criticism of the Uzbekistan government's "business as usual" approach in creating consent through intimidation and violence (for more on the Uzbek state's violence see, e.g., Atayeva and Belomestnov 2011; International Crisis Group 2011). Meanwhile, in order to protect its national values and traditions, in March 2011 the Uzbek government charged representatives of Human Rights Watch with "ignoring Uzbekistan's national legislation" and failing to understand "Uzbekistan's culture and traditions" and so shut down its office in Tashkent (Human Rights Watch 2011).

"National Islam"

In 2011, I saw a different Uzbekistan, Ferghana Valley, and Hovliguzar from what I remembered. That June, the country was preparing to celebrate the twentieth year of its independence from the Soviet Union. This event has been commemorated annually on September 1 through a national holiday that includes a vast and truly "spectacular" artistic performance in the capital (for more on the form and content of the celebration see Adams 2010). Great amounts of money have been spent to gather thousands of performers from all over the country into an epic nationalist production affirming the state's power, defining "correct" forms of cultural expression, and nurturing the citizen's compliance because a violent pacification of a population cannot by itself ensure the nation-state's normal functioning. This year, at the event attended by a number of foreign high-profile dignitaries, a display of Uzbekistan's culture and traditions, in their "correct" form, was going to be twenty times more "spectacular" than ever before.

Islam, the most potent national tradition and a symbol of national identity, also had to be expressed in "politically correct" and regionally authentic ways; as a part of the nation-building project a good Uzbek citizen had to have politically correct sensibilities, knowledge(s), and behaviors (for more on the religion and the nation-state, see Asad 1999). In line with national ideology incorporating

Uzbekistan's "Golden Heritage," "culturally authentic" traditions, and "a useable [Soviet] past," after the Andijon's tragedy the Uzbek government rallied religious leaders loyal to the state to help promote "national Islam" (see Adams 2010, 30; Rasanayagam 2010). In 2007, in order to establish doctrinal coherence corresponding to Hanafi Islam among local populations, these leaders were urged to tour the country and meet with their local informal counterparts and authorities.

The same year, in a public speech, while encouraging the official religious leaders' active participation in this process, the deputy chairman of the Muslim Board of Uzbekistan, Abdul-Aziz Mansur, linked national and religious ideologies and noted that the religious leaders should inform the people that "the state does not intend to enforce" its own ideology and that no one would persecute the people for "the proper observance" of religious rites at the mosques (quoted in Ferghana News Agency 2007). Like President Karimov, the deputy chairman portrayed "national Islam" as tolerant toward representatives of other religions, yet he also reminded Uzbeks that missionary activity by individuals representing faiths other than Russian Orthodox Christianity and Judaism was outlawed. He added that the "mosques" must be "places where people should be talked to and everything explained," including what "national Islam" is and how it should be performed. Yet these discussions did not have to include "the youth," whose main responsibility was to concentrate on their secular education.[3] Deputy Chairman Mansur urged religious leaders to forgive the youth who missed Friday prayers and to denounce as sinners those parents who encouraged their children to attend Friday prayers instead of going to school.

The government's domestic and foreign policies, and its discourse on "national Islam," however indirectly, affected the unfolding personal histories and life projects of individuals I am writing about. In

3. The deputy chairman was talking about young men and boys as "the youth" because women and girls did not attend mosques at the time.

turn these life projects created social effects that helped to articulate, however indirectly, these policies and discourse.

Nainahon, 2011

Upon my return to the Ferghana Valley in 2011, I spent a total of ten days at Nainahon's house. When I first arrived at her place, Nainahon was not at home. Her second daughter, who met me at the gate, said that she was at "fitness" (a fitness club). Nainahon's mother-in-law gave me a hug, while commenting that I was too slim and asking if I was healthy. In order to shelter us from the July heat of 115°F, she led me toward a *topchan*, an elevated, above-ground wooden structure that served as a table and a resting place in a shadowy part of the courtyard. On the way, she showed me her small flower garden and said that although she was slim too and too old to do anything, her spirit was still strong. While Nainahon's older grandchildren took my suitcases to a spacious air-conditioned room inside the house that was used for large *meropriyatiya*, her second daughter set up a *dasturkhon*, including tea, fruit, flat bread, honey, and candy on the *topchan*.

Nainahon arrived shortly. She was wearing a white and blue pantsuit and a semitransparent, loose, untied scarf that exposed her red hair, which was shorter than when I saw her last, and holding a *sotka* (mobile phone) in her right hand and another *sotka* in her left hand. While hugging me, she commented on how slim I was and immediately asked about the exercises and diet I have used to stay in shape. She, for a brief moment, returned to the conversation suspended in her right hand with "wait" and then asked me if my son, my parents, and my friends in Tashkent were healthy.

The previous eight years had been very eventful and challenging for all members of Nainahon's family. She had to pay for "four weddings in eight years"—two for her son and two for her daughters. They were very expensive. Her son's first marriage did not last, and he met his second wife while working odd jobs in St. Petersburg. According to Nainahon, there were more job opportunities for him in Russia than in Uzbekistan. His second wife's family members, Uzbeks who now lived in Ukraine, had, like her son, traveled to Russia for seasonal temporary work. They had showed him her picture. "He liked her," and Nainahon arranged their marriage. Several weeks after the wedding in Hovliguzar, her son left for Russia, where he shared a rented apartment with two other young men. Since his living accommodations were insufficient to house a family, his new wife stayed with Nainahon in the separate quarters at the same compound.

Nine months after the wedding, Nainahon's daughter-in-law gave birth to a healthy boy. In time, the relationship between Nainahon and the daughter-in-law became strained because they both were "hard-headed." One day, saying that she was tired of living without her husband, the daughter-in-law took her child and left for Ukraine to live with her brothers. This "broke [Nainahon's] heart." She locked up her son's part of the house, hoping that he would come back from St. Petersburg and get married again. And finally, "according to tradition," he, "the one and only son," would "stay put in one place" and "take care of his aging parents." I nodded in agreement even though I knew that her son, working at the time as a taxi driver, had stated in his most recent email message to me that he was not planning on returning to Uzbekistan anytime soon.

Two of Nainahon's four daughters had unhappy marriages. Her second daughter and her two children were living now with Nainahon. This daughter was twice married and twice divorced. The first husband turned out to be a drug addict, and the second one, according to her, was impotent. When she got married the first time, she had to leave college. Divorced a second time in 2010, she worked on a college degree. Then she wanted to get her master's degree, get a job at a local SNB office, and live in her own apartment with her two children. In this daughter's view, to work in the human resources department or as a secretary or an accountant or even an officer at a local SNB office was the best job for a single mother. It was more stable than a job in the private sector and had desirable social and retirement benefits. In Nainahon's opinion, her daughter's ideas were "just dreams." "A good husband" was all that this daughter "really needed in life." "Luckily," Nainahon knew of "one doctor needing a wife" and was working on marrying off this daughter to him.

Nainahon's third daughter almost died during her third C-section. Since she had gotten married, she had given birth to four children, one after another. Ten months after the second child, she had twins. Nainahon was very worried. She cried, prayed, and sacrificed "huge lambs," and she begged and bribed the doctors to assure her daughter's health. This daughter survived because it was, in Nainahon's words, "God's will." The only thing Nainahon regretted was not asking the doctors to "*perevyazat' trubi* [sterilize]" her (for more on Islam and reproductive health in the valley, see Peshkova 2005). A day before I arrived, this daughter had a fight with her husband; she was staying with Nainahon, waiting for the husband to come with an apology and take her and their four children back home. Nainahon's youngest daughter had married recently and was "so far happy." She lived in a nearby *qishloq* (village), and Nainahon's oldest daughter was married to a "good man" and resided elsewhere in the Ferghana Valley.

The sausage business Nainahon had launched in the early 2000s was successful for several years. But in 2007 the store downtown, which housed the largest sausage stand, burned down. In light of this loss and fierce competition with other businesses, Nainahon decided to return to shuttle trade. Like a decade or so ago, she traveled to Turkey to buy clothes (not fabrics this time) and resell them wholesale to local traders, who in turn sold them at local bazaars.

In order to advertise her products to other women, Nainahon wore the clothes she bought in Turkey, mainly pantsuits and fancy dresses, not a *hijab* and long dresses as before (although she did sell "Turkish *hijab*s" as well). She converted the guest quarters of her house into a store where she met her clients, and she housed guests in the large room for social events. Her business was slowly taking off, and mainly women wandered into her in-house store. Nainahon hoped that she eventually would not have to travel but could send money to the dealers in Turkey, who would in turn send the goods to her in Uzbekistan. Considering her previous experiences with Uzbek customs enforcement, these goods, she said, would go through customs offices other than those in Tashkent—"ideally" through those on the border with Kyrgyzstan, near Osh, where she had "some connections."

For years, Nainahon had financially supported herself, her husband, and her mother-in-law. Now she was also supporting her twice-married and twice-divorced daughter, her younger daughter, and all of their children. Although they could downsize, sell this house, and move to a smaller place, they all were "used to eating and dressing well," and she "could not throw her daughters and grandchildren out of her house onto the street."

In addition to—or as a result of—the economic challenges Nainahon had to face, one day she "looked in the mirror and saw an old woman." That day she decided to change her life: she "was not an old woman!" She joined a local fitness club, bought new facial creams, foundation, and eye shadows, and tried to follow "a healthy diet." In fact, during this year's month of ritual fasting, Ramazan, Nainahon was expecting to lose "five kilos [about ten pounds]." "Some things change," she said. "But some things do not," I thought. She was still full of energy, moving swiftly around the house giving orders to her two daughters and "a maid" (a hired laborer).

Nainahon was no longer going to religious lessons with descendants of the Prophet Muhammad because she was too busy making money for her "*ochen' bol'shaya* [very big]" family. She occasionally visited her favorite teacher, Ova. Ova's son, Tahsir, was still Nainahon's source of healing, and Tahsir's first wife, Onahon, stayed one of her best friends and clients. They met frequently during various *meropriyatiya* around town.

Despite being busy, Nainahon continued learning about Islam by herself at home. While focusing on her new business, fitness, and family matters, she read the Qur'an only in her free time but still prayed and performed ritual ablutions regularly and fasted every year; she tried to be "truly" Muslim to the best of her abilities.

Nainahon added that over the past eight years people's interest in "correct" Islam had not subsided. Local *otinchalar* trained the same number of students in 2011 as they did in 2002–2003; "if they taught a hundred then, they teach a hundred now." In her case, it was not the government's prohibition of teaching Islam informally at individuals' homes or disenchantment with Islam but her family's best interest that had led her to discontinue religious instruction with Ova.

In 2003, Nainahon had told me that if an individual really wanted God to hear her prayers, a holy person, such as her teacher, Ova, should intercede on her behalf. In addition to getting a religious education, this was one other reason she used to visit Ova and other "*svyatie ludi* [holy people]." But in 2011 she insisted, "You have to ask God yourself. It does not say anywhere that someone should ask God for you." This difference in her understanding of "correct" Islam, of a particular relationship between human and divine worlds, could have been a result of religious officials' insistence on the un-Islamic nature of mediators between the two worlds. It is more likely, however, that this difference reflected the fact that in 2011 Nainahon had a larger family to feed and less money to spend on a gratuity for others' intercession with God on her behalf. Therefore, within the range of discourses about "correct" Islam available to her and *in relation to* others, including her family members, she articulated the view that suited her contemporary situation the best. This view allowed Nainahon to pray and make requests directly to God. If and when she could afford it, she would ask the "holy people," those claiming to have a special connection to God, to pray on her behalf.

Nainahon asked me about changes in my personal life. She knew that things had been rocky for me but wanted the juicy details. I shared with her some of my stories, while she shared hers with me. She said she was upset with her husband for two reasons. First, since the sausage business had collapsed, Nainahon's husband had sold their family car and purchased farmland outside Hovliguzar. "This was *his* idea," said Nainahon. They hired labor to clear the land and planned to rent it out to local farmers. From the start, she did not like this idea but supported her husband as much as she could. As she anticipated, this land eventually became "a big problem": the local *prokhuratura* (prosecutor's office) was trying to find any possible reason to confiscate this land. According to Nainahon, "they [representatives of the prosecutor's office] sold this land" to someone else. She hired a lawyer and fought back. "But honestly," she said, "I am tired of fighting." While her husband saw the land as a good investment and was not planning on selling it anytime soon, she secretly hoped that he would change his mind and sell it, buy a good car, and invest the rest of the money in her new business.

Second, her husband always wanted another son. He had recently told Nainahon that he wanted to take a second wife to have more children with, but he would not get married without Nainahon's permission. Nainahon felt ambivalent. On the one hand, as a Muslim woman she thought she should not object to her husband's second marriage. But as a proud individual she could not allow it either. Her solution to this problem did not jeopardize her understanding of "correct" Islam. She thought she would resolve this dilemma in the "Islamic way" by allowing him to marry on one condition—he and his second wife would have to live elsewhere and not in this house, which Nainahon called "my house." This way she would not have to interact with the new wife in person; her husband's staying with the co-wife would be like sending him "*v kommandirovku* [on a business trip]." But before she gave him her answer, Nainahon wanted to secure the money her business was making for herself and her children, which in her view, was also "Islamic."

Despite the previous eight years of trials and tribulations, including the state's customs regulations and laws, the global economy, her aging body, her children's health, and her husband's desire to marry another woman, Nainahon was still optimistic. Against all odds, she was still trying "to make [her] own circumstance," as Nigel Rapport would put it (2003, 261). In the process, the choices she made in her daily life, including her choice of what to wear and the frequency of religious instruction, in her opinion did not diminish her faith in God but strengthened it. To her, being "truly" Muslim was dynamic and not static, and "correct" Islam was "about real life," pragmatic and not abstract. She was planning on getting Internet service "really soon" and buying a "big Apple computer." This would allow her to use Skype to talk to her business associates in Kyrgyzstan and Turkey, to me in the United States, and to her son in Russia. She also expected her new business to take off and grow, and as a result she would become wealthy. According to her, it was just a matter of time because "nothing was impossible" except for one thing, "a party," she said and chuckled. "If it were not Ramazan," she added while reminiscing about our dancing in 2003, she would throw a big party in my honor, where I could teach her some "new modern moves," and she could remind me of local "traditional" ones, which, she said, I had probably by now forgotten.

Jahon, 2011

Even though I had spoken to Jahon by phone at various times from 2003 to 2011, I had no idea how and in what ways the government's attempts to promote "national Islam" and establish doctrinal coherence among religious teachers and leaders had informed her life project. Our telephone conversations took the form of short updates on each other's lives. To my question "*Kak dela*? [How are you doing]?" she answered, "*Vse horosho, spasibo* [Everything is good, thank you]." Then she thanked God and said she was very happy. Then we talked about our families' news, and Jahon reminded me that she prayed on my and my son's behalf and that I should do the same for my son and myself. Every conversation ended with her inviting me to visit Hovliguzar and to stay with her and with me promising to do so as soon as possible. When I finally was ready to go back to the valley, Jahon enigmatically said, "Do not worry. I will do everything right. You will stay here. I will take you places. I will help you." I was not sure what to think about that invitation, in particular her promise to "do everything right." Because I had read about the government's firmer restrictions on religion and freedom of information, I was not sure if I heard in Jahon's voice a warning or a desire to share, to help me to learn some stories that I could share with others in Uzbekistan, Russia, and the United States. Maybe, despite increasing restrictions, there was a way to do it and do it right, as she promised.

Despite her invitation, in 2011 on the way to Hovliguzar I decided not to stay with Jahon. As a foreigner and a researcher intimidated by the state's law enforcement agencies in 2003, I was afraid to attract these agencies' attention to her activities. Little did I know that she was working for the government and that I would eventually lead representatives of a local branch of the SNB to her—or, perhaps, it was the other way around, that she would lead them to me.

After visiting with Tursun-oi following my arrival at Hovliguzar, I went to see Jahon. She greeted me and led me into the living room of her recently remodeled home, which still had some unfinished architectural projects. Eight years ago this room had a wardrobe, a table, chairs, and a sofa. Now, except for a low table and a couple of floor mats, the room was empty. I have learned since that day that not only the structural additions to her house, but also and more importantly career-related developments in her life affected the meaning and function of this room, which was now used for social events and meetings only.

Jahon offered me a seat on one side of the table on a floor mat, sat on a mat across from me, tilted toward me, and performed a *duo*. Then she smiled and said that there were many changes in her life. "First of all," her "soul" was now "happy and at peace." Islam "cleansed her thoughts and her heart." The second change, she said, was her family and her neighborhood. She had become "a better mother and a better," more patient wife—"not like I used to be before"—and a better friend. She "loved and respected" her friends, neighbors, and elders and cared for the sick. She called them and stopped by to check on their well-being. As a result, although she had not become independently wealthy, her soul was greatly enriched.

"I Am Not an Otincha, but an Otin"

"I meant to tell you, I won the competition," Jahon said. "What competition?" I replied, unsure what she was referring to. "To be a regional *otin* [*otincha*]," she answered. "Remember, I wanted to compete with others, to compare our knowledge about Islam. I will tell you more later," she added with a coy smile, waving her right hand in the air.

Although during our subsequent conversations, Jahon used the words *otin* and *otincha* interchangeably, she told me from the offset to refer to her as "an *otin* or *otinoy*," not "an *otincha*." Earlier that day Tursun-oi, too, had told me that "in Islam we do not have *otincha*; we should have *otin*, *otinoy*, or *otinlar*, [or] *illimtolib*, a human looking for knowledge. We all are *illimtolib*. We can never know everything." Jahon explained that *otinchalar* were women who did not have her level of ethical behavior and religious knowledge. In her view, this change in preferred terms of reference also signaled increased social respect toward *otinlar* (the plural of *otin*), toward women like her. Even though she would never become an official scholar of Islam, "like the learned men from Tashkent," her family and the members of her community and the local *hokimyat* (city hall) respected her "more than before."

Jahon chuckled and said that she had not become wealthy but had become "a well-known *otin*;" she *could* make plenty of money by presiding over various *meropriyatiya* but turned "many invitations down" because her husband, who used to drive her to and from social events around the valley's towns and villages, had gone to Russia "to make money." "Of course," he would not object to her taking a cab to attend *meropriyatiya* regionally, but she "could not" do it "out of respect" for him. She also had a reputation to uphold. In her *mahalla*, Jahon said, some people would not understand why a married woman, while her husband was far away, would travel by herself accompanied by unknown men, taxi drivers. She decided that she could travel regionally only when her husband had made enough money and finally returned home to Uzbekistan.

During our first conversation, Jahon mentioned several times that after her husband's return from Russia, she wanted to perform the hajj. In order to be able to do so, she had to put her name "on the list." She said that every year only one person from each *mahalla* was "allowed [by the Uzbek government] to go." She was the thirty-first person on the list. Jahon did not want to bribe officials in order to move up the list, like "others" did, and she tried to be patient and a better Muslim, to do more "good deeds," for which God would reward her and help her to complete the hajj at some point in less than thirty years.

Although Jahon understood that not everyone could perform the hajj—that some could not afford it, and that others, like her, were "too far down on the list"—ideally, she believed, everyone should have an opportunity to go on the pilgrimage because "the real hajj changes your whole life and your whole family." She said that she was grateful that President Karimov had "opened for Muslims the road to the hajj" and "allowed Uzbeks" to travel overseas to earn money. She chuckled and added, "They [the president and the government] opened all the roads. The first time my husband went there [to Russia], [he did it so that we could] change our car from a Zhiguli [a Russian car] to a Nexia [a car model made by GM Uzbekistan]." "Now," she said, pointing around the room, "[he has gone to make money] to fix this house." There were more job opportunities in Russia than in Uzbekistan, people's salaries were much higher, and "a Russian ruble was worth more than an Uzbek som."

Jahon made other plans. After going on the hajj with her husband, she would marry off her two youngest daughters, and only then would her husband drive her to *meropriyatiya* in Hovliguzar and the valley so that she would finally be able "to bring change" to other parts of the region and "maybe even to become wealthy." Her mission of changing others and becoming financially successful was important to Jahon, but not essential. For her, as for Tursun-oi and Nainahon, family always came first, and social changes started at home, with an individual and her family.

Jahon's Solutions to Women's Problems

Later that day Jahon told me that in 2008 she had met with local imams and the ulama (Muslim legal scholars) from Tashkent, who, in order to establish doctrinal coherence among religious teachers and leaders, were touring the country. Among "two hundred women," she faced a selection committee made of four ulama. The committee members asked each one of these women three questions about "Hanafi *mashab*'s position regarding this and that." She answered these questions better than anyone else. As a result, out of the two hundred women she was appointed "*hokimyat otin* [the city's *otin*]." This committee initially offered her the position of "*oblastnoj*, *viloyat* ["provincial" in Russian and Uzbek] *otin*." She turned down this position "for personal reasons for now." As a *hokimyat otin*, Jahon focused on the local—her family and the families in her *mahalla* and her city—not on a regional community or the whole Uzbek society. She was also invited to the Hovliguzar *hokimyat*'s monthly meetings, where she brought "women's problems," such as *mnogozhenstvo* (polygyny) to the local government's attention and advised on how to solve these problems.

According to Jahon, *mnogozhenstvo* was one of the main problems afflicting Uzbek society, affecting women and children negatively. She stated unequivocally that in Uzbekistan polygyny had nothing to do with Islam; local men had other than Islamic reasons to marry a second wife. Some wanted more children; others were very wealthy and so getting new wives was "like getting new cars." Yet others married a second wife because their first wife failed to become an interesting companion and stay sexually desirable. This last reason, she believed, was the easiest one to address. "I began thinking what we [women] can do. Because this is a problem that women *can* resolve."

In synch with her understanding of ideal marriage as a companionship based on gendered complementarity of spouses, who are biologically and ontologically different, solving the problem of polygyny, in Jahon's view, required cooperation among women—in particular mothers-in-law and daughters-in-law. She believed that men's main social responsibility is to provide for their families, but one of women's responsibilities is to be sexually desirable. This made sense to Jahon because she said that men's sexual desires are a part of their biological nature and that women are endowed with a biological ability to satisfy these desires. Thus, it is only "normal" for a husband to look for other women if his wife fails to satisfy his natural sexual urges.

Jahon's solution to polygyny was contextual. In her neighborhood, as in other *mahallas* in the valley, patrilocal and joint (or extended) residence, where a (youngest) son, his wife, and children resided with his parents, and an extended family structure that included in-laws and sometimes siblings as well as the husband's kin were prevalent. She observed others and knew from personal experience that *kelin*s (daughters-in-law) often did all the work around the house "from early morning until late at night." As a result, they had "no time or *sili* [strength]" left to develop intellectually and stay sexually desirable for their husbands. Hence, she encouraged mothers-in-law to "allow your *kelin*s to rest more" so that they could "stay [physically] clean" and visually "attractive" and thus stay sexually desirable to their husbands.

But marriage was not only about satisfying sexual desires; it included companionship, where the spouses could share "interesting conversations." Even though men liked to socialize with other men, wives' ability to converse about various topics with their husbands, to be their companions, only strengthened marriages.[4] To fashion themselves into interesting conversational partners for their husbands, Jahon said, the *kelin*s should have enough time to educate themselves, to read books. Because daughters-in-law are expected to have "no idle moments," gaining time for their personal development

4. The view of marriage as companionship was historically persistent in the region (see chapter 3).

required encouragement from their mothers-in-law. If mothers-in-law and daughters-in-law were to cooperate and follow this model, husbands would be happy in existing marriages and "would not look for other women, for other wives." Jahon added that the children too would be happier knowing that their father's attention is not divided between them and the children from his other marriage(s). Furthermore, the husband's income, so important in their contemporary economic context, would not have to be divided between two or more families. As a consequence, she concluded, there "will be a lasting peace among all family members."

This solution made Islam's universal ethical paradigm, which included gendered creation and gender-specific propriety and responsibilities, relevant to pragmatic daily concerns and experiences. Because she claimed that men had other than Islamic reasons for polygyny, this solution did not include any reference to the Qur'anic verses often interpreted as sanctioning polygyny (e.g., Qur'an 4:3). Instead, the solution she proposed stressed the importance of sexual rights and obligations (e.g., Qur'an 2:228, 4:129) and cooperation and peace within a family (e.g., Qur'an 30:21, 7:189), which, according to her, were fundamental Islamic values. But, more importantly, Jahon fashioned this solution from what she knew best—namely, her own situation. Her personal experiences, not just religious knowledge and her analysis of intrafamily dynamics and the existing socioeconomic context in Uzbekistan, formed a foundation to her solution to polygyny.

Jahon claimed to be happily married. Her husband was often gone to Russia, but every time he came home, he wanted to spend "all his time" with Jahon, "just me and him, no children." The two of them often visited popular tourist destinations in the valley. He brought presents from Russia for her and the children, gave her money to buy religious books, and encouraged her to seek medical help if she had any health problems. He had five very close friends; each of them had two wives. "Why did my husband not get one?" Jahon answered her own question: "Because I am a good wife"; because she loves and sexually satisfies him; and because, owing her ongoing self-education, she "always" has "something new to talk about." Inasmuch as love and respect have to be cultivated and sustained, companionship and sexual desirability too require individual efforts. She reminded me of a friend who had taught her how to be "the one and only wife." "You know," Jahon said,

> our women go and work with cows and then with this smell go to their husbands. I am sorry—they smell like cows. Their husbands then start looking at other women. This one woman taught me how to live. I tried to be good so that my mother-in-law and my father-in-law liked me. I worked hard [did chores around the house and got a job for wages outside the house], and at night I was tired. I had no time for my husband. Dildorahon taught that this was not right. She taught me how to dress [to wear visually enticing lingerie]. . . . She taught me, and I taught my daughters. Thanks to her. So you see there was always someone who taught me, and I teach other people. Without it [knowledge], you cannot live. You need to know. I do not only want it for myself; I need to teach it to others.

Jahon's relationship with her husband was informed by the knowledge about how to do the right thing, which was not separate from but very much a part of their daily lives; it was experiential and existential, shaping not only their "hereafter," but also their "here and now." This knowledge was participatory, applied in relation to others and the self, and shared. Jahon learned from others, including Dildorahon and Tursun-oi. In order to ensure continuous circulation of this knowledge, without which "you cannot live," she had to pass this knowledge on to others.

Another "problem in Uzbekistan," Jahon said, were frequent *ehsons*. Similar to Nainahon, Jahon stated that some individuals spent "too much money on such feasts" to "show off" their wealth in a *mahalla*. This "wrong" intention invalidated *ehson* by making it a sin and not a meritorious act. She advised her neighbors, friends, and acquaintances to spend money on books, on education, and "on a happy life" instead of on ceremonial feasts. For instance, "recently one woman," Jahon's neighbor, complained to Jahon that her son had gone to Russia to make money but failed to send her money to buy a lamb for an *ehson*. Jahon replied that God would not help her son in finding a good job as long as his mother was unhappy with him. She told this neighbor that there was no need for making a special *ehson* because as "a mother, a Muslim woman, and through her daily work" around the house she already performed seven or eight *ehson*s a day.

The first *ehson* was "sending the daughter-in-law to work [and taking care of the house while she was gone]." The second *ehson* was "raising her grandchildren." Making food and keeping the house tidy were *ehson*s as well. These were not what Jahon called "open *ehson*s," but "covered *ehson*s" because no one except God knows about them. But this is precisely why they are "the best *ehsons*." Therefore, in Jahon's view, the *ehson* does not have to be a ceremony or a feast; it might be an individual's ethical behavior in relation to others, which is often overlooked and taken for granted in daily life.

According to Jahon, as a meritorious act *ehson* is always already there in the form of care for others—in relation to them—such as a mother's care for the members of her extended family. Therefore, daily gendered activities, duties and responsibilities that women are expected to perform in accordance with their ontological and biological differences from men, are also intentional meritorious acts rewarded by God in this life or in the next life or in both.

In Jahon's view, religious efforts, such as ritual prayers, are not divided from or superior to other efforts to be good because "correct" Islam is not external to human life, but practical; it provides moral direction for daily mundane affairs and offers pragmatic solutions to daily problems. Some of these solutions Jahon had devised, and others she had experienced. Some of them might have worked, and others might have failed. But her creativity, her intrasubjective relations with God, and her increasing knowledge about God's universal ethical paradigm, the final goal of which was for human beings to be good toward each other, guaranteed limitless configurations of possible solutions.

Competition and Negotiation

During our first meeting in 2011, Tursun-oi, referring to her former students, said, "They compete and feel jealous. I am treating them the same, as if they all are my children, but they are still jealous. I am like their mother, but they still want to feel special." Jahon, too, wanted to feel special. Among Tursun-oi's students she had a rival, another *otin* in Hovliguzar, Dilbaropa, who used to be a professor at a local institute. In the early 2000s, Dilbaropa and Jahon took lessons from Tursun-oi together. By 2011, each of them had her own followers and students. Even when Jahon and Dilbaropa were still Tursun-oi's students, they had a thorny relationship, which, Jahon said, I had failed to notice. Apparently, after I had left in 2003, many of Tursun-oi's students split along Jahon/Dilbaropa lines. Jahon said, "Dilbaropa's group has more knowledge than ours. [Our] *ustoz* [Tursun-oi] put them this way [treated them as more knowledgeable]."

Despite being very knowledgeable, Dilbaropa was rude in Jahon's view and experience. Knowing (about) the universal ethical paradigm is not the same as living it. This knowledge becomes valuable only when applied in relation to someone or something else, not just to the self and God. If rudeness toward others is a vice and kindness a virtue, then, according to Jahon, Dilbaropa was not *really* knowledgeable; she failed to establish a correspondence between her thinking, feeling, and acting and therefore had not achieved an individual mastery of Islamic knowledge.

One day Jahon wanted to attend a ceremony Dilbaropa was going to preside over in order to hear her recitation of the Qur'an and *masalas*. But she had learned that Dilbaropa did not like this idea. "Dilbaropa said"—lowering her voice, Jahon tried to imitate her—"What, am I supposed to pass an exam in front of Jahon?" Jahon felt offended. "I just wanted to know if their [Dilbaropa and her followers] knowledge was better than ours. Our *ustoz* put them above us [Jahon's followers], and now she [Tursun-oi] regrets this," she added.

When Jahon became a *hokimyat otin*, her teacher, Tursun-oi, told her "to put *our* women in each *mahalla* because they know

[Islam] better [than other existing *otinlar*]." Jahon telephoned some members of Dilbaropa's *mahalla*. As it turned out, those people she spoke with did not want Dilbaropa to become their *mahalla*'s *otin*. "They do not respect her. They do not love her. How could she lead and change people if these people do not want her? I do not know," said Jahon.

Jahon insisted that in order to effect change in others, "you need to be kind" to them. If an *otin* is supposed to teach others about how to do the right thing and live a life well led, which is a slow relational and not unidirectional process, her community has to respect this *otin*. The community has to have confidence not only in her "correct" knowledge of Islam, but also in her ability to relate to others in a way that reflects this *otin's* moral character and virtues of patience, respect, love, and care. Dilbaropa, according to Jahon, did not have her community's confidence and respect.

Dilbaropa continued to dislike Jahon because Jahon, not Dilbaropa, had "won a competition [on both the city and regional levels]." Dilbaropa had even called the *hokimyat* to find out why Jahon had successfully passed the exams. "But I won, [and] I am proud," repeated Jahon, tilting her head to the right side and raising her eyebrows.

Unlike Nainahon, Jahon reported that local *otinlar* had more students in 2003 than in 2011; "if [an *otin*] used to have twenty-five, now she has two." Jahon also noticed that the student body as a whole "used to be older, now [it is] younger." She said that Miriam, Tursun-oi's current favorite student, was relatively young. She was "a very simple girl from a nearby village" and was about twenty years old. Because "they [Miriam's family] live[d] a rural life, her soul [was] pure." But despite this purity and Miriam's knowledge and recitation skills, there was one thing about her that Jahon disliked.

> I think that she [Miriam] is very knowledgeable, but [at one *ehson* attended by Jahon] when she came [inside the room], she took a *toga* place—the highest place [she took a seat at the head of the table usually taken by the oldest individuals, an honorable place].

> This is a minus. The older people should take the high places. We read that if you are older and I am pious—read *namoz*, do *tahorat*, talk to Allah 302 times a year—I still cannot be higher than [superior to] you.[5] I tell my women [the *otinlar* she supervised and her students, although she denied having any] that they should not do it. There are both plus and minus in her [Miriam]. Even though you read and understand [have religious knowledge], you should not think that you know [everything]. We do not know. This girl is like an academic. [She behaves as if] "I know everything. All should listen to me." I think this is a minus. She is about twenty. She is very young. She is not married. She is a virgin. There are both plus and minus in her.

Because an *otin's* ability to effect moral change in the lives of others is informed not only by what she knows and teaches but also by how she behaves, in Jahon's view being knowledgeable in religious matters does not excuse an individual from the gendered and generational hierarchy that is or should be observed in relation to others. Whether you are Muslim or non-Muslim, male or female, a learned individual or not, you are expected to demonstrate respect toward elders because respect, an Islamic virtue, is also a part of historically continuous local discourse on generational hierarchy. According to Jahon, the proper behavior that reflects this discourse and Islamic virtues should be taught to children from an early age.

As in 2003, Jahon continued to believe that religious education should not be limited to adults (see the discussion of Jahon's views on this topic in chapter 3). In order to live Islamically, an individual has to have at least a rudimentary understanding of Islam. Therefore, children have to learn about Islam as well, but from qualified teachers, not just anyone. Jahon did not have her own students, but she had heard of "one local *otin*" who taught children even though

5. There are 354 or 355 days in the lunar or Islamic calendar. Jahon subtracted 52 days, during which women menstruate and should not pray because their prayers would be considered invalid.

she was not registered as a teacher. The students would make a stop at this *otin*'s house on their way home from school. "They come with books, and they leave with the same books [so no one would be suspicious]," she noted. "We [knowledgeable Muslims] are not supposed to leave anyone without knowledge. Her students are, maybe, in the sixth, third, and fourth grades. Who knows, maybe they will be famous *qoralar* [reciters of the Qur'an] one day. Young people have a good memory. I think they read the Qur'an in Uzbek and in Arabic." "They come [to study with that *otin*] with their shoulders uncovered, wearing *lyamochki* [tank tops], just like they go to school," Jahon added. "She [the *otin*] does not tell anyone. She is afraid of *proverka* [an investigation of her activities by SNB agents]."

In 2011 in Uzbekistan, sartorial practices were as important as they had been eight years earlier, particularly if an individual wanted to receive and provide religious education inconspicuously. The law enforcement agencies, endowed by the government with power to curtail any untraditional forms of Islam, were operating under the assumption that religious instruction unsanctioned by the state fostered political opposition to the existing government (see Mahmood 2006). This opposition was manifested, among other things, in an individual dress code, whereby sleeved shirts replaced sleeveless ones, and the scarves tied at the back of the neck were retied to cover one's neck and shoulders. In such context, what might be perceived locally as immodest dress became safer to wear than a modest outfit because it signaled a lack of exposure to religious instruction that was unsanctioned by the state.

In this context, *otinlar*, such as the teacher of youths whom Jahon described, had to be creative. In order to effect change in their immediate context, such women's "correct" Islam had to be practical; their own understandings of Islamic piety had to be negotiated in relation to the views of others. They had to teach minors about an ethical paradigm defined as universal and Islamic without encouraging their students to change existing sartorial practices, which these women otherwise might have defined as immodest and un-Islamic.

Jahon said that over the previous eight years, although the number of official educational centers in Uzbekistan providing knowledge about Islam had increased, it was still insufficient locally.

> The state has more [educational/learning centers]. People teach less at home. The state [in general] has more, but in *mahalla* and in the city [Hovliguzar] less. The government does not trust [those who teach at home]. I do not trust these teachers either and reprimand *otinlar* who teach [at home]. They [have knowledge but] do not know how to give this knowledge. I love some of these women, but I reprimand [them]. Our *hokimyat* now has special *kursi* [courses] that teach *otinlar*. *Qorihona* [home school] is a secret. There are many. The *hokimyat* knows, and the SNB knows. But the government cannot close all of them. They trust [you] if you go the right way. They check, and they trust [she smiled]. *Bol'shoe spasibo* [a big thank you] to them! [She smiled again].

In Hovliguzar, some local *otinlar*, the majority of whom had signed the document promising not to teach minors, felt morally responsible to share Islamic knowledge with others. Although the teaching of Islam to minors by teachers unregistered with the state was strictly prohibited, in 2011 these feelings ensured the continuance of private religious instruction. But this was changing too. If an *otin* took the *hokimyat*'s "special" courses about Islam and became certified, she would no longer be breaking the law by teaching others, although she would still have to deal with a local tax department. If the tax department considered this form of tutoring a private business, she would have to charge for her services in order to pay taxes. That is why Tursun-oi continued teaching informally; in her view, a view shared by Jahon and Nainahon, religious instruction is not merchandise in a global marketplace of ideas, but a universal individual need, duty, and a right (see chapter 1).

According to Jahon, over the previous eight years, the availability of educational sources and tools for learning about Islam had also increased. For instance, one of Hovliguzar's bookstores offered a wide variety of books about Islam. Some local merchants also sold religious literature, computer programs teaching one about Islam, and what Jahon called "a pen Qur'an." This playback device, like the one that Tahsir's mother had, was shaped in the form of a thick pen, which, when tapped on the text of the Qur'an that came with the device, replayed prerecorded Qur'anic recitations with *tajweed* (see chapter 2). Jahon had one and said that she recommended everyone to buy it as a present for elderly parents, particularly those with impaired vision; if they could not read, they could still listen to the Qur'an. Like Tursun-oi, Nainahon, Tahsir, and others, Jahon believed that the Qur'an is a miracle and that its auditory experience, its internal sound universe, is magical (for more on the auditory experience of the Qur'an, see Sells 1999). In addition to generating the divine light, listening to "the beautiful recitations" of "the holy Qur'an" stimulated a feeling of knowing that an individual is "made by God to be good," in order to have a life well led together with others (see chapter 4).

While demonstrating this pen Qur'an to me, Jahon said, "Is it not beautiful? These [the Qur'anic reciters] are professionals." As she closed her eyes, slightly rocking her body side to side, she instructed me, "Listen to the sound."

Being an Otin

I asked Jahon to explain to me and exemplify what it means to be an *otin*. She responded like an anthropologist by saying that there are different ways of being an *otin*. She felt she had disappointed her *ustoz*, Tursun-oi, who wanted Jahon "to teach Islam" the same way Tursun-oi did. Instead of teaching, Jahon chose "a different approach of providing care," one resembling pastoral care, to the members of her community and presiding over religious ceremonies (for more on different leadership roles among Muslim women, see Mattson 2008; Peshkova 2009b).

Unlike in 2002–2003, the religious ceremonies Jahon officiated over no longer included such propitiatory rituals as Bibi Seshambe and Bibi Mushkil Kusho (see chapter 3); these rituals venerating female saints, Jahon now said, were *shirk* (idolatry). As a result of her persuasion, as far as she knew, the members of her *mahalla* no longer conducted these ceremonies. In order to curtail their performance in other *mahalla*s in Hovliguzar, Jahon repeatedly told other *otinlar* that these ceremonies were un-Islamic.

The *meropriyatiya* Jahon presided over included recitation and explanation of parts of the Qur'an and *masala*s. She also performed *hikmatlar* like those by "a local saint, Ahmed Yassawi" (on Yassawi, see Dzhumaev 1996; Sultanova 2011). She said that these hymns and verses, written by famous regional poets, were considered "traditional" and were "liked very much" by local people. Like *masala*s, they "touched people's souls" (see chapter 4). In order to learn *gazali*, a poetic form, she had recently purchased *Devon* (The book) by Boborahim Mashrab (published in 2006 in Tashkent). It included poems in the Uzbek language, which she planned to recite at the ceremonies.

By 2011, Jahon had been an *otin* for almost fifteen years and felt "happy" to be able to contribute to "positive changes" in her local community. While presiding over ceremonies and counseling others, she focused not on disseminating religious knowledge per se but on promoting ethical behavior. In order to affect thoughts and behaviors of others, she had worked on changing herself through self-critique and evaluation into a better mother, wife, and friend. Like Tursun-oi, this work on the self allowed Jahon to learn from and use her personal experiences in addition to her knowledge of the Qur'an, *hadislar*, and other literature written by famous Islamic scholars and poets (see chapter 1). She could show others that "if I can do it, they can do it too."

Tursun-oi taught Jahon that one was not born an *otin*; one has to become an *otin* (on a hereditary religious status of *otin*s see Fathi 1997). An individual's ability to change others is not a given and has to be cultivated. Before Jahon could give advice to or criticize others, she had to become a moral example for them. For instance, in order to promote love and respect toward others, she had to learn how to accept and love all her neighbors despite their faults. She always greeted them, thanked them for doing little things for their community, such as "planting flowers on a street," tried never to turn down anyone seeking advice, and always had time for the people needing her help. Treating others with kindness, patience, and respect eventually paid back. Others came to respect Jahon to the same extent that she respected them. This mutual respect, according to her, was a result of her ethical behavior toward others, of her working on herself and living Islam daily and *practically* in relation to others.

Mediating conflicts between daughters-in-laws and mothers-in-laws, wives and husbands, and parents and children was also one of Jahon's responsibilities. It was not a part of her job as a *hokimyat otin*, which so far had no clear description. Rather, she felt she *had* to do it; it was her moral responsibility and part of her life project that afforded her life a particular meaning and directionality (for more on directionality, see Rapport 2003).

Jahon knew that many families in her *mahalla* kept their problems to themselves, and she thought this was wise. Yet these conflicts contributed to individual unhappiness, which in turn contributed to social unhappiness. She thought that, with God's help, she could help to resolve some of these conflicts. Instead of expecting families with problems to seek her out, she called them to inquire about their lives and to offer her help if they needed it. Her mobile phone was "very handy"; by reaching "anyone, anywhere, at any point of time," digital technologies helped to facilitate a life well led together with others. Jahon believed that as a result of her active engagement with the members of her *mahalla*, they "complain[ed] less" and had "fewer problems" than families residing in other *mahalla*s in Hovliguzar.

As an *otin*, Jahon's main duties included listening to others, leading discussions, and giving advice often in regard to the mundane problems of the individuals she wanted to change. This change was necessary because her contemporary society was "ill." Jahon recalled that a young woman whose third marriage had failed had recently come to visit her. Inconsolable, this woman was blaming herself, crying, and saying that she wanted to kill herself. Jahon advised her to try and "think differently," not to focus on what she "did not have, but on what she had." According to Jahon, if this young woman were to change her perspective, she would see that she had everything—wonderful children, a place to live, both parents living, and a job. "What she lacked was a bad husband." Therefore, happiness was always already there; in order to feel happy, the young woman had to recognize it by changing her perspective. Instead of death, she had to focus on life. Instead of thinking about herself as a failure, she should remember and realize her goodness.

"'Why would you want to die?' I asked her," said Jahon. "If people knew how to be kind to each other," she continued, "many" daily problems could be avoided. But, according to her, "it was easier to break than to make." Her role as an *otin* was to help them figure out how to make. She did so because, she said, to be truly Muslim "is not just about loving Islam as an idea, but about making it *real*, by living Islamically." She urged members of her community not to "offend each other, not take somebody else's money," but to "help each other." According to her, this is "a good road." She told them, "If you want to have friends, you should love God and act kindly toward others, and you will have a good life and good friends. Islam is not about difficulties. Islam should be easy and beautiful—love each other!"

Neither difficult nor impossible and centered on the message of love, Jahon's "correct" Islam was practical, "easy," and "beautiful." Caring for the elderly exemplified this practical Islam because this was an important individual duty, a part of leading "truly" Muslim life. In her view, in every Hovliguzar's *mahalla* elderly people needed "additional attention." She claimed to encourage children and young adults "to visit with" their elderly relatives and unrelated elderly people in their *mahalla*, to "talk to them," and to "bring them small presents." In order to set an example, she did it herself.

In addition, Jahon claimed to visit sick people and be particularly attentive to and patient with teenagers. She recommended that members of her community do the same. "Recently" Jahon had heard a rumor that there was "a new *hazrat* [holy person]" in the valley.

He "helped people, built roads, and sponsored poor families' weddings." But he turned out to be "just another human [*chelovek*], only a relative of the president's wife." He could afford "to do whatever he wanted." In Jahon's view, any individual, whether a relative of the president or not, could become a *hazrat* if she or he loved others and acted in a corresponding manner; both love and care toward the self and others, as a daily practice, not just abstract ideas, are part and parcel of "correct" Islam.

Regulating Religion

In Uzbekistan, the 1998 Law on Freedom of Consciousness and Religious Organizations, among other things, forbids wearing religious garb formally used by religious officials only, limits religious officials to those recognized by the state, prohibits religious instruction outside of official educational centers, bans missionary activities, and requires compulsory registration of all religious organizations with the Ministry of Justice and certification of all individuals teaching religion. The registration process includes an approval issued by the Council of Confessional Affairs, which is financially supported by the government. The Muslim Board of Uzbekistan is a member of this council and receives government funds. The administrative relations between the Uzbek government and the Muslim Board of Uzbekistan provide venues for the government's (in)direct control of individual religiosities, which are expected to correspond to the form and content of "national Islam" promoted by the government and the board.

The board's members represent various provinces. They are responsible for the curriculum and the quality of instruction provided at educational institutions, such as madrasas. The board supervises mosques' operations, provides the content of sermons to the local mosques, and appoints imams, who are expected to follow the standards of worship and preaching issued by the board. If the imams' personal understanding of Islam diverges from the government's understanding, their criticisms of the government's discourse on Islam are often self-censored as a result of their administrative connection to the state.

Scholars observe that despite the state's efforts through selective retention and activation, individual practitioners do not blindly imitate but interpret and inhabit the state's discourse on "national Islam" (see, e.g., D. Abramson 2010). I propose a different way of thinking about "national Islam." Unless one adopts a theological position, the state's discourse does not exist a priori, outside of human bodies, and cannot be reduced to a book (such as the Qur'an) or an ideology advocated by the Uzbek president, government, intellectual secular elites, or representatives of the Muslim Board of Uzbekistan. In order *to be*, any discourse has to be articulated, comprehended, and attributed meaning to by human beings. Therefore, I argue that in the context of their daily lives individuals such as Tursun-oi, Jahon, and Nainahon do not just inhabit and interpret but *create* discourse on "national Islam" in Uzbekistan. Various strategies, including interpreting the state's discourse, are practices of individuality that signal their active participation in the process of co-creating an authoritative but contested discourse on "national Islam" in Hovliguzar, the Ferghana Valley, and Uzbekistan.

Tursun-oi: The Old and the New

Before my arrival in Uzbekistan in the summer of 2011, Tursun-oi and I talked on the phone several times. When during our last phone conversation in May 2011 I informed her about my plans to visit Uzbekistan, Tursun-oi asked whether this visit was "*po rabote ili otdihat'* [business or pleasure]." My first answer was "*i to i drugoe* [both]." Tursun-oi must not have heard my answer or was not satisfied with it and repeated her question. I replied that the reason for my visit was to meet my old friends and teachers and to see "for myself" how their lives had changed over the past eight years. She chuckled and said that my teachers were now "*stariki* [elderly]" and that they were no longer teachers because teaching Islam at home was prohibited: "we are not getting together anymore at all; I am too old, and they [the state] do not allow it." But she added that she would be happy to see me.

The day after I arrived in Hovliguzar, Tursun-oi was standing in front of me in her newly renovated courtyard wearing a long colorful dress and a light scarf tied at the back of her neck. Her poise always impressed me. She emanated confidence, wholeness, and resolve. These qualities were contagious. Next to her I felt at peace, parted from worries and anxiety, internally coherent and aware of my own body, my own self. After the greeting pleasantries, she invited me into her "new school."

The courtyard was secluded from the street with windowless walls and a new large wooden gate that had elaborate carvings. A little pool, finished with floral tiles reflecting the sun entangled in the running water, made the yard look larger and brighter. A new room with a separate entrance had been added to one side of the house during the renovation. Tursun-oi called this room her "new school." This bright room had three large windows opening out to the front inner yard; it smelled of fresh paint and was twenty-five by fifteen feet at least. A long low table that was used in her old classroom and cotton floor mats around it marked the center of the room.

Sitting at the table across from me in her "new school," Tursun-oi said that during the previous eight years she had greatly enriched her religious knowledge by reading "new" books about Islam and rereading "old" ones. According to her, no one locally could teach her because no one had as much knowledge as she did. She could learn only from books. "My teacher is a book," said Tursun-oi. Some new books she had gotten from Tashkent, and others she had bought locally at a new large bookstore in Hovliguzar. She said she read each book at least twice, wrote down a summary of each and explained it "in simple words" to her current and former students. Thus, the statement she had made in May, "we are not getting together anymore at all; I am too old, and they do not allow," did not adequately describe what was happening in her daily life and her role as a teacher.

Making Changes

According to Tursun-oi, eight years earlier the lessons she had offered were different, both in form and in content. She no longer held large classes, explaining this change both in terms of her "old age" and the state's strict prohibition of informal religious instruction, which she continued supporting. Just as during our meetings eight years earlier, she unequivocally stated, "If our president has decided to prohibit [homeschooling of Islam], he knows what he is doing. Some teach good and correct Islam, but there are others who teach wrong [things]." She added that she was no longer a teacher, but a tutor; tutorship was not prohibited. Possessing an expert knowledge of Islam, she was tutoring individuals in order to prepare them for entrance exams to the Imam al-Bukhari Tashkent Islamic Institute and for personal moral development. Unlike local tutors of languages, science, and math, she did not charge for her services.

As a tutor, Tursun-oi used a methodology both similar to and different from her teaching of Islam during 2002–2003. Back then, memorizing and reciting the Qur'an were central to educational process at her home school. In 2011, however, before her students were ready to study the Qur'an, they had to master the fundamentals of Islam, including the six *kalima*s.[6] She said, "First, I ask my new students what is *imon* [faith], Islom [Islam], *kalima*s. They need to learn these by heart. I ask them what is '*La ilaha illa Allah*'? I make them write and learn these by heart and tell me what they have learned during the next meeting. I ask them, 'What should you say when you wake up? What should you say when you go to work? What should you say before you eat? What should you say after you sneeze?' I do not teach them Arabic until they know all the answers. Only then I

6. The first *kalima* is a statement of pure belief. The second, in some ways similar to the first, is the affirmation of faith. The third praises Allah, the only one worthy of worship. The fourth is an affirmation of the oneness of Allah. The fifth seeks forgiveness for sins committed intentionally and unintentionally. By pronouncing the sixth *kalima*, one has rejected disbelief and falsehood.

teach Arabic letters [and the foundations of *tajweed*], then the suras. I explain why [reasons for the revelations] and when and where. But first I teach them about [daily] life."

In the educational process, Tursun-oi always used religious books written by famous theologians and scholars in addition to the Qur'an. In 2011, she put even more emphasis than before on the importance of such literature because "the Qur'an is one, but each [person] understands it differently." These divergent understandings, in her view, were a problem. In order to understand Islam "correctly," students had to learn *tafsir* (Qur'anic exegesis) and *hadislar* and consult other religious books such as *Hadith va Hayot* (see chapter 1).

When Tursun-oi read this book the first time, she was surprised that "this knowledgeable man, a sheikh, used 119 different books to write this one." Because "this famous sheikh" was Tursun-oi's role model, she followed his example and encouraged her students to do the same. According to her, books such as *Hadith va Hayot* helped her students to understand Islam and enhanced their ability to live according to "our *oqim*—Imam Azam [Hanafi *mashab*] *ahlus sunnah* [people of the Prophet's tradition]." The Hanafi *mashab* is "the best," she said, because it follows "the Prophet Muhammad's *ibodat* [religious observance and obligations] and life [mundane affairs pertinent to everyday life]."

During 2002–2003, instruction in the Arabic language was at the core of the educational process of Tursun-oi's home school. In 2011, however, she downplayed the importance of Arabic and insisted that religious education should be performed in her native, Uzbek language. She said, "I did study Arabic after the *Mustakilliq* and even found mistakes in my teacher's questions [at the Culture Center]. She gave me a diploma, and I then examined other students. But when we don't speak it, why do we need Arabic? We should learn [about Islam] in our Uzbek language."

Tursun-oi's emphasis on the importance of the Uzbek language, the Hanafi *mashab*, and literature other than the Qur'an was similar to the discourse on "national Islam" promoted by, among others, the government, Deputy Chairman Mansur, and the touring ulama in 2007–2008. Yet she did not just iterate or inhabit this discourse (assuming there was a significant level of agreement among those learned men on what "national Islam" should look and sound like and how it should be lived). She thought about and articulated *her own* "correct" Islam in light of her personal experiences and while interacting with her immediate human and nonhuman environment, which included historical and contemporary discourses on Islam advocated by the representatives of the Muslim Board of Uzbekistan.

In Tursun-oi's view, supported by the opinions of theologians, teachers, and writers she respected, Hanafi Islam and the Qur'an's relevance to daily life, not only its devotional iteration, help to create a shared understanding and historical continuity of the universal ethical paradigm. She said, "Some students have studied with me more than fifteen years. They have read the Qur'an five or six times. And every time I explain the meaning [of the Qur'anic verses] because we cannot just read the Qur'an but also have to understand it." Over the previous eight years, from her experiences as a student and teacher of Islam, Tursun-oi discovered that learning about this paradigm was more efficient and effective in Uzbek rather than in Arabic. Hence, her "correct" Islam reflected knowledge(s) she acquired from books, her former teachers, and her experiences as a student and a teacher of Islam.

Tursun-oi claimed that an increased level of Islamic knowledge among local individuals led to considerable changes. She was particularly proud of the decreasing popularity of the practices that she, like the representatives of the Muslim Board of Uzbekistan, considered to be idolatrous. "For example," she reported, "we do not do Mushkil Kusho—we told the people that it was *shirk* [idolatry]." As a result of local *otinlar*'s efforts, local communities celebrated "the Bayram [which marks the end of the annual observation of the month of fasting] differently, Islamically." If previously "some people in *mahalla*s went to other people's homes to read prayers and sing hoping to receive money or whatever," according to Tursun-oi this was "in general" no longer the case. "Our women used to wail at a *maraka* [memorial service] very loud." In her and her students' *mahallas*, this did not happen "anymore" because they taught others that "this [behavior] is *odat* [a customary practice] and not Islam." She also observed that "our old and young men now understand that Ramazan is a reason to get together to read the Qur'an and pray [e.g., during the day or after the evening meal], not to party."

Like the *jadids* during the late nineteenth and early twentieth centuries (Khalid 1998) and the current government and religious officials (Kandiyoti and Azimova 2004), Tursun-oi was critical of *ehsons* that could turn into marathon feasts. Unlike them but like her student Jahon, Tursun-oi did not condemn *ehsons* per se; rather, she criticized the manner in which some of them were conducted. Whereas the *jadids* and politicians perceived these feasts as sites of decadence and conspicuous consumption and the law enforcement agencies saw them as suspicious social gatherings, she was more concerned with the intentions of the *ehsons*' participants. Wrong intentions, such as a desire to impress others by displaying one's wealth, made such social events sinful, un-Islamic. In order to ensure meritorious, "Islamic" *ehsons*, Tursun-oi told her students and those seeking her advice to carry out what I would call "pragmatic *ehsons*," which included investing whatever money the families could spare in their children's religious and secular educations.

For instance, one local woman whose husband had died recently visited Tursun-oi a couple of days before our first meeting in 2011, asking advice on what would be "an Islamic thing to do" with the gold she had amassed during her lifetime: Should she spend it on an *ehson*, "a feast," in his honor? Tursun-oi told this woman not to spend her gold on a feast but to sell it and set money aside for her children and grandchildren's future. "This would be a real *savob* [meritorious act]," said Tursun-oi.

Tursun-oi advanced her understanding of "correct" Islam through former and current students. Some "graduates" of her home school, now local *otinlar* teaching others and presiding over ceremonial gatherings, continued to come to her for advice and knowledge.

Among other things, she helped them to answer the questions raised in the audience during *meropriyatiya* they officiated at.

For instance, while presiding over "one *meropriyatiya*," one of her students, Zulfiahon, "wished them [the attending women] happy New Year." In response, some of the women criticized her by saying, "The New Year is a Russian and not an Islamic holiday." Zulfiahon came to consult with Tursun-oi on the issue, who reasoned that since "Christians and Jews are the peoples of the book [mentioned as monotheists in the Qur'an and *hadislar*], Muslims should respect their holidays." She added that there were two calendars, the Gregorian and the lunar, "an Islamic one"; if Christians are "the people of the book" and follow the Gregorian calendar, where the New Year "is a holiday," then although this holiday is not Islamic proper, it is not prohibited, not un-Islamic, either.

Like Tursun-oi, the government and religious officials promoted interfaith coexistence and tolerance as hallmarks of Uzbekistan's "national Islam." For example, the deputy chairman of the Muslim Board of Uzbekistan, Abdul-Aziz Mansur, was quoted as saying: "We Muslims are very tolerant, and we are never aggressive toward worshippers of other religions, since the Holy Koran and Hadith [*sic*] teach us to be respectful toward them. . . . One of the Hadith says on behalf of Allah, 'If anyone hurts a follower of another religion, you shall know he hurt me'" (quoted in Yaniseyev 2011). Even though the deputy chairman's and Tursun-oi's statements about religious tolerance are similar, Tursun-oi's answer to Zulfiahon's question was really *her own*. This answer was informed but not determined by Tursun-oi's knowledge and experiences as a Soviet citizen and a social leader working with people of different nationalities, who, as she said, were "like a family" to her (see chapter 1). She fashioned her answer also *in light of* her understanding of Islam as a peaceful moral self-formation, with final adjudication of right and wrong individual sensibilities and behaviors being the sole prerogative of God.

According to Tursun-oi, Islamic education is a quintessential part of human development; it enables individuals "to follow the right path" toward achieving the goal of human individuation—a voluntary genuine submission to God. Although Islamic education is critical to leading a good life, it is not a substitute and has to come in tandem with what she called "regular education," "*shkolnoe obrazovanie* [education at school]," which was also secular. "A human," she said, "should have all kinds of skills."

Tursun-oi's emphasis on secular education's importance was not idiosyncratic, but historically continuous. While insisting on the importance of secular education, the *jadid*s argued that at primary and secondary schools students' education should not be limited to Qur'anic studies but include geography, science, and languages (Khalid 1998). In 2007, Deputy Chairman Mansur, too, emphasized the importance of secular education in his speech about "national Islam" and insisted that Uzbekistan's "youth" had to focus on secular education, even if it had to be done at the expense of attending Friday prayers at the mosques (Ferghana News Agency 2007).

Despite these similarities, Tursun-oi, I argue, offered her own view on relations between Islamic and secular education. The latter was very important because it provided an individual with the skills necessary to acquire and implement the former. Tursun-oi knew it all too well. Her secular education fostered her desire and enabled her to learn more about Islam (see chapter 1). Her emphasis on secular education also reflected the age of her current students; she reported that over the previous eight years (2003–11), overall her student body had become younger. During 2002–2003, her students already possessed secular education acquired at the Soviet schools and some at the Soviet institutes (of higher education, similar to colleges and universities); they were prepared to acquire Islamic knowledge and behaviors. Her current students, the "younger students" she tutored, had to continue developing necessary skills associated with secular education in order to be able to master "correct" Islam. Such skills as reading and writing and knowledge about history, geography, and foreign languages had to precede an Islamic education, which she took to be more advanced than a secular one.

The changes that occurred in Tursun-oi's life and her teaching of "correct" Islam cannot be fully explained by social changes in the country, the Uzbek state's discourse on "national Islam," and the government's control of individual religiosities. Rather, these changes reflected her experiences and a persistent desire to further her life project of helping others to become "truly" Muslim. This desire informed changes in her teaching methods as well as changes and continuities in her understanding and articulation of "correct" Islam.

Discourse and Its Creators

Following John Conley and William O'Barr, I take the term *discourse* to refer to the broader "range of discussions that takes place within a society about an issue or set of issues" (1998, 7). According to Rapport, these discussions do not exist a priori, and they require discussants, whose unique individual experiences inform "[a] plurality of [individual] interpretations" and result in "a diversity of meanings" (2003, 88). As a result, there can be no singular uncontested discourse. In Uzbekistan, individual discussants produced a range of discussions about an authoritative yet contested discourse on "national Islam" by attributing meaning to this discourse, interpreting existing historical artifacts—such as the Qur'an, stories about monumentalized personalities such as Sheikh Naqshband, the Law on Freedom of Consciousness and Religious Organizations, and the deputy chairman's speeches—and devising creative solutions to their daily problems.

While analyzing sociality in the Soviet Union, Johan Rasanayagam aptly observes that performance of Muslim ritual privately, in domestic space, does not oppose but is "outside" the public performance of the "authoritative discourse that reproduce[s] [the individual] as a 'correct person'" (2010, 79). During the first decade of the twenty-first century, Tursun-oi, Jahon, and Nainahon claimed not to interfere with or resist the Uzbek state's authoritative discourse on "national Islam." But they were not "outside" it either. They co-created this discourse in their own terms in relation to and in light of other terms, experiences, and discourses available to them. Their strategies, including compliance, avoidance, interpretation, and advocacy, did not signal their inhabiting of the state's regulations of private religiosities and its discourse on "national Islam" but were formative of both the regulations and this discourse.

For instance, during 2002–2003 Tursun-oi advocated for certification of all *otinchalar* (see chapter 1), and Jahon, in order to demonstrate her mastery of "correct" Islam, desired to participate in a "competition" among *otinchalar* (see chapter 3). These women's desires were not constituted by the state's discourse on "national Islam" but were a part of their personal life projects that included leading "truly" Muslim lives, combating "wrong" Islam, and promoting "correct" Islam. These women intentionally and consistently pursued their life projects; as a result, some of their desires came to be actualized, even if imperfectly.

The certification that Tursun-oi supported was animated by the efforts of the touring ulama to establish doctrinal coherence among Muslims in the valley. In the process of the ulama's examination of local *otinlar*'s knowledge, which Jahon called a "competition," she demonstrated the highest level of "correct" Islamic knowledge; she "won" this "competition," which *really* took place, and became a *hokimyat otin*. And, according to her, in 2011 Hovliguzar's *hokimyat* was now offering courses to informal religious practitioners that would lead to their certification, just as Tursun-oi had suggested several years earlier. Both Tursun-oi and Jahon actively contributed to these processes, regulations, and practices as well as to their concomitant discourses.

In 2011, Nainahon, too, rethought her understanding of a particular relationship between human and divine worlds, deciding now that it did not include intermediaries. Her "correct" Islam no longer required systematic attendance of religious lessons and was no longer symbolized by a particular modest dress code she had adopted upon her return from the hajj in the late 1990s (see chapter 3). In relation to her immediate environment and the problems it presented, she developed creative solutions that were not historically discontinuous, but really hers. They were not finalized and somewhat ambivalent, like her "Islamic" solution to her husband's request to marry a second wife.[7] But these solutions were not "outside" the state's and religious leadership's (contested) discourse on "national Islam." She co-created this discourse, which reflected the ambivalence of the state's, the religious leadership's, and public's contested views on polygyny (for more on polygyny and tradition, see Farhadi 2010; Tabishalieva 2000). Jahon, too, was contributing to existing contested views on polygyny, "a problem that women *can* resolve." As a *hokimyat otin*, she navigated the city government's attention to this problem and proposed a potential solution.

Jahon was not "outside" of but an active participant in making an authoritative but contested discourse on "national Islam." Her life project included the hajj, her daughters' marriages, her and her husband's happiness, and her career plans. These personal interests and desires, particular forms of religious observance, and her understanding of relationships between spouses and parental duties and social responsibilities were also part and parcel of her discourse on "correct" Islam. By emphasizing faith in God, the value of companionship, the importance of children's upbringing, women's problems and the (pragmatic) solutions to these problems, and the virtues of love, respect, and care for oneself and others, Jahon co-created, inbodied, and embodied "national Islam."

The women I am writing about were among the *discussants* producing and actively participating in the range of *discussions* about how to be "truly" Muslim. Nainahon's pragmatic decision making, Jahon's work within her community, and Tursun-oi's efforts to educate others demonstrate that "national Islam" in Uzbekistan was not just a discursive regime, a system of power and regulation, or an ideology inhabited by individuals. These women's stories show that, as a practice of individuality, their participation in the broad range of discussions about "correct" Islam and being "truly" Muslim was not just iterative of the government's discourse on "national Islam," but

7. The *jadids* in general upheld polygyny, although they criticized it as depriving other men of wives (Kamp 2006, 46).

also formative of it. The women co-created "national Islam" through their individual articulations of "correct" Islam, which stemmed from their consciousness and bodily experiences.

Created in relation to human and nonhuman others, in the process of interacting with organic and inorganic environment, these individual discourses on "correct" Islam were not discontinuous from but instead resembled other discussions about Islam in Uzbekistan (and elsewhere) (as in Hafez 2011; McBrien 2009). For instance, Tursun-oi articulated "correct" Islam in relation to her experiences as a Soviet social leader and as a religious teacher, to stories about history she learned, and to other existing views of "correct" Islam, such as the one from the "Arabiston" (see chapter 4) and the one advocated by the Muslim Board of Uzbekistan. Her "correct" Islam was at once continuous, but also really hers; it was thought of, interpreted, articulated, felt, and enacted by her. So were Jahon's and Nainahon's "correct" Islam. Understood this way, "national Islam" in Uzbekistan was *really* personal Islam, formed and attributed meaning by individuals pursuing their goals and desires in the environment created by themselves and "by the intentions of others" (Rapport 2003, 250).

During the first decade of the twenty-first century in Uzbekistan, "national Islam" was learned and taught during lessons at private homes as well as in sermons at the mosques, books, Internet programs, and radio and television programs. Both individual and diverse but also continuous and shared, "national Islam" was attributed meaning, articulated, in-bodied, and embodied by individuals in light of their experiences, dreams, and personal life histories and in relation to their surrounding environment. Therefore, not only the government and religious officials but also ordinary Muslims articulated and effected changes in "national Islam."[8]

8. Because non-Muslims are part of Uzbekistan's social environment, they too affect the contested discourse on "national Islam" by articulating their views about it.

6

From a Unique Uzbek Nation to a Unique Individual

Proposition: Individual existential power to change the self and others is relational; the actions of others do not determine this power but inform it, and personal faith in God does not negate it.

Hovliguzar and Tashkent, August 2011

I try to be friendly. I ask the Civilian about his family. He replies that he has a wife and a child, but we are here to talk about me. He says that he knows everything and that I am here to collect materials for a book. "What kind of a book?" he asks. "Who told you that I am writing a book?" I reply. "We have our sources," he says. "A novel, a story, what difference does it make?" I ask. He answers that it makes a huge difference. "What are you going to say about Uzbekistan in this book?" he continues. "The truth," I say while trying to smile. "Only good things," I add. He responds with a series of questions and statements: he says he has a copy of my dissertation on the table in his office, and if I wanted to tell the truth about Uzbekistan and only good things, then I am talking to the wrong people, the "street people," asking them all kinds of questions about religion. He asks what I want him to think; from where he stands, it looks as if I am collecting information for someone. Why do I want to learn about Islam? Are these street people giving me information, or am I teaching them about Islam? Did I read the Qur'an? He adds that I flew from the Caucasus, and there are Islamic terrorists in the Caucasus. For whom am I really collecting this information? The

Americans? The Russians? I met with a hokimyat otin. *Why? Why do I want to know about the local government? He says that religion and politics are important matters that should not be discussed with the street people: "If you want to write about Uzbekistan, why not ask knowledgeable people? Why not ask learned people, such as our imams in Tashkent? Why not ask history professors?" I reply, "I am familiar with professors' opinions. As an anthropologist, I want to learn about and from ordinary people." "This is wrong," he concludes, "very wrong."*

He asks me to name all the people I've met with on this trip and adds that if I have difficulty remembering who, he has a full list. He wants to know if I am going to tell him the truth. "This is kak examin *[like a test]," he says and smiles. I give obvious names, the people with whom I stayed in Hovliguzar and those with whom he, by now, surely knows I had visited. "All of them are my friends. Please leave them out of it; they have nothing to do with me, my questions, or my book," I enunciate every word, making sure he hears me. He says he can name them for me and that I should trust him. He says he is not my enemy and not an enemy to his people; he is only "doing his job." Surely I can understand that. Peace in Uzbekistan and his people's happiness are his only goals. Therefore, he has to make sure that no one is spying around, trying to collect the "wrong" information about Uzbekistan and use it to misrepresent this country abroad. "What should I think about you? You keep on coming back here. Why? You were here in 2001, then in 2002, and then in 2003, always curious about Islam. Why? What are we going to do? How can you help me? How can you help us?" "Who are 'us'?" I ask.*

This bombardment of questions is exhausting. I have to interrupt him. Although I have no time to come up with a strategy that includes a rhetorically persuasive story, I know that I need to take him and the government seriously. I begin by asking the Civilian, "What do you want me to do? What do you want me to say? You asked me to be honest; I am honest. I have nothing to hide. I did nothing criminal. Is it criminal to talk to people, to ask them questions? Is it criminal to meet old friends?" I pause to breathe, and, oddly enough, President Karimov's speeches about Uzbekistan with which I am familiar come to the rescue. I begin, "Is not Uzbekistan a free country? Is that not what the president says? Is it not what they are celebrating on the first of September, freedom and democracy? I want peace in Uzbekistan, too. I want to write a book about the changes in people's lives since Uzbekistan's independence. I want to write an honest account, which shows that the valley is not a dangerous place, that it is not that different from other places in other parts of the world. I want to write about religion in order to show that religious radicalism does not define the valley and its people, that there is more to their lives than often assumed. This too is probably a result of freedom of religion pioneered by the president and the government. I want the rest of the world, not only Russian- or Uzbek-speaking audiences, to learn more about these changes and about the Uzbek people. Maybe that is why I keep coming back; I do not know. I hope I am not going to regret it now. Oh, yes, by the way, the first time I came to Uzbekistan in 1998, I was an assistant to an American professor who taught a course on international law and human rights at President Karimov's Academy for Social Construction in Tashkent, and . . ."

"Maybe you should move to Uzbekistan and live here in Hovliguzar if you like it so much," he interrupts me with a clever remark. "You recorded your conversations with the street people, did you not? I know you did. Where are your camera, computer, voice recorder, and telephone? If you have nothing to hide, we need to see them; we need to see your computer files. We want to be sure that you describe Uzbekistan correctly and truthfully, that you do not have any sensitive information about our country's national security." While thinking how oxymoronic it is to pair up "correct" with "truthful," I object, "These are my personal possessions, and I hide nothing, but if you want to search my belongings, you need to tell me what I am charged with, and you need to have a warrant." He responds, "Believe me, you do not want this. Do you know what can happen to you if we were to discover that you are spreading

antigovernment propaganda or, worse, collecting information for your government? Which one is your government? Russian? American?" He says that he is sure that I understand the consequences of kachat' prava *(insistence on my rights). He asks, "What are you, a* pravozashitnik *[person who defends human rights]?" Coming from him, such a defense sounds like a felony, yet I answer that I do understand and will defend my rights. He repeats that he is just doing his job and adds that he does not want to harm his people or me. "It is getting late. Just let us see your computer, camera, telephone, and a voice recorder, Sveta-opa," he pauses, standing next to me, chain-smoking his cigarettes.*

After a long and tedious "discussion" and a whole pack of cigarettes, after multiple questions about who I really am and whom I'm really working for, and after never-ending reassurances of the innocence of my intentions, late this August evening the Civilian returns my purse. He keeps my passport, looks through my mobile phone's address book, and calls the Uniform, who shows up in ten minutes. They drive me to my friend's place, the one who came with me to the OVIR branch today. Apparently they have already decided that I will stay overnight at my friend's and not at Rashida's because my friend has already brought my bags from her place. He might have been instructed to keep an eye on me, but, strangely, I am glad of that. I feel safe with him around; he is still my friend.

By the time we get to his house, his parents are gone. He says they decided to visit relatives in the nearby village. But his wife, kids, and sister are at home. We barely talk. Their silence is very telling—we usually have very lively conversations. They probably do not want me here. Nor do they want me talking. I am no longer a friend but a liability. I am too tired to care. I have nothing to say to them, either, except "Thank you" and "I am sorry."

The Civilian and the Uniform write an official statement noting that my computer, camera, and voice recorder were confiscated and will be returned to me tomorrow, as soon as they are inspected. They bring in a witness from the street, a second one in addition to my friend. We all sign the statement. They leave. My friend leaves with them and later returns with a photocopy of the statement. "Here," he says, "let's eat."

After dinner, I talk to my mother and my son, who by this time normally would have been asleep, on Skype. "What else can we do? Who else can we call?" She says she feels helpless but is trying her best to stay calm. I am glad. I do not want to infect my son with the ominous fear I hear in her voice, the same fear that is lurking in my own as well. "Is there anything on your computer, you know, that they would not like, any compromising pictures or files?" she asks. "Compromising who? What would they not like?" I retort. I always do this. When I am frustrated, scared, or tired, I become easily irritable; I snap. My poor mother. I hope she knows how much I love her. "Can I see my son?" I ask. He enters the frame. "I love you, baby, and will be with you soon," is all I can say. I keep it short in order not to cry in his presence.

Then I call Rashida. "I am sorry you got mixed up in this ordeal." She says that no matter what happens, I am her best and brightest student, even if I failed to be fluent in Uzbek. I say, "I am sorry, sorry, sorry"; I can never apologize enough. She says that there is nothing to be sorry or worried about. She says, "Fuck them!" "Fuck them," I repeat.

I try to sleep but cannot. I walk outside. Grape vines and a swimming pool. Outside feels good. It is still unbearably hot during the day, but cool at night. I think about my son and about the people I have visited on this trip. Has anything happened to them, to Jahon, Tursun-oi, Nainahon, and Tahsir? Should I call them? I want to, but what if SNB agents are listening to my phone conversations, which, by the way, both of my parents are sure they are doing. Everything is possible in this surveillance state. If the agents did not think it necessary to question these women and men, my phone call might bring them unwanted attention. No more phone calls. Maybe tomorrow I can use my friend's phone.

I feel guilty and scared. What will happen to the people I have learned about "correct" Islam from and my friends after I leave?

That is, if I leave. This is my fault entirely. Did I erase all the files from the computer and the audio recorder? How geeky are the SNB agents? It is not that difficult to recover the files. How about my personal audio notes? What do I say in them? I did not erase pictures showing people I've met with. My son. Oh, how I miss my son. Am I going to leave the valley tomorrow and Uzbekistan a day after? I try to think about those who will stay behind in Hovliguzar and Tashkent, but my thoughts keep turning back to my son and myself. Scared, guilty, and selfish, I go back to bed.

The phone rings at about four in the morning. It is Jahon. She says she knows. She was questioned yesterday, early in the morning. "Ne bespokoisya za menya *[do not worry about me]," she says and adds that I should worry about myself. She worries about me, too, and will pray for me and will not stop praying until I am safe.*

"Did we do anything wrong, anything criminal?" she asks. "No, we did not," I answer. "How is Tursun-oi? Did they question her?" She replies that the "esenbeshniki *[SNB agents]" will not question Tursun-oi. She, Jahon, asked them to leave Tursun-oi out of it, and they promised. I do not believe them but say otherwise: "Thank you and thank God." She pauses for a moment, then states, "If we did not do anything criminal, we have nothing to worry about.* Vse projidet *[It all will pass]. God is with us." "And you need to get some sleep," she adds. I promise I will and end our conversation with, "I am so sorry. I will call.* Bobter *[Bye]."*

She is safe. I am relieved, but, oh my God, what did I do? Why did I not leave the valley a day earlier? And why did I come back to Uzbekistan knowing that THIS might happen? Was not what happened in 2003 enough for me?

In my amateur attempts to psychoanalyze myself, I conclude that my "death drive"—the idea that I sabotaged my own interests—brought me back to Uzbekistan. My "death drive" has social effects. What can I do for the people I have affected? Anything? Nothing? I feel like a criminal. I am supposed to protect those I work with and learn from; at the least I should do no harm, but I have failed. I have let them down. What a mess! I need to get out of this country. I need to get back to my son. I need to get my stuff and get the hell out of here tomorrow. It is tomorrow already.

At about ten in the morning, I get my computer, voice recorder, and camera back in return for my photocopy of the statement they wrote yesterday. "We checked everything," the Uniform says and adds, "You have to pay a fine, Svetlana." "What fine?" I ask. "This fine. You broke the law," he responds and gives me the innocuous-looking document in Uzbek that I signed yesterday. Today it has a number on the back of the page right above my signature—5,720,000 soms. "What kind of fine is it? This is ridiculous! That's almost three thousand dollars. Why? You said it was just a formality, a warning; this is why I signed this form." Now I feel really angry, mainly at myself. The Uniform suggests settling it here. He wants one thousand dollars. "I have only three hundred dollars cash," I reply. "This is not enough," he says. "You should leave for Tashkent immediately," he adds. Now he is angry, mainly with me. He makes a point to remind me that he and "his friend," the Civilian, saved me from a two-year or more jail sentence and that THEY are letting me go because the twentieth-anniversary celebration of Uzbekistan's independence is approaching and because I am a woman, of course. He says that they like me. But he adds that I will have to pay a fine—if not here, then in Tashkent. Otherwise, I will not leave Uzbekistan. He asks, "What did you expect?" He answers himself, "You broke the law! This will be a lesson to you." "Such a condescending prick," I think and ask out loud, "Which law? Whose law? Yours?" "Oh, do not start again," he replies and walks away.

In the afternoon, my friend finds a car that will take me to Tashkent. It is over, finally, or is it? The same white car that followed me the day before yesterday follows us all the way to the border with the Tashkent Province. The driver and I do not talk much. Maybe he is one of "them," I think. I ask him to stop the car next to a cotton field so I can pick a branch of cotton with cotton balls on it for my mother. Back in Russia she asked me for it in response to my question about what present I could bring her from the valley.

At Tashkent's provincial border I get out of the car to register at the police checkpoint. The white car stays in the Ferghana Province, while we drive on. I feel somewhat relieved. Is it finally over?

We enter Tashkent's city limits. I call and book a room in a hotel because my Tashkent friend with whom I usually stay did not call yesterday or today—not a single time. I could not reach her either. As if responding to my thoughts, the phone immediately rings. It is this friend, but she does not sound friendly. She says she is calling to tell me that I have created "serious problems for her family. My husband is furious. The Tashkent OVIR officers are here now! They say you owe them almost three thousand dollars. We are not going to pay it for you. You better take care of it as soon as possible. We do not want to be dragged into a court hearing. Use your credit card if you don't have cash."

I am glad I have booked a hotel room; I understand I am not welcome there. I ask her to give the phone to one of the officers. An officer tells me that the Hovliguzar branch of the Bureau of Internal Affairs called them and faxed the paperwork. "You have signed a paper stating that you have broken Uzbekistan's registration law and agree to pay a fine for it," he adds. I ask the officer to please leave this family alone; I will not be going there and give him the name of the hotel I will be staying at instead. We can meet and talk there. I continue, "I do not have three thousand dollars, and the document in Uzbek is fraudulent. I signed it without an interpreter, not knowing what it said, and the amount of the fine was added later, after I had signed it." I add, "I have to leave Uzbekistan early tomorrow morning. It is too late to do anything today. I have a ticket, I must leave." The officer listens and responds that these are serious allegations and that Hovliguzar's office has a different story. They will be waiting for me at the hotel. "We will settle it there," he says. "Good," I reply and hang up.

The driver feels bad for me. He understood the conversation because he speaks flawless Russian. He says he worked in Russia for several years until he made enough money to buy this car. He liked it in Russia but has a family to take care of here in Uzbekistan: "The law does not work here, but this is my rodina *[motherland]."*

I walk into the hotel lobby and see four young men sitting around one of the tables. They are not wearing uniforms, but I still feel nauseated. I think I have developed a particular allergy to law enforcement officers. I look at them. They look at me. What am I going to do? In whose office am I going to end up today? They are slowly becoming a blur because I can barely hold my tears. The "why" and "why me" questions generate self-pity, which spawns tears. I walk toward the reception to check in. A concierge offers me a glass of water, which helps me to swallow my tears. I do not want to cry in front of the officers. I check in and walk toward the table. They know that I know who they are. After brief introductions, I ask them if I can take my stuff to the room and freshen up. They say I can, but on one condition: "You have to leave your passport with us." "My passport? My passport." I do as they say and go up to my room.

I want to see my son. I have to *leave tomorrow. What should I do? I do not have three thousand dollars. I suppose I can get cash from my credit card. But it is a weekend and the banks that I know of are already closed. From the room, I try to call the Russian consulate, figuring that because I am a Russian citizen, they may be able to offer some kind of assistance; but, of course, only the guard answers me. I Skype my mother. She is shocked but tells me that everything is going to be all right: I WILL get back to the Caucasus and to the United States. She says she'll fix it. It sounds like a promise, which I really need to hear. I do my best to try to compose myself before going downstairs.*

The officers insist that I have nothing to worry about, that we will settle this matter somehow. They say that they understand my frustration. They are frustrated, too. This office in Hovliguzar, they complain, always creates unnecessary difficulties for Tashkent's officers. But there is no going back; the documents I had signed make it clear that I was in Hovliguzar for a week without registration. I have to pay this fine.

They insist we drive to the Tashkent OVIR to try to figure out who will loan me 5,720,000 soms today if I want to leave tomorrow. We get into a cab and in twenty minutes arrive at the office. I use my phone and call around. No result. The friends in Tashkent who would have this amount of money handy do not answer my calls. News spreads quickly, especially bad news and especially within one's social circle. By now, I guess, they all know about the fine and the potential problems I can bring into their lives. I am not surprised. I am an outsider who will leave, but they will have to stay in Uzbekistan. They have too much to lose. Yes, they have money, which they probably earn in less than honest ways and so do not need the additional police scrutiny that an association with me can bring. But, more importantly, they all have families, and Uzbekistan is their home. To jeopardize these things for the sake of a long-distance friend, someone who is more like an acquaintance, makes no sense. I understand completely. For me, too, as for many people I met in Uzbekistan, Russia, and the United States, family always comes first.

My phone rings. It is my mother, who says she will wire money to me tomorrow through Western Union. She says I have nothing to worry about; even if I am a day late, I will be with my son soon. I feel somewhat relieved. Now I have to reconcile myself to the fact that I am not leaving Uzbekistan until I pay this fine. An officer's voice brings me back to the present. While looking through the documents, he says, "A copy of this set of documents is at a local court now. And, as I see, you have signed all the papers, including the one stating that you have violated the registration regime, that you will never do it again, and that the officers in the valley treated you fairly and that you have NOTHING TO COMPLAIN ABOUT." *"Yes, I know what it says," I reply. "But let me tell you why I wrote and signed them. I had to if I wanted to leave the valley." I add, "I am sure you know what I am talking about." Another officer responds that nothing can be done now and that all of them are sorry.*

I have a feeling they understand what really happened. They look at each other and offer me another option—not to pay the fine and to go in front of the judge in court on Monday and demand justice. This would probably mean spending a week in jail, and then the judge would probably decide to deport me because I have no money or friends vouching for me. If it is, indeed, a matter of principle, this is the only way I can avoid paying this fine. If it were up to them, they would rather deport me than worry about the money; in fact, the OVIR in Hovliguzar should have informed me that I had a choice, to be deported or to pay the fine. But since by signing the documents I have chosen the fine, I have to pay it. "But they did not tell me about other choices," I protest. I can repeat it only so many times. The thing is, I feel sincerity in these officers' voices. Maybe they do sympathize with me. Maybe there is no other option, no justice. Or maybe this is *justice. Not thinking carefully through the political implications of this research project has a price. And this price is the least I can pay for my mistakes, for not taking my premonitions seriously, not working with the state's academics, talking to the "street people," asking questions about Islam, and not hiding my political views better. It is time to face the consequences.*

Of course, for me the option of another week in Uzbekistan and probably in jail is not an option. I need to get out of this country, whatever the cost. I want to see my son as soon as possible. I do not care about my own or anyone else's principles at this point. Of course, I will pay this fine. "I will do it tomorrow when Western Union and the banks are open," I state with resolve.

Civilizing Mission

I was initially uncomfortable with the civilizing mission of women such as Tursun-oi. By resenting their seemingly condescending attitude toward *avom khalq* (uneducated people) and their audacious insistence on possessing "correct" Islamic knowledge and a blatant criticism of others for possessing what they considered "wrong" knowledge, I was judging them for judging others. But as I got to know these women and observed their patience and determination in assuming responsibility for moral individual and societal change,

I came to admire them. They may not have been humble, but their civilizing mission was a humble endeavor because they did not consider themselves to be "essential" but rather "instrumental" in the process of change (terms used in Marranci 2009, 112).

These women's civilizing mission also had personal risks. Despite an ongoing prohibition of homeschooling Islam and the persecution of those who did not comply with this prohibition, Tursun-oi continued teaching others into 2011. These policies mattered less than what she felt she *had* to do—to share knowledge, which she did not want to take "to the grave" (see chapters 1 and 5). This knowledge, she hoped, would lead others to examine the correspondence between their thoughts, feelings, and actions and as a result would help them to become "truly" Muslim.

While teaching others how to question and improve their lives and the social world around them, Tursun-oi did not impose on them her own model of a life well led. Although she was an example for others, she was not essential but instrumental to their personal self-formation. Her role was to persistently and purposefully remind individuals about that which was always already there, about the human ability to become good by following God's guidance. Pursuing her mission, she extended herself into her community through teaching those who would teach others (in their own ways), including unrelated individuals and family members.

Jahon sought to change others through her personal example, advice, care, and storytelling. She shared with them her knowledge about Islam, how to fix broken lives, and about feeling happy. Using the Qur'an, *hadislar*, poetry, and her personal experiences, she counseled those seeking advice on how to behave Islamically toward others and presided over ceremonial events that always included a pedagogical component—didactic stories. Her didactic storytelling addressed, among other subjects, children's upbringing, education, and housewives' care for and of themselves by making themselves into desirable sexual and intellectual companions and caring mothers, wives, and daughters-in-law. Jahon reached out to her local community by inquiring about its members' health and problems and by visiting the elderly and the sick. She also engaged Hovliguzar's government by advising its members on religious matters and offering solutions to women's problems. While actively extending herself into the social by consulting, advising, providing examples, and creating stories, she wanted to change her "ill" society. She knew that this change could happen only as a result of individual moral self-formation and that she was instrumental and not essential to the self-formation of others. To achieve this goal, she (repeatedly) invited people to change their lives and join her in an effort to become "truly" Muslim.

In order to satisfy her desire to teach and change herself and her family, Nainahon continued to increase her knowledge about Islam, either with the help of the teachers or by herself. This knowledge made her "feel the *nur* inside"; her soul "became clean" and enabled her to be an *otincha* for her family members and thus to lead them by means of personal example and persuasion. She knew intellectually and experientially that despite her tribulations, such as failed business ventures and her and her children's health and marriage problems, God was always with her. God, she said, gave her everything: relative wealth, many children, grandchildren, and multiple opportunities to see the world outside Uzbekistan. But she had to do her part, including changing her family members by sharing her knowledge of Islam and inviting them to lead "truly" Muslim lives. Only God knew if they would follow her example because she was only instrumental and not essential to changes in their personal lives.

In 2003, after witnessing a street protest in Hovliguzar, during which the protestors demanded gas and electricity and amnesty for political prisoners, I asked Jahon how an individual could distinguish between good or bad government, and if the government was bad, whether it should be changed. She responded by saying that the state is like a family; in a good family, each partner has to work on her or himself. Therefore, in order to have a good ruler, an individual herself has to be good, to behave morally, with correct intentions toward others. She said, "If you are good, your rulers will be good. If you are bad, your rulers will be bad. Our rulers have houses and cars, and our people do not. I'm not going to advise that the rulers be punished. I would advise that we be punished. We deserve what we get. If *we* were good, our rulers would be good. Everything starts with a person, with a family. If I am good and my husband is good, then my family is good. . . . But you need to work on becoming good." I inferred from her answer that social change in the state or in the family starts with the individual; although only instrumental to changing others, individuals are essential to changing their own selves and their own personal lives.

Organisms and Environment

Nigel Rapport suggests that social scientists should learn from the animal-physiological world, because individual humans, like individual worms, are not just groups or species, but "'architects and engineers of their environments'" (2003, 225, quoting Rapoport 1998, 486). From a physiological standpoint, organisms, such as worms, "structurally" modify their environment; in the process, they extend "the range of homeostatic conditions [e.g., the organized delivery of temperature, nutrients, oxidants] necessary for their form of life from inside their 'bodies' to outside, adapting their environment to themselves (as themselves)" (Rapport 2003, 222). In other words, organisms, including humans, do not just adapt to their environments; they also and always adapt their environments to their own needs.

The stories recounted in this book demonstrate that despite existing structural constraints in Uzbekistan, including economic instability and various juristic prohibitions, individuals such as Tursun-oi, Jahon, and Nainahon persistently orchestrated change in their environment, including themselves and others. They did so *not* by adapting to the existing "ill" society (in Jahon's words) that exhibited "signs of the end of the world" (in Tursun-oi's words), but by trying to change the society from what it was into what it *is supposed to be*, into what it *has to become*, by trying to change one individual at a time. Purposefully and persistently, however successfully, they were attempting to adapt their environments to their visions of a life well led together as a community.

These women knew that engineering and building a different society is a slow process and that their abilities to change others were limited. They did not aim at radical social changes but continued doing what they did the best on a small scale, at an individual level, within their immediate environment because they felt it had to be done. For instance, Jahon wanted "to see" others "as Muslims"; she stressed that she had to "show you a good road, the right way, God's way" (see the introduction). Moving toward a different, Islamic society, showing "a good road," and going "the right way" is a process extending into the future but originating in the past because, according to these women, one's ability to modify one's environment for oneself as oneself is always already there, created by God at the beginning of time.

Tursun-oi, Jahon, and Nainahon did not self-identify as social reformers. They were not part of a social movement. They did not protest on the streets or run for Uzbekistan's Parliament. They had no official accreditation, known as *ijazah* (authorization or permission to transmit knowledge), and none of them, except for Jahon, held an official leadership position.[1] Rather, they felt content with and proud of their discipleship; Tursun-oi was a disciple of Sheikh Naqshband, Jahon of Imam al-Bukhari, and Nainahon of local *turamlar* (a family descended from the Prophet). But as previous chapters demonstrate, in order to effect change in their own and others' lives, these women did not have to be imams or sheikhs or descendants of the Prophet Muhammad or *pir*s. They led others in the process of moral self-formation without seeking conventional political authority, official titles, or existing forms of spiritual leadership. They were often *other* leaders in *other* places.[2]

1. An educational authority, whether the state or an individual religious official or a well-known teacher, can issue the *ijazah*.

2. Among the women I discuss, only Jahon assumed a position of administrative leadership. The effects of this position on her ability to lead others were at the time unclear.

As other leaders, these women effected change at a local level in what I call "a self-reflexive manner" by first changing themselves and then working on changing others. They enacted leadership in other places, such as individual homes, including and starting with their own homes. This leadership took on forms that were equally important to but not exactly the same as that of the imams at local mosques or the ulama representing the Muslim Board of Uzbekistan (Peshkova 2009a, 2009b). While addressing and mediating small, immediate, but often significant problems and teaching about "correct" Islam, they extended into the social through public life in private spaces.

Each one of these women had a mission, a "life project," that afforded her life "directionality and force" (Rapport 2003, 34). While pursuing their life projects, they claimed to experience change and to have changed the lives of others around them. Through practices of individuality, which included creating their own discourses on women's rights and "correct" Islam, they desired, expected, and moved this change forward; they did so purposefully, not accidentally or incidentally. These assessments are both my *etic* (researcher's) conclusions and their *emic* (authors') claims.[3]

Nainahon claimed to have changed her husband; he quit drinking. She changed her life by starting new business ventures or by persistently restarting old ones. She changed the lives of her daughters by facilitating their marriages or their divorces. In order to challenge both time and gravity's effects on her physical body, she joined a fitness club, among other things. Distraught by her husband's infidelity in 2003, Nainahon insisted she could change it. She may not have achieved her husband's full fidelity, a desired outcome, but she certainly affected his behavior. Instead of dating different women, in 2011 he told her of his desire to have more children. Nainahon did not want to get pregnant (even if she were able to do so biologically

3. In the argument I am advancing, whether their claims corresponded to the empirical truth is less important than their ability to make such claims.

at that time in her life); she had plenty of children and grandchildren of her own. In order to satisfy his desire, he decided to marry another woman, "to take a second wife." Although ambivalent about this marriage and probably deeply hurt, Nainahon remained optimistic about her future. She made plans, some of which no longer included her husband. Instrumental and not essential to his moral change, she might have decided not to change or challenge him anymore; but, whatever her decision was, it was really hers. Despite others' desires and against all odds, she continued pursuing her life project by moving it forward, as she said, "with God's help."

As a social leader in the Soviet Union, Tursun-oi had effected change in the lives of others as well as in her family, community, Hovliguzar, and the Soviet Union (see chapter 1). As a religious teacher in Uzbekistan from the 1990s into the second decade of the twenty-first century, while learning about and teaching "correct" Islam, she changed her self, her family, and students. Through her students' engagement with their local communities, she even affected the lives of some remote others. Her life project was not to amass knowledge, but to share it and call others to willingly receive it. In the summer of 2011, despite stating that she was too old to teach, she was not ready to give up her mission of slowly changing "uneducated people." Possessing an abundance of knowledge, she called others to volunteer and take the "bags" that her knowledge would "fill full."

In 2011, Jahon claimed that she had become "a better person," while the members of her *mahalla* (and beyond), with her help, had also become better people; they "complain less than others" (see chapter 5). Earlier in her married life, she had refashioned her self as a desirable companion for her husband and as a more caring and patient mother to her children. Consciously and purposefully, she set out to excel in these qualities.

By the end of the first decade of the twenty-first century, Jahon and Tursun-oi teamed up to change other communities in Hovliguzar, not only their immediate environment. Tursun-oi advised Jahon, now a *hokimyat otin*, to place Tursun-oi's students as the leading *otinlar* in the city's other *mahalla*s. Through these women, Tursun-oi and Jahon hoped to reach more individuals, share their knowledge of "correct" Islam and how to do the right thing, and continue helping others to become "truly" Muslim.

From their personal experiences, Tursun-oi, Jahon, and Nainahon knew that humans not only undergo but also and always create change within and around themselves. As a result of their increased knowledge about and understanding of "correct" Islam, they believed that by following the universal ethical paradigm encapsulated in the Qur'an, supplemented by *hadislar* and explicated by more knowledgeable individuals (such as *otinlar*), humans can achieve a different, Islamic society built on the moral principles of love, respect, and care for oneself and others. This future society is not immediate, fictional, or ethereal, but rather imminent and achievable, maybe tomorrow or in ten years or in the next generation. They believed that this change is slowly happening because individuals, as God's creatures aware of their purpose in this earthly life and believing in the promise of justice in the afterlife, do not just constitute but create such a society.

These different women and their different life projects also shared a methodology of how to (re)make the existing society. They believed in God's omnipotence and the goodness of humanity, and, if I understood them correctly, they saw the ethical and religious instruction of individuals (whether during religious lessons or through *masala*s or by providing advice to others or teaching one's children) as an impetus of social change. A fundamental assumption behind their methodology is the idea that societal change has to be propelled by individuals acting on their own volition, which reflects God's will. To paraphrase Rapport (2003), individuals have to enact change for themselves as themselves *and*, in these women's view, with God's and others' help by following "correct" Islam.

According to Tursun-oi, Jahon, and Nainahon, this "correct" Islam is simple, easy, and beautiful, and a "correct" Islamic way of living is clear and straightforward, founded on a relation between cause and effect. God, the Creator, is the cause of everything, including human actions, and every human action has consequences, if not in this life, then in the next. Yet even though God created humans and their actions and sent (repeatedly) the message meant to guide them how to have a life well led together, the choice to follow this guidance, *the choice to make a right choice*, is still an individual's choice.

These women were someone's students and disciples as well as teachers and leaders for others. As "good" teachers, they hoped that the students would follow their teachers' examples and eventually cultivate their own moral selves (for more on educating for a moral life, see Garfield 2007, 286). These women's mistakes, ambivalences, and compromises, described in the previous chapters, demonstrate that in the process of moral self-formation, one can make mistakes and unknowingly or knowingly sin. Nainahon openly admitted failing but did not give up on trying to be such a moral example for others, and all of them acknowledged that as human beings they were not perfect; some of them wanted fame or money, others a personal legacy. But from personal experiences and by increasing Islamic knowledge, these women learned that being imperfect is not a problem as long as an individual aspires to do better, to be a better Muslim, learns from his or her mistakes, and continues cultivating his or her own moral self despite them.

In their different ways, Tursun-oi, Jahon, and Nainahon taught others that in order to achieve God's plan for humanity—for each person to learn how to lead this earthly life well together with others as an aggregation of individuals—each person has to purposefully extend herself toward God and others in *her own* way, capitalizing on her talents, just as they did. Jahon, in her didactic stories, called others to extend themselves through care, respect, and self-reinvention—to become "a human who never complains, everything is good for him, a human who has enough *sobr* [patience]." Tursun-oi called on others to focus on education and personal transformation in order to become knowledgeable people, *illim khalq*. This focus came hand in hand with moral comportment toward God, the self, and others. Empowered by her faith, Nainahon helped her family members to become better Muslims and in response to pragmatic daily concerns and pursuits continued to affect her own condition and the lives of her relatives to the best of her abilities in the context of daily life's structural constraints.

Despite what others, I included, thought of them, these women's civilizing missions, their daring and persistent endeavors, consisted of changing their selves, their existential condition, and the lives of others. Different leaders and different individuals who effected moral change in different ways, these women agreed that social change starts with an individual, who in order to become "truly" Muslim—in light of increasing knowledge of the universal ethical paradigm built on the virtues of love, respect, and care for the self and others—thoughtfully, experientially, and patiently makes her self into a better human being, voluntarily submitting to God's guidance.

Knowledge and Existential Power

The previous chapters demonstrate that in Hovliguzar, as much as in other places, not only politicians and religious activists but also "ordinary Muslims" actively participate in defining "the moral and political direction of [their] contemporary Muslim societies" (Hirschkind 2006, 2). There, in spite of persecution, some Muslim men and women, such as Nodiraopa (see chapter 2), affected the moral and political direction of their society through political protests, and others did so through an ongoing emphasis on religious devotion, individual salvation, and social responsibility (on women's protests see Khamidov 2008). Moral self-formation facilitated by ethical instruction offered by women such as Tursun-oi and Jahon was as political as overt political protests, but in unusual ways and in "unusual places" (Mahmood 2005, 192). Aimed at teaching an individual to think critically about the self and others in light of the universal ethical paradigm, this ethical instruction—as much as politics in usual places, such as street protests—was meant to achieve social change. This change did not come through a revolution, but through individual evolution into a moral subject capable of influencing and remaking not only her self but also her immediate context through her existential power.

In the case of the women I am writing about, this power was exemplified by and further developed through individual meditation on the correspondence between thoughts, actions, and feelings and their successive mediation. In the process, the God-given capacity to become what God intended an individual to be—namely, a "truly" Muslim human and a part of the social universe—was developed into an ability to change the self and others. This ability was not constituted but rather enhanced by the knowledge of the universal ethical paradigm—"correct" Islam. For Tursun-oi, Jahon, and Nainahon, the change within themselves, in accordance with their understanding of how to do the right thing, was essential to the successive and successful unfolding of their life projects, which included changing others.

I take this existential power to be a conceptual kernel of human agency. Addressed by numerous scholars of the social sciences and humanities, human agency is variously defined as "a capacity [not necessarily synonymous with empowerment] to exert some control over the conditions of one's existence" (Gomberg-Munoz 2010, 297) or as "the intentional and motivated capacity to act" (Hay 2010, 260) or as "a correspondence between one's desires, the effects one's actions have in the world, and the ability to manage the reception of those actions by others" (Greenberg 2011, 89). Writing about pious Muslim women in Egypt, Saba Mahmood (2005) provides an in-depth review of the literature on agency and argues that the political agency of women such as Tursun-oi, Jahon, and Nainahon cannot be understood "without a proper grasp" of their "ethical agency" (2005, 35).

Although "ethical agency" is important to understanding social and political effects of Islamic instruction, my goal in this book is not to debate agency, whether and why it exists or what its modalities, meaning, and origins are. My aim is less ambitious and more general. Building on the work of other social theorists, including Mahmood (2005), I, following Rapport (2003), want to add to existing understandings of social dynamics in Central Asia by focusing on the existential power that individuals possess (see also Cohen 1994). Inasmuch as Islam or Islamic instruction does not produce Muslims (Marranci 2009), nationalism does not produce nations (Adams 2010), and an "ideology of national independence" does not produce Uzbeks (Rasanayagam 2010), this individual power is existential and creative. It originates within an individual and is not constituted or produced by power relations, but rather produces them (for a critique of social ontology, see Marranci 2008; Milton and Svasek 2005). Therefore, social dynamics in Central Asia are also created, not constituted, by individuals.

The kind of analysis I advocate is not unique. Its various iterations have been criticized as products of the "Western" ideology of individualism, atomism, Enlightenment, and liberalism and thus utterly inapplicable to "the East" because of "the East's" unique communalism (on a "Western" philosophical geneology of "modern" individual identity, see Taylor 1992; on conceptualizing an individual as a relational being, see Gergen 2009). In this book, I challenge this inapplicability.

Individual and Society

A number of existing interdisciplinary scholarly works argue or assume that the concepts of "the self" and "the individual" are historical precedents, that they are inventions created "during a period that we now view as the Enlightenment" (Gergen 2009, xiv) and therefore belong to thc "Anglophone" (Rabinow 2008, 56) or "Western" or "European" or "modern" or "Christian" world (e.g., Foucault 1972 and Mauss 1954; for how Foucault changed this view in his later works, see Laidlaw 2010, 374). These works explain sociocultural differences and changes, including different political and economic systems, as effects of this precedent, which naturalized individualistic forms of life and established the ideology of individualism (e.g., Max Weber's argument about connections among Protestant ethics, individualism, capitalism, and northern Europe in Weber 1978; see also Seigel 2005 and Taylor 1992).[4] In such analyses, personhood, agency, and integrated independent individuals are treated as sole possessions of "the West," of "modern society," whereas the concepts of "collectivity" and "the social" are associated with "the East" or "Eastern" countries, where populism, communalism, and religious sensibilities are (apparently always) prioritized over individual desires (see, e.g., Dumont 1994, 27; Tudge 1991, 132).

Over time, the repeated use of the terms *Western self* as normative and *non-Western self* as its opposite resulted in a kind of epistemological confidence that the non-Western self is "unbounded, not integrated, dependent, unable to set itself reflexively apart from others, unable to distinguish between the individual and a role or status that [the] individual occupies, unable to pursue its own goals independently of the goals of a group or community" (Sokefeld 1999, 418). Construed as a negated Western self and always subordinated to the social or the transcendental or both, the non-Western self is "denied a self at all" (Sokefeld 1999, 418; for subordination to the transcendental, see, e.g., Bruce 2000 but compare Marranci 2009). This epistemological confidence continues to inform analyses of "non-Western" societies, which often give prominence to collective identities and cultural forces; these analyses focus on community, history, and religion, whether the latter is understood as a social glue, a system of symbols producing agents without independent agency, or discourses that have their own techniques and law (for such analyses, see Durkheim 1915; Geertz 1968; Foucault 1980, 685; Huntington 1996). For instance, Slavoj Žižek (2002), in his analysis of the

4. Kenneth Gergen (2009) argues that despite the Enlightenment's claims, individual selves are not bounded but co-constituted. He proposes that we do away with the concept of the individual as a freely choosing agent and start social analysis with the concept of "relating," an emerging process whereby the conception of an individual consciousness should be derived from a relational process (not the other way around). Adopting this approach, Gergen argues, will rid humanity of individual psychological suffering (abuse, isolation, loneliness, and lack of morality), materialism, and environmental degradation (xxii).

terrorist attacks in New York City on September 11, 2001, portrays Eastern or Third World individuals—Muslims specifically—as very different from other, mostly non-Muslim individuals living in New York and Europe. He concludes that these Third World individuals are "ready to risk anything" for a transcendental cause (40; for a powerful critique of such neo-Orientalism, see Almond 2007).

Similarly, many existing studies of post-Soviet Central Asia focus on collectivities such as "Muslim women," "the *mahalla*," and "the family" or on "Muslim men," "ethnic groups," "clans," "nations," and "members" of social and religious movements, such as Hizb-ut-Tahrir (e.g., Abashin 1997; Corcoran-Nantes 2005; Fathi 1997; Karagiannis 2006; Poliakov 1992; Snesarev 1974). In some of these works, we hear individual stories, but these individuals are nevertheless constituted by the social or substituted by the transcendental, and they do not create either.

From a Unique Nation to a Unique Individual

Collective exceptionalism and particularism of "Eastern" values also underline the ideology (idea) of "national independence" advocated by the Uzbek president, Islam Karimov. By co-opting cultural relativism and culture talk and using them as techniques of state craftsmanship, this ideology describes Uzbeks as a nation forged by a unique "national Islam" and an "Uzbek model" of gradual democratization. In this ideology, "national Islam" is explained in terms of "traditional" Central Asian Sufism and the heritage of Hanafi Islam (Louw 2007); and the "Uzbek model" of gradual democratization is presented as the logical outcome of the unique Uzbek traditions and the country's particular history (Adams 2010; Rasanayagam 2010).

An excerpt from the transcript of President Karimov's speech in 2011 at the celebration of Uzbekistan's twenty years of independence from the Soviet Union illustrates the focus on the importance of the gradual nature of the democratization process and on the need to sacrifice individual freedoms for the well-being of the collective:

> On the way to improve the quality of life of the people, the principal priority for us is to gradually accelerate the pace of democratic renewal, the liberalization and modernization of all spheres of life. I think I speak for all present at this majestic square [who are] attending this ceremony, for our wider public, for all the people, if I say that this is the surest way that has fully justified itself for the twenty years of our country's recent history, the path that has acquired an extensive acknowledgement around the globe as the "Uzbek model." . . . The honorable duty of every one of us is to be ready to devote ourselves entirely and if necessary to give our lives for the future prosperity of the land dear to us all, in the name of its well-being and a great future.[5]

In this speech, individuals in Uzbekistan are portrayed as both a collective engine and recipients of the benefits of the unique "Uzbek model," but not as its creators. The model is always already there. Articulated and emplaced through juristic means and national policies, it precedes and is expected to constitute every Uzbek citizen.[6]

The powerful dichotomies of "the East" and "the West" do not stand by themselves. They are connected to an array of ideological qualifying adjectives: "the West" is democratic, individualistic, capitalist, free, liberal, and so forth, whereas "the East" is authoritarian and despotic, conservative, communal (if not Communist) and is built on family values and individual unfreedom (for a criticism of this rhetoric, see Varisco 2007). I do not argue that the unfreedom of individuals does not exist in the Eastern Hemisphere; Uzbekistan is but one of its global instantiations. Nor do I suggest that these and other ideological adjectival qualifiers should be

5. President Islam Karimov's September 1, 2011, Independence Day address is available at http://uza.uz/en/politics/2117/, accessed Sept. 5, 2011.

6. Although in one of the publications attributed to President Karimov he uses the concept of "the perfect person," this concept does not refer to a unique individual, but to dependent elements meant to populate a larger unique collective "Uzbek model." For a thorough discussion of the passage on "the perfect person," see Rasanayagam 2010, 110.

reversed—although the United States and European countries, as much as Central or South Asia, are populated by individuals who self-identify as conservative and uphold "family values." Rather, I contend that to limit preoccupation with the self and individual to "the West" is to fail to question this duality's own historicity and to deny "the reality of our experiential lives," in which, irrelevant of geographic location or historical time, humans act as "agents with transformative powers" (Sugarman and Martin 2011, 285).

The concepts of the self and individual are not at all unfamiliar in "the East." They were fundamental to the fifth century's development of Buddhism in northern India and utilized by Chinese, Central Asian, Russian, and Soviet philosophers (see Carrithers, Collins, and Lukes 1985, cited in Laidlaw 2010, 370). In the Central Asia of the tenth and eleventh centuries, Ibn Sino (Ibn Sina or Avicenna) contemplated the soul's individuation and individual perfection through (individual) unification by the means of love with the divine ("the First Cause" or "the Absolute Good") (Ibn Sina 1945, 227, and 1974). In Russia during the nineteenth and twentieth centuries, Nikolay Berdyaev articulated the philosophical concepts of personality and creativity (see Berdyaev 1943, 20–22). In his work, creativity is not just a gifted person's ability; it is an ability to be and create that adheres to every person (see also Ingold and Hallam 2007). In the twentieth-century Soviet Union, Mikhail Bakhtin developed the concepts of the dialogical personality and "I-for-myself," where dialogue is a creative encounter between two or more personalities, with others and within oneself (see Bakhtin 1981; Emerson 1990, 117, and 1997, 158). None of these thinkers denied the importance of the social. Yet even if they attributed the cause of being to the Absolute Good (as Ibn Sino did) or to God (as did Berdyaev), they affirmed free personalities in the sense that these personalities are not alienated or alienable from themselves into any kind of "exterior collective body" but "individualized" in each person (Berdyaev 1943, 41–71; Emerson 1990, 124). Their works, among others, exemplify both interest in and creative thinking about the relations among individuals and between an individual and God as well as about the role of the individual in society.

Because "an individual" and "a self" are not synonymous with "individualism" and "the West," and because there are no essential differences between humans—we all have physical bodies, with their complex neurological systems and ecological emotions—in any part of the world at any historical period, nothing should preclude us from starting the social analysis of a particular society with the individual—by focusing on the individual self (Marranci 2008; Rapport 2003). Such analysis helps us to understand the forms of knowledge created by women such as Tursun-oi, Jahon, and Nainahon as well as their self-formation and its social effects. Surrounding relational processes, social forces, history, and religion either enhanced or hampered these women's decisions and actions, but they cannot fully explain those decisions or actions.

These women's stories show that their decisions, actions, and feelings were neither reactionary nor socially scripted (concepts discussed in Goffman 1971). In Uzbekistan, those who were resolved to teach Islam did so despite the prohibition; those who protested on the streets did so in spite of the horror stories of detention and beatings; and those who launched business ventures did so regardless of (even if partially enabled by) systematic and systemic corruption. Neither reducible to nor solely conditioned by the enabling or constraining social strictures, these decisions and actions exemplify individual existential power to follow a life project—and all within an "Eastern" context.

Women such as Tursun-oi, Jahon, and Nainahon did not see themselves as being atomistic and would certainly argue against the ideology of an individualism that is, in their view, incompatible with the universal ethical paradigm created by God and advanced by them or with the traditional cultural values promoted by multiple actors in Uzbekistan, including intellectual and religious elites and themselves. The previous chapters demonstrate that these women saw themselves as persons created by God with different bodies, tastes, voices, talents, and aesthetics, who in order to have a life well led together with others had to in-body and embody the knowledge of how to do the right thing *individually*.

If I understood them correctly, they believed that before there was any social structure (society, social relations, states, governments, or movements), there was God, who created humans, humans' life projects (what they were or ought to be or become), and a capacity to actualize these projects. They also learned and taught others that human life is sacred and unique and that God endowed humans with a capacity for and a right to self-formation, which, in turn, helped to further develop individual ability to create, perform, and change or to willingly stay the same against all odds. Reflecting their understandings of a particular relationship between the human and divine worlds, these women insisted that social change is possible only if willed by God, but that it is initiated and carried out by an individual who first has to undergo change herself. As Tahsir said on March 13, 2003, "It is all from Allah. But we have to do our part." Tursunoi's, Jahon's, and Nainahon's personal lives and stories illustrate that while following a set of normative (Islamic) principles and the moral example provided by someone else, every individual can develop his or her God-given capacity for self-formation into an ability to do the right thing. Everyone can cultivate his or her own moral style according to her personal yet not historically discontinuous understanding of God's plan.

Such personal understandings are created in relation to and in light of historical precedents left in the "physical remains of past practices" (Rapport 2003, 59) in one's organic and inorganic environment. The physical remains, which provide important resources for historical continuity, include the Qur'an and *hadislar*, stories about the Soviet past and the Great Patriotic War, privatization, the hajj, and national icons such as Sheikh Naqshband. Without human individuals, however, these stories and artifacts would be meaningless: neither the sheikh nor the Qur'an nor the Soviet past would matter. By attributing meaning to them and while pursuing their life projects, human individuals reactivate these practices, stories, and memories and create historical continuity and social relations within, with, and in relation to this organic and inorganic environment.

Toward Relational Existential Power

To insist that "*the power of the individual*" engenders "*his or her own becoming*" and that self-knowledge is "the source of, and route to, self, world and other, is not the same [as to claim] that individuals are naturally or necessarily solitary or self-contained" (Rapport 2003, 36, 33, italics in the original). There are always others who create an environment within which self-formation takes place, individual stories become meaningful, and choices and actions matter. Previous chapters show the importance of the social environment in which the book's characters actualized their "capacity for and a right of self-authorship" (Sugarman and Martin 2011, 287), transcended sociocultural boundaries, and "exercise[d] the power to make their own circumstance" (Rapport 2003, 261).

For instance, Tursun-oi's mother played a very important role in her daughter's life project. By helping to take care of Tursun-oi's children and house chores, this woman enabled Tursun-oi's continuous education and helped to build her successful career. Tursun-oi's rise to be the director of the silk factory, her husband's position in the local government, the factory workers' labor and efforts, and the Communist Party's emphasis on the necessity of local women's involvement in the industrial sphere and in the party's leadership in 1970s also contributed to Tursun-oi's thriving career as a social leader. By making her life project possible and assuring her "continuing capability to be responsible for interpretations made, relations entered into and actions taken" (Rapport 2003, 6), this social environment created by other individuals increased Tursun-oi's chances of success.

The agentive personhood of the individuals I am writing about was always enacted in an environment and cannot be explained *entirely* as an artifact of self-determination. In order to understand why and how Tursun-oi, Jahon, and Nainahon (or Tahsir and others) continued to follow or changed their life projects in their unique ways, we should include environment (social, physical, virtual, historic, and so forth) in a relational analysis of their existential power.

Rapport argues that "in order to" achieve certain goals, individuals create and participate in social relations and affect the social (2003, 52). But if relations need participants, then to be a participant is to be *in relation to* someone or something else. The women I am writing about and I myself had unique life projects that were imagined and unfolded always in relation to someone or something else, including God, husbands, children, friends, business partners, religious leaders, natural disasters, wars, SNB agents, and dreams, as well as in relation to ourselves as aging or pregnant, ill or terrified physical bodies. In this sense, our existential power was always relational.

If we accept that social relations have no life of their own but are created through interactions between individuals and with their environment, including themselves, and that these interactions are critical to self-formation and daily life, then I find what I call "relational existential power" to be a useful analytical tool. This concept aids in understanding self-formation, its social effects, and the forms of knowledge (such as the experiential knowledge of empathetic sociality discussed in chapter 4) that emerged in the process of learning how to do and feel the right thing as facilitated by local *otinlar* through didactic storytelling.

While moving their life projects forward, individuals always encounter others, who also have different or similar yet clearly distinct directionalities; some of these individuals further their life projects "irrespective of others or at other's expense" (Rapport 2003, 254). For example, the corrupt local officials from the prosecutor's office sold Nainahon and her husband's land to someone else, and her "hard-headed" daughter-in-law's actions "broke" Nainahon's heart. The hurtful words of envious individuals, such as Dilbaropa, who were also in the process of moving their life projects forward, added to Jahon's distress, and my interest in religion led to her interrogation by SNB officers in August 2011. Because some advance their life projects at the expense of others, the social environment, created by an aggregation of individuals, is not limited to but includes individual suffering, pain, and injustice. Rapport (2003) points out that in such an environment the pursuit of an individual life project does not have to have a happy ending. The negative possibility calls for, in his words, "the diagonal line . . . between autonomy and sympathy" (2003, 257) or, in Marranci's words, for empathy (2008, 75–78).

From their personal experiences, their intrasubjective relations with God, and their increasing knowledge of the universal ethical paradigm, Tursun-oi, Jahon, and women like them learned the importance of empathizing with and feeling for others, and so they considered empathetic sociality to be a fundamental part of the self-formation they advocated (see chapter 4). The forms of knowledge that emerged through *stories well told* by them and other *otinlar* made an individual who heard these stories feel that which is right, good, and true in addition to pointing out correct choices of action. These stories helped the listeners to experience, to in-body, an empathetic, proximal, and *nonabstract* ethic in the context of storytelling and, it was hoped, to embody it in daily life. As part and parcel of the universal ethical paradigm, this empathetic and proximal ethic was necessary both theologically, as decreed by God, and pragmatically because daily life was always lived in relation to others.

In these women's views, working on the self and developing respect and love toward the self and others are prerequisites for one's ability to be what God intends one to be—a part of the social universe; self-formation *always* has social effects. To borrow Rapport's words, God willed that in a social universe distinct individual directionalities come together, "not treating others instrumentally, as one's means, and not treating oneself disrespectfully [and] irresponsibly" (2003, 257). The forms of knowledge these women helped to create fostered an individual ability to imagine and embody a future based on the virtues of respect, love, and care for the self and others, while recognizing the irreducible value of each and every human life. In their view, to develop this ability is essential to self-formation because an individual's capacity to actualize her potential to be good (to be loving, caring, and respectful) and her right to self-authorship as an ethical subject are God given; this capacity has a transcendental ontology, not a social one, and therefore is not only a right, but also a responsibility. Jahon reminded others and me again and again that even though humans may not have been made equal, they all have been "made [by God] to be good."[7]

Individual, Society, and God

Tursun-oi's, Jahon's, and Nainahon's personal faith in God informed the existential power they exercised in relation to themselves and others. According to these women, there *is* something beyond matter and the individual life force. This other force is not society or state, but God, who can, if God so wishes, steer an individual life project in a particular direction or annihilate it completely, whether through the actions of others, natural disasters, or illness. Reflecting their faith in God, these women also believed that even though a unique individual mind cannot fully (or really) be known to others, it is always known to God. In addition to private knowledge (as "I" know myself) and public knowledge (as "others" know me), there is always a third knowledge: the divine knowledge (for more on an Islamic perspective on relations between the self, divine, and the other, see Wadud 2007). This knowledge mediates human inability to fully know the other because the other, inasmuch as the self, has been created by God to be good, whether this goodness is actualized in this earthly life or not.

At the same time, Tursun-oi's, Jahon's, and Nainahon's faith in God did not cancel out their individual existential power. Rapport argues that faith in God is an example of "bad faith," a projection of the self in a cultural form, in order "to make more concrete, comprehensible and resolvable what is awesome and fluid in our lives" and to find someone or something to be "responsible for our bodies and experiences" (2003, 56). Because human symbolic interaction is

7. The stories shared in the previous chapters show that these women rarely evaluated their society as "good"; they understood that it had a long way to go to be good.

impossible without projections, being human is impossible without "bad faith." This, however, does not mean that individual actions toward the self and others are constituted (or substituted) by the transcendental.

Tursun-oi, Jahon, Nainahon, and women and men like them were self-relational individuals, themselves "the potentiality of relations" (Pedersen 2012, 60). They created relations with others on an intersubjective level and with God and themselves on an intrasubjective level (see chapter 1). As a part of their surrounding environment, God became a part of their sense of self and identity, a process by which they made sense of their autobiographic selves as Muslims. In such an environment, their faith in God and desire to become "truly" Muslim exemplified "relational transformation" (Pedersen 2012, 63), a process by which instead of focusing on relations with others, they first focused on relations with God and within themselves.

Their work at learning about "correct" Islam and their individual experiences provided numerous opportunities for the practice of thinking, feeling, and acting, which increased their self-knowledge, strengthened their relations with God, and enhanced their understanding of God's plan for humanity. This plan required social change, a long-term process that started intrasubjectively with individual self-formation. Then, without abandoning their work on their selves, these women and men tried to modify others purposefully and persistently, while others modified but did not determine them, their stories, life projects, and desires for change. In this process, faith in God enhanced their relational existential power by articulating it not only as a capacity that should become ability, but also as the *responsibility* of every "truly" Muslim human.

According to the individuals I am writing about, a human cannot "study up" to God's level, nor would God ever "come down" to a human level. In 2002, Tursun-oi told me that no one can know or learn *everything* about God and God's message. She exemplified and embodied this inability. In the summer of 2011, she was still learning about Islam from books, which continued to be her teachers. That year, while discussing Tursun-oi's young apprentice Miriam, Jahon insisted that only God can know everything: "you should not think that you know [everything]." In 2003, Nainahon told me that "Islam is like science, and no one can ever master it all. No one can say, 'I am finished [learning about Islam].'" Although these women claimed to respect other (previous) messages, such as Christianity, sent by God to humanity, none of them agreed that God became human. A human can never *really* know the Creator and therefore can never *really* have a personal relationship with God.

In our conversations, Tursun-oi, Jahon, and Nainahon insisted that theologically the Creator is of a different order, unfathomable to humans; God is beyond human relations in the sense that God is prior to humans and thus prior to their relations.[8] These women learned from personal experiences and through their increased knowledge of "correct" Islam that in the human world created by God—in the created order—human individuals also are and can and ought to be creative in a moral and physical sense. Jahon wanted to teach her community's members to create, to make rather than to break human relationships. Not single-handedly, she and Tursun-oi created stories about how to do the right thing, about "right" and "wrong" thoughts, feelings, and actions. Nainahon wanted to teach her family members how to live Islamically and how to create a moral space conducive to their self-formation into "truly" Muslim humans; her new business ventures were part of her attempt to create such a space for herself and her family. These women's faith in God, their "bad faith," did not cancel out their existential power to be, become, change, and create. Rather, this faith affirmed their God-given capacity to develop and self-form, which they *had* to exercise in relation to others, including themselves.

Tursun-oi told me in 2002 that the Qur'an, *hadislar*, and didactic storytelling demonstrated that God rewards moral deeds in the afterlife, but also in this life. Nainahon and Jahon echoed this view (see chapter 3). These rewards, material and spiritual, augment the

8. Tahsir held similar views (see chapter 2).

individual's ability "to be responsible for interpretations made, relations entered into and actions taken" and, as a result, further her individual project (Rapport 2003, 6). By rewarding good and punishing evil, all-powerful God does not simply manipulate humans: God endows every human with a capacity to learn how to distinguish correct actions and to create social relations. *Each* individual, not a collective, will be rewarded or punished by God for developing this capacity into an ability to shape her own and others' circumstances in ethical ways (for more on predestination and free will in Islam, see Hourani 1985 and Tomson 1950).

Therefore, the transcendental ontology of human experience and faith in God do not terminate but require individual responsibility and ability to learn how to do the right thing in relation to the self and to others in order to have a life well led together with them. To put it differently, even though an individual acquires the capacity and the right of self-authorship through God's creation (God has created the individual's soul and body and hence this capacity), self-authorship or self-formation—the ability to evaluate, be critical of, and be able to change the self and others—is still individual. Even if God has created right and wrong choices for action, a human being herself picks and embodies her individual choices.[9] She is neither constituted by the social nor substituted by the transcendental, but creative of the former even if she believes herself to be created by the latter.

9. This view of self-formation, shared by the women I am writing about, is in agreement with the Islamic theological doctrine of free will and predestination (or the divine decree). George Hourani offers a briefer version of famous Islamic scholar al-Ashari's Doctrine of Acquisition: "God creates every human act and enables [the] human to do it, but [the] human makes a choice and thus [is] responsible for outcomes" (1985, 8). He also describes a different position by theologian Maturidi that allows for a greater human ability to act independently: "[the] human makes a choice how to act, God creates an act, [the] human acquires it, and hence [is] responsible. God is the only creator" (9; see also Watt 1948).

7

Is It Over?

Not a Conclusion

Proposition: Individuals create the society and state by pursuing their life projects intentionally and purposefully.

Tashkent, Uzbekistan, August 2011

The next morning one of the OVIR officers accompanies me to a local branch of the Western Union. His cough is driving me crazy; he must be sick or a heavy smoker. When we get out of the cab next to the Western Union, he suddenly says, "I wish I could help you, but I cannot do anything. It comes from the top." He rolls his eyes up. "I have no idea what you are talking about," I snap. "Let's get the money."

I get the money by 11:00 a.m. He helps me to exchange American dollars for Uzbek soms and to carry the bag full of soms. "It IS heavy," he says. We take a cab to a bank to pay the fine and to get a receipt to close my delo *(case). The bank manager spends more than half an hour running paper banknotes through the counting machine. "Finally, it is done. I even broke a sweat," he says and smiles. I turn to the officer and look straight into his eyes. He understands. He gives me back my passport.*

In the cab on the way to a travel agency, the officer says he is sorry that I have missed my flight. He says he is sure I will be able to get on another one. "I know, I need to get out of this country," I reply.

In the travel agency, the sales rep tells me that there are no tickets available to Russia till the very end of August. "Gastarbeiteri," *he adds smiling. Before I say anything, the officer shows his* udostoverenie *(badge) and tells the sales rep that I am being deported and that he, the sales rep, has to find a ticket. The sales rep responds, no longer smiling, "I understand."*

The badge helps. I get a ticket to Sochi, a Russian city on the shore of the Black Sea. Although I am not flying back to the Caucasus, and it will be an eleven-hour drive to the town where my son is, I do not care. I will no longer be in Uzbekistan. That is all that matters. I feel somewhat relieved. The ticket is for a late-evening flight tomorrow. "Thank you," I tell the officer.

After I pay for the ticket, the officer takes my passport from the sales rep and says that he will keep it safe until my departure: "If you do not have it, no one can take it from you." "Someone still wants my passport?" I am dumbfounded. In response, he breaks into an endless hacking cough again. "Oh, no. I hope he does not have TB," I think. His telephone keeps on ringing. Again and again. He does not answer. "Why don't you answer it?" I ask. He smiles in response to my question and says, "Let's go to lunch."

At the café, he orders lunch, and I—coffee and cigarettes. "You know, I quit in 2006," not sure why I tell him. The officer says that I should not smoke if I was able to quit. Then adds, "I understand what you are going through." "Do you?" I retort. He changes the subject and asks me if I am married and have children. "Divorced and a seven-year-old son," I reply. He notes that he grew up with his mother in a single-parent household, too. Although I do not ask him about his family, he tells me that he is married and has a son also, much younger than mine. I nod. He asks, "Is this his picture?" looking at the wallpaper on my mobile phone screen. I nod again. "Handsome and big, a real lad [patsan]*," he replies. "I do not have a picture of mine, but he is handsome too," he adds, smiles, and coughs again. "I am sure," I agree and nod. But all I can think behind my constrained responses is: Why is he kind to me? Why did he help me to get the ticket? What are his orders? And why did he take away my passport? Who can still take it away from me? But I say sympathetically, "You really should take care of your cough."*

He smiles in response. I have asthma. I know what the never-ending cough feels like.

I spend the night at the same hotel and all the next day at the OVIR. The same officer comes to pick me up at the hotel in the morning. He tells me that I will see my son soon and should focus on this. He adds, "You will be safer with me than in the hotel," and smiles. Of course, he could have been instructed to keep an eye on me so that I leave the country without contacting anyone else. But who cares, as long as he is friendly?

We take a cab to the OVIR. My belongings are locked in the office next door. Except for visits to the bathroom, I am never alone. The officer is with me all the time. I guess he has adopted me; I am his "case [delo]*."*

He plays a Michael Jackson song for me on his mobile phone. It is a nasheed, *a religious hymn. "It does sound like Michael Jackson, but why would he be singing a religious hymn?" I ask. The officer says that before Michael Jackson died, he converted to Islam. "Are you sure? I haven't heard anything about that," I reply. "Of course, why would they tell you that their famous singer converted to Islam? Don't they hate Muslims?" he asks. "There are always people who hate other people, but not all, not everywhere, and not all the time," I reply. "Americans do not hate Muslims, but some Americans use hate as means to achieve political ends, and others do not know how to channel their fear," I add.*

The officer says that he likes Michael Jackson but prefers Sharali Dzhuraev, a famous local singer. He tells me that the Uzbek government no longer favors Dzhuraev. The officer adds, "He sings traditional songs, and here [in Uzbekistan] there is no one as good as him." We listen to Dzhuraev for another half an hour before his phone's batteries run out. Plugged into the wall, the phone sits silently on the table while we talk about travel and education and share stories about our families. Two more officers join us. Tea, Coca-Cola, pasties, their jokes and questions about America and the Caucasus, and my talking about Times Square, American police, law, banks, education, and daily life there make me feel better. Their curiosity and empathy, which to me feel genuine, make a big difference. Although I am still upset about the whole ordeal, I am no longer afraid of them.

Late that evening, the officer accompanies me to the airport. It is almost over, I hope. It is hard to believe. Who knew I could be so happy driving to the airport. The officer gives me back my passport. I handle my passport with care, as if it is fragile and precious, and put it in my handbag. I love my passport today. It feels like an extension of my body. It makes me real and legal and able to cross borders. It makes me exist and count. It makes me someone. I've never thought about my passport as a defining element of my identity. They say you don't know what you have until it's gone. Now I know.

Standing at the center of the main hall, I fill out the customs forms to show Uzbek customs that I am not taking more money out of the country than I brought in. In order to avoid the crowd, the officer checks in my luggage and me. He is patient with me, almost protective. I look around. Video cameras, bright lights, and occasional ads look back at me.

The customs stand is across from the entrance of the main hall; a passport control booth is behind it, then the long corridor through the terminal and duty-free shops. I realize that I am so close to what I think of as a "neutral zone." I can see it from here. Then the plane and then Sochi and then—my son. I am well on the way toward him. I am almost out of here. Almost there. I just need to get through customs and passport control.

"Here you are, Svetlana Alexeevna!"[1] *I hear my name and turn around. Two young men in civilian clothes are approaching me, smiling. "We have been waiting for you. Let us help you through customs," one of them says. Dressed as civilians, helping me through customs, they must be SNB officers. Oh god, not again! The officer*

1. Here I am addressed by my first name and patronymic, a formal way of addressing an individual.

from Tashkent's OVIR—the one who brought me to the airport, the one who played Michael Jackson for me, carried my heavy bag full of Uzbek banknotes, and fed me lunch—comes toward me. He looks somewhat perplexed. He shakes hands with the two other officers, looks at me, and lowers his gaze.

Earlier today he said that I should not think that all law enforcement officers in Uzbekistan are assholes and that he was sorry my friends in Tashkent did not help me in time and that this happened to me in general. He told me that he knew how to be a friend. I had a feeling that he was not an asshole. But then, what do I know? Is he really a friend? Does it really matter? The Tashkent SNB found me anyway.

These two men in civilian clothes "help me" through customs, meaning that the customs officer does not ask any questions and signs my papers without even looking at me. One of these men in civilian clothes picks up my passport from the customs station. It all happens so fast. My passport, which in the past four days has changed so many hands; my passport, which has been pocketed and locked up in a safe; my passport, the absence of which has kept me hostage in this country till now. One of these officers says that my carry-ons and checked-in luggage have to be carefully searched. I ask, "Why? What did I do? Why me?" Another one answers, "Because we have to make sure that you have no heroin or psychotropic substances on or with you." "HEROIN?! ON ME?! This is not happening. THIS IS NOT HAPPENING!" I know what it means. It means a strip search. But, more importantly, I know what the outcome might be. In order for them to find heroin, you do not need to have it with or on you. In a matter of seconds, I go from angry to terrified. I want to scream but cannot. Arrested by terror, my dry throat cannot make a sound.

They lead me into the room right in front of the passport control. What if they planted heroin inside my voice recorder, camera, or my computer in Hovliguzar or inside my clothes in the Tashkent OVIR? If it happened to others, it can happen to me. What if this know-how-to-be-a-friend officer did it earlier today during one of my bathroom trips? I knew it. I knew I could not trust him. I can trust no one, not even myself. I already see myself behind bars. I will never get out of here. I will never leave this place. What if I will never see my son?

The room they are taking me into is so close to the "neutral zone." It is fifteen steps away. If only I could magically be transported to the other side. Or if I could run. Run. I should run. But I will never get through the passport control officers without my passport. Where would I run? Into a "neutral zone"? There, too, I will not be safe. This is madness. I am crazy even to think about it. You cannot run away from the state; it is everywhere.

A million thoughts are jammed inside my skull. They are a legion trying to get out in weird ways and all at the same time. I have to focus, but I cannot. My ears burn. My fingers—I see but cannot feel them. They are no longer just cold; they are numb. My body is lost to terror. Like a virus, it spreads fast from my mind into my spine and extremities. But I cannot let terror paralyze my thinking. Not now. Not here.

The SNB officers walk out, leaving me with a female officer in the room where she is to conduct the strip search. I turn my head, watching them sit down on the bench right in front of the room. I hear one of them saying, "Prohodite razdivaites' *[Come on and take off your clothes]." The other one smiles. He finds it funny. "Shut the door," the female officer commands. I obey.*

"We have to perform a personal'ni dosmotor *[strip search]," she begins. "Do not worry, there will be witnesses," she adds. "Just to let you know," she notes, "unlike the United States, we in Uzbekistan do not have sophisticated equipment to do it." How does she know that I am from the United States? I am flying to Russia. My passport is Russian, and the ticket is for Sochi. Both are on the table in front of her. Oh, god! They probably have a camera installed in this room too. They will be watching my body being searched. I feel like something is growing inside me, ready to rip me apart. It is a scream, but all that comes out is a pitiful, "Why are you doing this to me? Why me? What did I do?" She answers, "I am not sure. Do*

you have heroin or psychotropic substances with you? We have to be sure that . . ." Her voice fades away.

While she replies, I remember Uzbekistan's horror stories turned into black humor. One story I had read goes: "On Tashkent's Independence Square, a man murders a woman in cold blood . . . [in front of many] people and a few cops. The murderer easily works . . . [through] the crowd and disappears. The crowd raises hell and begins to curse at the cops. A while later they call on the Ministry of Internal Affairs to intervene. Upon finding out what happened, a commanding officer from the said ministry immediately appears at the scene and lashes out at the cops: 'You do-nothings, why didn't you detain the murderer? You sons-of-bitches! I'll fire all of you.' The cops then respond: 'Comrade General, we're sorry, but the fact is that today we forgot to take narcotics and Hizb-ut-Tahrir leaflets with us.'"[2]

I gasp for air. What if they did not forget to bring heroin with them today?

"The witnesses," the female officer says, pointing toward two women who have just come into the room. They are dressed in neat blue airport janitors' uniforms. "Your names?" she asks them. "Undress," she tells me. "Konkretnoe unizhenie *[real humiliation],"* *I hear one of the witnesses saying to the other one.*

The human brain is amazing. It is like a huge movie theater with multiple movies playing at the same time. Blue-uniformed women and the female officer are in one of the movies in my head. Another one is about Umar. I met Umar in September 2002. I remember thinking that he looked like a ghost. A shadow that was there and not, he was soft-spoken, slim, and tall. I do not remember ever making eye contact with him. He was always looking at the floor. Responding to my request for his personal history, he said that in the mid-1990s he was a playboy and a drunk. His first wife left him. He

2. I read this story in Russell Zanca's article "'Explaining' Islam in Central Asia" (2004), which he read on the Ozod Ovoz website.

married again. That wife left him too. He married again and decided "to get on the straight path of Allah, to follow His law."

In order to learn more about Islam, Umar studied Arabic at a local Culture Center; he wanted to read the Qur'an in the language in which it was revealed. After two years of study, he got a certificate that allowed him to teach elementary Arabic. Umar also began regularly attending Friday prayers at a local mosque, where he asked the attending imam questions about Islam because he wanted to understand the Qur'an better.

In 1999, while fasting during the month of Ramazan, he decided to go on a pilgrimage to Bukhara. He knew that during this month, in addition to fasting, it was a great merit to travel to a holy place in order to demonstrate humility and respect toward God. Umar and his three friends left the valley and went to Tashkent and then to Bukhara. He did not return home that year or the next one. While he was gone, his third wife left him.

In truth, Umar spent only three days in Bukhara. The next two years he spent in prison. While on the pilgrimage, he and his three friends met other young men coming from different parts of Uzbekistan to visit Bukhara's holy places. They slept at a local mosque and prayed together for two days. On the third day, a police officer came by and took their passports in order to register them in Bukhara—or, at least, this is what Umar and his friends were told. In a while, the officer came back and said that they needed to pick up their passports at the local OVIR.

They were told to get their belongings and board a police truck. Then they were driven to a building where they were kept the rest of the day. Their personal belongings were confiscated. The officers asked them to name everything that they had in their bags. They did. Then one by one they were taken to another room, where their bags were opened and personal possessions pulled out. In one of Umar's shirts, the officer found six grams of opium. Umar had no idea how it got into his luggage except the obvious—the officers planted it. He was set up.

Umar was furious. He tried to argue, but it was useless. One of the officers warned him that he could be charged with not just using, but trafficking, which had a lengthier prison term, so he should be grateful and shut up. The same destiny awaited Umar's friends. That same night they were taken to a local narcotics department and tested for drug use. The results of the test stayed undisclosed until the court day. On the court day, Umar was told that the results of his and his friends' drug tests were positive. He was shocked. Umar did not have the money to hire a good attorney. His public defender was useless. The only thing that he could do was pray.

At the trial, Umar was sentenced to two years in prison. There he was prohibited from praying and was not allowed to read the Qur'an. He had to learn how to be ceremonyless, how to perform ritual prayers without all the necessary movements, how "to avoid the wardens' eyes" and to stay sane. The latter was difficult. He felt angry and betrayed by the law because, according to him, he was innocent and was being punished unjustly. These feelings drove him crazy. In order to survive, he had to change his perspective and learn how to accept this punishment as a test from God that was meant to make him a stronger believer.

In almost two years, during one of the president's amnesties Umar was paroled. He was allowed to go back to the Ferghana Valley, to Hovliguzar, where he had to check in monthly with a local police department. When he returned to Hovliguzar, he met and married his fourth wife. He said that she was an orphan and a true Muslim. Umar knew that meeting her was a sign from Allah. They were meant to be together. She performed ritual prayers with him, wore hijab, *and respected and loved him and others; she lived according to the shariat, in fear of and love for Allah and her husband.*

Umar told me that from personal experience he learned that in this life no one but Allah can assure you security, stability, happiness, and justice. Although he had serious financial difficulties and had four children from his previous marriages to support, he trusted in God and continued to humbly walk this earth doing handywork here and there. He knew that not only Allah but also the local police were watching him. Every step he made, he made very carefully in order not to endanger himself and those near him. He said that his life was in a way similar to that of the Prophet Muhammad, who also was persecuted for his devotion to God.

As I undress, I wonder, Am I going to repeat Umar's story? Who can I rely upon? Where did they plant narcotics this time?

My body hides nothing, I know this. And now they know this too; they find nothing. I get dressed. Two more officers wearing white uniforms, just like the officer at customs, come in. They look through my documents and bag again and again. Then they take me to a room across the hall to search through my luggage. They bring in a black cocker spaniel. The dog sniffs through my carry-on bags, my computer and camera, and the bag that I, or rather the officer, checked in.

These two officers look through the computer applications and files, camera, and then my voice recorder. What are they looking for? All that could be erased has already been erased. They look through every piece of my clothing, through all my personal possessions. Any one of these items could have narcotics planted inside them. My face and ears burn. I feel as if my body weighs a ton. I need to sit down or lie down. I lean on the wall. I cannot pass out. I need to watch their every move. And their every move is torturous. I cannot hide my panic behind my large sunglasses. I hear myself talk. I hear this disgusting, shaking, high-pitched voice, "Please, just let me go, let me leave Uzbekistan." It is not me; it is my fear speaking.

They find nothing. I am relieved, but the damage has been done. There is no safe place in the land of fear. I get back my carry-on bags and my passport. My check-in luggage goes to the cargo. Clutching my passport in my hands, shaking, and barely controlling my tears, I somehow make it to the passport-control booth. In front of it, I see the officer who brought me to the airport, who said that he knows how to be a friend. He puts me in front of the line. While my passport is inspected, he shakes my hand and says, "I am sorry, I am so sorry, I really am. You will forget." Looking straight into my eyes and holding my hand in his, he continues, "Text me when you are in the plane and when you land in Russia, please."

I am confused. I can barely comprehend what is going on. But suddenly, in a moment of sanity, I feel something for him—something that makes me warm for a moment and sad. I feel he feels it too. I want to hug him, really hug him. But instead of this hug, not really sure why, I squeeze his hand and finally feel my fingers. They are no longer numb. I feel them in his hand, enveloped by his fingers. I want to tell him how sad I am that I will never get to know him, to really know him as a friend, and that he will never get to know me, who I really am. But instead I say, "I will text you," and let go of his hand. My fingers feel numb again. I turn toward the booth, get back my passport, and step through the gate that divides him and me, there and here, Uzbekistan and what I think of as a "neutral zone." My passport has been stamped. I have left Uzbekistan. I have entered a "no country," no country yet. For a moment I turn around. The officer is gone.

My father told me on the phone yesterday that I need to be very careful and vigilant because "they" can take me off the plane and no one will know where I am because officially I have left Uzbekistan. My father knows about a "no man's land." He speaks from experience. He was a national security officer in the Soviet Union.

I need to get on the plane, and the plane has to take off. I have to hold it together until then somehow, even if in fragments.

On the Plane, August 2011

Scared, humiliated, feeling sorry for myself and guilty for being selfish—this is how I am leaving Uzbekistan. An additional fifty bucks buys me a seat in business class. A shot of vodka and tomato juice, and the lights of the big city are slowly disappearing beneath me. I cannot wait to see and remember nothing about Uzbekistan, its SNB, OVIR, and Bureau of Internal Affairs. But neither Uzbekistan as the state nor its agencies act, people do. I want to forget the people too. They may have different needs and interests—God or money or career or all of the above or something else entirely. Despite their differences, they all know that there is something wrong about big banners depicting smiling children, women, and elderly people in Uzbekistan. They know that what holds all of them together, as the state, is not only love and trust, but also lies and fear. They know it. They know that I know it too. They are guilty. They are complacent.

Maybe I do not want to forget all of them. I certainly will not forget individuals such as Umar, Nodiraopa, and Marifat. Their stories mark the new national history of every post-Soviet state, not just Uzbekistan. Even though the attempt has been made to erase these marks and write over them, as palimpsests these stories will continue to haunt us because it is impossible to erase every story, not on the wake of the celebration of twenty years of independence, not on any other day. Someone will remember and tell the stories that Umar, Nodiraopa, Marifat, and others like them are a part of. I mix vodka and tomato juice in a plastic glass. I call it a "Spontaneous Bloody Mary."

Do I have regrets? I do. I was one of the main agents of my own undoing. I brought the tools of destruction into this state: a computer, a voice recorder, a camera, and questions about Islam. In 2003, I was accused of distributing Hizb-ut-Tahrir's leaflets; in 2011, I was accused of violating the registration law and suspected of promoting antistate propaganda, spying, and drug trafficking. As a result, several people I met with—I know of two—were detained and questioned by the SNB agents, and the Hovliguzar SNB got pictures of others, who were spared, at least for now. But will they be spared forever? My eyelids get heavy. I have various flashbacks—flying to Uzbekistan in June, my trip to the valley in the car through the Kimchik pereval, *my son's silly face on the plane from the United States to Russia, blood gushing from the neck of the rooster sacrificed on my family's behalf by a man claiming to be a descendant of the Prophet Muhammad, my hotel room in Tashkent with a chair securing the door the night before. "You will forget," the last Uzbek officer in charge of me said. I wish. But before this happens, I fight to stay awake and write about my memories. As an anthropologist, I cannot throw the data into the abyss of my desire to forget.*

Two days ago my mother called the Russian Ministry of Foreign Affairs. Whoever she talked to said that in Uzbekistan the people who represent the law enforcement agencies are human beings, too, and not monsters with two heads. Considering my latest experiences, I would disagree, except I did meet some of those not-two-headed monsters. They, too, know that in Uzbekistan people—including themselves—have no rights. They told me so. Maybe by telling me that, they did not want to become or to be remembered as two-headed monsters. Or maybe they resisted forgetting that their personal lives could be different. Maybe they wanted one head and the ability to use it as they wished and not to worry about adverse consequences of their thinking and actions. I met those not-two-headed monsters, I have come to think, and not just once.

I remember the images of monsters from the children's book Where the Wild Things Are *by Maurice Sendak. I read it to my son not long ago. Maybe the two-headed monsters are, like the Wild Things, figments of my imagination sustained by horror stories. Maybe those whom I think of as monsters are who they say they are—human beings simply doing their jobs. Or maybe they forgot that they matter, that they can change, that they create and not simply play the monsters' roles.*

I feel cold. The air-conditioning is mixed with my distilled fear. I ask for another blanket and for more vodka. I need to stay awake and write a beginning after the end of research and probably the end of my travels to Uzbekistan. I look through the airplane's window. Darkness. We fly through and over it. Why do I want darkness instead of memories of the past four days? This desire not to remember is generated not just by self-pity but also mainly by the guilt I feel for not developing a better strategy to protect the people I lived among this summer, a better strategy that might have allowed me to come back to Uzbekistan in the future. In the end, my motivations may not have been selfish overall, but they were selfish nonetheless.

I needed to know and did not think of the price of this knowledge, particularly for others.

I turn off the overhead light. I look at the computer screen, which lights the whole first row of business class, but do not see my reflection. This feels good. I cannot look at myself. I want to be a different self, a self-written one, innocent and optimistic. I wish we could fly faster, fly away from this self.

I hate flying. Tonight, however, I love it. I love the air pressure inflating my head, pushing on my frontal lobe, bringing a sharp pain in the ears and leading to moments of deafness. I love turbulence. I would even love noisy neighbors if I had some. Love and hate are relative and situational. I guess it depends what and whom you are flying toward and what and whom you are flying away from. I am flying toward my son. I want to be absorbed by his embrace as if he can liberate me from the feelings of shame and guilt. I am flying away from Uzbekistan, away from fear.

Surely this fear will not be the last in my life; it is not the first, and it could be, always could be, so much worse. But, for me, this fear is nonetheless significant, different from the fear I've experienced in other places and at other times. The past few days were like a runaway train, which although still far away is bound to crash. Nothing can stop it. This train ran through Hovliguzar's downtown; Jahon's, Tursun-oi's, Rashida's, and my other friends' lives; the Tashkent Province's border; the airport, and it chases this plane because I still have no idea whether it is over for those who surrounded me in the valley, for those who shared with me their stories, for those who opened their homes to me, and for those who shook my hand. My inability to help them and my cowardly retreat are terrifying.

How in the period of four days did I become a liability to those in Tashkent whom I've managed to stay friends with for (almost) a decade? If I look beyond self-pity and recognize the importance of my self-interests, I see the answer. I see their fear and desire to protect themselves and their families, just as I want to protect my family and myself. One way or another, they, too, heard about or saw the two-headed monsters and wanted nothing to do with them, and that is why they wanted nothing to do with me. In Uzbekistan, the monsters and I came hand in hand. The tears run uncontrollably down my checks. . . .

I wake up an hour before the end of the flight and look out of the window. The darkness outside is pierced with the lights below. Ironically, it is Grozny, the capital of Chechnya—a place close to my mother's home and, now that I think of it, the city where she was born. I wonder what would happen if I were to pursue my dissertation research in Chechnya. How would my research about freedom fighters, militias, or what-have-you end? Where and in what darkness? What would I regret then? Which monsters would I find there? What horror stories would I learn? And what fear would I be running away from and writing about? We fly over Grozny toward Sochi, the home of the 2014 Olympics, a growing megalopolis on Russia's Black Sea shore. My father is waiting for me there. My mother and my son are waiting for me in the Caucasus.

I feel not only regrets but also—and this is absolutely inappropriate—some pride, some indignant dignity. I did type up the last interviews, emailed them to myself, and erased them from the voice recorder before it was taken away from me. At least, these erased interviews cannot be used against the interviewees. I lived though the strip search and a detailed luggage search, constantly thinking that heroin or psychotropic substances might be planted among my possessions in my luggage. Agonizing about the possibility of the officers finding what they were looking for, I did manage to hold it together, somehow. I managed to get on this plane. Now if I only could get rid of this one annoying thought: Is it really over?

After I get to Russia in the morning, in my father's car for the eleven-hour drive from Sochi to the Caucasus, I pull out the Uzbekistan SIM card in my cell phone, put in a Russian one, and send a text message to the officer who was my "last friend" in Tashkent: "ya v rosii spasibo drug *[i am in russia thank you friend]." He responds:* "da nezashto. ti pozhalysta izveni mena chto ya teby v aeroporty ne smog provodit bez nih. ti znaesh ya postoralsya. ya specialno ne podnyal trobku no oni vseravno nashli nas. ti ponimaesh ochem ya?

izveni drug *[there is nothing to thank me for. please forgive me that i could not see you off at the airport without them. you know, i tried. i did not pick up the phone on purpose, but they still found us. do you understand what i am saying? forgive me, friend]." I remember his phone ringing several times, playing the same morbid tune with a male voiceover saying, "It is time to get to work! Your superior is calling!" This is what he meant when he said the day before I left that "it" comes "from the top." Whoever was at that top wanted me to experience all I have experienced because I asked the "wrong" questions, met with the "wrong" people, and would potentially be publishing "incorrect" information. I text back,* "ya ponimau beregi sebya lechi kashel moi drug *[i understand take care of yourself and your cough, my friend]."*

The Caucasus, Russia, August 2011

We drive into my mother's courtyard. I get out of the car and want to run, but I cannot. I do not know why. I am happy to be back in the Caucasus, but my happiness is not full; it is half empty. Or maybe I am simply tired of running—if not physically, then mentally. I walk down the stairs and into the living room. I see my son. He says in Russian, "Privet moya mamochka *[hello, my mommy]," and continues in English, "You told me that you would come back on Sunday; it is Wednesday." His embrace is my home. I give him the stuffy I got at the Tashkent airport. I cannot lie to him. "Problems with police in Uzbekistan," I say. "Okay," he nods his head and turns toward the TV. I sob uncontrollably on the way to the bedroom upstairs.*

After I wash off my tears, I come downstairs, where my son is watching a movie, Magical Voice of Gelsomino *(1977), directed by Tamara Lisitsian, based on the children's book* Gelsomino in the Country of Liars, *by Gianni Rodari, published in 1958. The story has a simple plot. Gelsomino, a boy with a magical voice, leaves his village and eventually finds himself in the Country of Liars ruled by the pirates' leader Gakomon, who claims to have magical golden hair. According to Gakomon's law, the people in the country must call everything the opposite—"good night" instead of "good morning," "hotel" instead of "jail," the cats are supposed to bark, and so forth. Everyone is accustomed to lying. Gelsomino exposes the lying by reading what is truly written on the walls and saying what should truly be said. The people find out that the ruler is bald and that his magical golden hair is a wig, and they eventually rebel against the regime. Gakomon is overthrown, and the people's celebration of the victory concludes the movie.*

I watch this movie with my son and think how profound this children's story is. I know every state we live in is really us. If we make this state daily, we can certainly break it at any time. The question is: What do we, each one of us, have to gain or to lose from this breaking? Maybe it is the fear of change that allows and enables my own and others' pretending that the king is not bald, whoever the king is.

On August 23, my son and I fly to Moscow and then to the United States. On the plane to New York, my son is talking about his cacti. He is curious if they survived the summer. "Surely they did," I reply. He also wants to know what would happen if he were to jump off the plane now. "Mommy, will I get stuck in the clouds?" he asks and gives me a coy smile. I say that I hope he would get stuck in the clouds, but I do not want him to jump off the plane in order to see if he will. I tell him that I, too, know something about the clouds. I admired them on the way to Tashkent this summer. Although they exist, they can be very deceptive. They cannot hold our bodies, only our dreams and memories. I kiss his head and try to smile. Then I take a tranquilizer. Catching up on the war in Libya with a newspaper, I fall asleep.

We land at JFK. As we are getting ready to go through the security for our flight to Boston, a powerful seismic wave shakes the terminal, which triggers the terminal's lockdown. The security check is halted as well. I pull out my computer and search for information online. As long as it is not a bomb, I think, we will be okay. My son is glued to my stomach. "Wow! Mommy, what was it?" he asks. The earthquake was in Virginia, 5.8 on the Richter scale. It is almost as powerful as the one in the Ferghana Valley in July, but this earthquake feels much less intense because New York City is a few hundred miles away from Virginia. While we are standing here, at the airport, in the United States, waiting to get through the security, life goes on, including the preparations for the twentieth anniversary of Uzbekistan's independence from the Soviet Union. I will call Uzbekistan next week or next month. I cannot talk to anyone now. Maybe I do not want to know what happened to the others.

Another flight and another bus ride. One of my friends picks us up at the bus station. I feel delayed, deflated, detached, and unreal. My son keeps me going.

The State Where "Nothing Happens"

In a phone interview in October 2011, Marfua Tokhtakhodjaeva, a famous Uzbek scholar, feminist, and writer, told me, "We do not have news [in Uzbekistan]. In this big country nothing happens. We have about thirty million people. But there are no events. Every channel shows the same seminars, concerts, and movies. This is abnormal."

In order for nothing to happen, *something* must be going on. Dr. Tokhtakhodjaeva suggested that in Uzbekistan this *something* was the ruling elite's effort to entrench "kleptocapitalism" by traditionalizing Uzbek society. She continued:

> From the 1990s we have a new ideology, a different propaganda. It is absurd. It is neotraditionalist. Our scholars are engaged in social begging [having to praise those in power to maintain their careers]. Corruption is rampant. What we have in Uzbekistan is capitalism, but a criminal kind of capitalism. It is a kleptocapitalism built on stealing and not on a long-term investment. In Uzbekistan, this capitalism is wild with elements of feudalism and nomenclature capitalism. This is why our official leaders would like people to focus solely on traditions. The result is a full degradation of social consciousness. There are no *gumanitarnih* [humanitarian] interests. These are ignored. . . . In our country those who are in power hijacked culture and religion. Our country and people are poor, but if you look at Uzbekistan, all you see are shiny colors.

According to Dr. Tokhtakhodjaeva, the state where "nothing happens" was intentional. A focus on culture and religion obscured the reality of economic and intellectual degradation, and an appearance of happiness covered up a lack of freedom of information.

While I was conducting research in Uzbekistan from 2001 to 2011, during interviews and personal communications some people I met with openly criticized economic corruption and a lack of freedom of association and expression in the country. Their stories demonstrated the violence committed by the state agents in connection to one's religious sensibilities, knowledge(s), behaviors, political views, or financial achievements. The political nature of "the religious" and "the everyday" was all too obvious in the individual accounts of the state's persecution and in a social commentary critical of the existing illusion of democracy and people's rights in the country. Yet there were several individuals, such as Tahsir, who praised the government, the president, and the new post-Soviet freedoms, including what they took to be freedom of religion. If taken at face value, this praise can be used as evidence of social change in Uzbekistan—its movement away from the Soviet state, now defined as repressive and colonial, toward a new relatively democratic state. So how do I reconcile criticism of the Uzbek state by some and praise of it by others as well as my personal experience of a lack of freedom in the country?

Assuming that the democratic changes in the Uzbek state are really a fraud, one way to understand praise of the government and the country's post-Soviet freedom is to take it as an expression of the false consciousness of people duped into believing in a particular ideology. This approach, however, still does not answer the question why some individuals have been duped and others have not. If this ideology is that effective, then why is there such a diversity of opinions—from praise (Tahsir in chapter 2) to criticism (a businessman from the valley and a representative of one of Tashkent's Bureau of Internal Affairs offices in the introduction) to fear (me) to condemnation (Marifat in chapter 2)? In order to understand the simultaneously existing praise and criticism of the Uzbek state, we should read between the lines, while being particularly attentive to what is obvious and what is obscured, to what is said and how it is said, as well as to what is not said (as done, e.g., in Navaro-Yashin 2008).

The Unsaid

Focusing on the unsaid, I recall that in 2011 my "new Uzbek" friends and acquaintances—the nouveau riche of Tashkent and Hovliguzar—and I did not talk about several subjects, such as what would happen if President Karimov should die or what happened and how many people died in Andijon in 2005 or in Osh in 2010. We did not talk about why certain websites, such as al-Jazeera and the BBC, were unavailable to the citizens but available in Arabic and English, not in Russian or Uzbek, in the hotels for foreign tourists; why information about the Arab Spring was so hard to come by; why Uzbekistan's citizens had to get "exit visas" to travel abroad; why foreigners had to declare all electronic equipment they brought into the country; and how many people really died during the earthquake that we all experienced in July 2011. These topics were among the unsaid.

In the valley, during our first meeting in 2011 Nainahon expanded my understanding of the unsaid. When I asked her about the Andijon events of 2005, she answered that they were among the subjects "not talked about," which we also did not talk about. I take the unsaid, including individuals' *not talking about* certain subjects and their recognition of the existence of subjects *not talked about*, to be "a practice of individuality," a symbolic act that denormalized the rubric of everyday life in a "democratic" Uzbekistan (see Rapport 2003, 48–49). The not talking and the existence of subjects not talked about, as much as open criticism, effectively undermined the discourse on democracy, freedom, peace, and prosperity in Uzbekistan. The political is implicit in such intentional silences about and omissions of these subjects.

The unsaid, the subjects not talked about and the not talking about them, could also be a "fetishist disavowal," an intentional act summarized by the following statement: "'I know, but I don't want to know that I know, so I don't know.' I know it but I refuse to fully assume the consequences of this knowledge, so that I can continue acting as if I don't know it" (Žižek 2008, 53). In Uzbekistan, this fetishist disavowal allowed individuals to keep what Michael Taussig (1999) calls a "public secret" about the existing lack of freedom. In the state of prohibition and surveillance, this "public secret" is sustained by the fear an individual experiences, particularly when this person has something or everything to lose or a desire to maintain control of her life in a state that—unlike some of the neighboring states—works, however imperfectly. In such a state, the unsaid is intentional. As such, the unsaid is an expression of individual ability to understand and evaluate social dynamics around the self and to create purposeful silences that betray this ability.

But a "public secret" is never stable. In Uzbekistan in the first decade of the new millennium, this instability was manifested in slippages and glitches, like silences and pauses, and in the purposeful (mis)recognition of unfreedom by friends, acquaintances, and strangers. Some of these silences might not have been intentional, but others were certainly deliberate. In a March 2011 Skype chat, Navruz explicitly warned me about the state's increased control of *otinchalar*'s public life in private space and said that I had to be "very careful" with my research topic (see chapter 1). She added, "Do not go to their [the *otinchalar*'s] gatherings" and "do not be a part of the group." In the context of the Uzbek government's claims about post-Soviet freedoms enjoyed by the citizens, these warnings were particularly telling.

Post-Soviet Freedom and Prosperity

During my research in Uzbekistan, both official and unofficial discourses divided the country's macrohistory and individual microhistories into Soviet and post-Soviet periods; the former was colonial, oppressive, and economically devastating, but the latter symbolized freedom and prosperity and national uniqueness. The date September 1, 1991, marked the turning point in Uzbekistan's history from its Soviet republichood to its post-Soviet statehood (although

Uzbekistan sovereignty was declared in June 1990). This turning point is celebrated annually (see Adams 2010 and chapter 5).

The discourses on post-Soviet prosperity and freedom and unique national traditions disguise Uzbekistan's political and economic dependencies on its Soviet Union's former counterparts and obscure the role of the Soviet Union in the ideological and ethnographic production of the now widely celebrated cultural heritage and ethnotraditional characteristics of local peoples. Johan Rasanayagam argues that in addition to "the primordial concept of ethnicity" and the model of "the ethnonational state," the post-Soviet Uzbek government inherited from the Soviet Union "the Soviet concept of citizenship," which was not "founded upon the rights of [the] sovereign individual" (2010, 109). Hence, if scrutinized, history and the contemporary state of the Uzbek state challenge the image of rupture between the Soviet and post-Soviet epochs capitalized on in official historical discourses and articulated in individual ones.

Tahsir's opinions about freedom of expression in and the growing economic prosperity of Uzbekistan discussed in chapter 2 exemplify individual discourses that connect the Soviet versus post-Soviet differentiation to a radical shift from Soviet unfreedom and economic stagnation to post-Soviet freedom and prosperity. I contend that such individual annunciations of post-Soviet democracy and prosperity were not self-referential, self-obvious assessments of Uzbekistan's sociopolitical and economic context during the first decade of the twenty-first century. These statements were not just a reproduction of an authoritative yet contested official discourse on post-Soviet individual and economic well-being and freedom. Rather, they were individual rhetorical strategies that revealed as much as they obscured. As such, their analysis should begin with questions: Why did these particular people make these statements in conjunction with discussions of their everyday lives? What did the individuals who made these statements stand to gain or to lose by describing post-Soviet Uzbekistan as free, democratic, and prosperous? Finally, if taken as individual strategies, what can these annunciations tell us about the state of the Uzbek state?

To answer these questions, following Yael Navaro-Yashin, I focus on "the passing comments, exclamations, statements made out of despair, sighs, interrupted sentences, ironic phrases, laughter, and the like" (2008, 182). These behaviors animate individual power to define, interpret, and evaluate the state of the Uzbek state and the individual ability to write against the social by using its own discourse. Because I did not *really* know what motivations and desires each individual had at the moment he or she made these statements, I used my own sense and experience-based knowing when rereading and re-membering the interviews in light of Navaro-Yashin's advice. My ability to understand the meaning of these behaviors was not only a consequence of my and the narrators' geographic and historical proximity. Following Marranci (2008), I accept that in order to empathize with and understand what was said and not said and how it was said or not said, I did not have to share the same experiences with the narrators. By engaging with my own (organic and inorganic) environment, I have already learned how to love, hate, pretend, make fun, suppress, and self-censor. I have already felt and experienced justice and injustice, dignity, happiness, violence, fear, doubt, and a definitional freedom. Thus, during the analysis, I could use my existing experiential knowledge and associate my feelings with the feelings of others.

Knowing and Sensing

On the initial drive from the Tashkent airport to Hovliguzar in 2011, I sensed in the taxi driver's comments about peace, protection, and corruption the sarcasm and slight desperation that denormalized the state's discourse on democracy, peace, and prosperity (see chapter 4). Paula Salvio notes that sarcasm "is an effective rhetorical strategy for piercing the skin and hitting a bone" (2007, 37). If a deep cut can expose the bone, then the taxi driver's sarcastic comments, too, could expose the state of the Uzbek state.

The driver told me that the president, "our Karimov," wanted the provincials "to stay in their towns and villages" and wanted "this city clean and protected." The president did not want "large groups of people, young men in particular," because "they say something might happen on August 31." The more I thought about the driver's statements, the more questions I had: Why did people from villages and towns surrounding Tashkent, young men in particular, have to leave or stay away from the city? How and in what way would they threaten purity and peace in Tashkent? What and who should the city be protected from?

I gathered from this driver's comments that to leave Tashkent or to stay away from the capital, to stay in their towns and villages, was not these young men's choice, but the president's desire. The way the driver talked about the president, enunciating his last name, was analogous to talking about one-man's-land, ruled by one person, where everyone is following that one leader, the One. This obviously did not fit the image of a new Uzbekistan with its democratically (re)elected (again and again) president and parliament.

In referring to the president, Islam Karimov, and his oldest daughter, Gulnara Karimova, the taxi driver noted that they, "our grandfather and his daughter," wanted citizens of Uzbekistan "to live in peace." *Dedushka*, the Russian word the driver used for the president, which I have translated as "grandfather," connotes, among other things, old age and a certain fragility, the need of help in crossing the road, getting out of bed, or leading the state. Such a reference to the president and his daughter destabilized the government's discourse on the "national" Uzbek model of gradual democratization linking the government's claim of being a powerful protective patriarch to its claim about existing democratic governance (see chapter 6). The driver recognized that Karimov was the leader (the president), a patriarchal one (a grandfather), but he was also an old man whose power and authority were no longer his alone but shared with someone, such as, at the time, his oldest daughter (in 2014 she fell out of favor).

After declaring that these two individuals were fighting corruption, the driver added a statement that could have been avoided, "But corruption is even greater than before." This statement, a passing comment, was left open-ended. Not followed by "because," it continued to beg the question "why?" leading me, as the audience, to two conclusions: either something was wrong with the efforts put into the war against corruption, or "the enemy"—"the Corruption"—was too strong for the claimed-to-be-powerful Uzbek government to fight.

In 2003, in response to my observation that some of Eminem's songs were about social issues, Nainahon noted, "Our singers cannot sing any political songs" (see chapter 2). Then she added, "They sing only about their love for mothers, women, our people, and for our motherland." Tahsir agreed with her: "True." This could have been Nainahon and Tahsir's view of the national art scene in Uzbekistan, including the thematic preference of Uzbekistan's artists. Yet, like the taxi driver's statement about corruption in July 2011, the first part of the sentence about singers' inability to "sing any political songs" was not avoided but included in what Tahsir agreed with.

This statement revealed that the current government policed individual choices in Uzbekistan and was just as oppressive as the Soviet Union's government. Nainahon's statement and Tahsir's agreement also clarified that which was obscured by the government's emphasis on unique national traditions and Uzbekistan's unique path toward democracy: while mothers, the people, and the motherland were expected to be loved and glorified, expressing political dissent was prohibited. If this prohibition indeed was a national tradition, then by definition it was antidemocratic.

At the beginning of the US war on Iraq in the spring of 2003, I was told that during one of the faculty meetings at a local institute, members of the administration instructed the faculty members to behave as if nothing had happened, as if there were no war. The faculty members were also instructed to terminate any discussion of the war among the students and report the most curious students to the administration, which, in turn, would report them to the "appropriate official organs," such as the SNB. This was a description not just of a faculty meeting with administration, but of an insider's knowledge about and experiences of internal workings at a state institution, which was purposefully imparted to me. This information carried an implicit evaluation of the state, where political questions and discussions were prohibited and the violators reported to the "appropriate official organs"; this post-Soviet state was not different from a Soviet Union cast as colonial and politically repressive.

When at the end of March 2003 I was asked about the reasons for the US war on Iraq (see chapter 2), one of the women in the audience at this social gathering preempted my answer. She said that they could not criticize America because it was at the time providing humanitarian aid to Uzbekistan in exchange for the use of military bases. But this woman did not stop there. She turned to me and whispered, "This is the official position. How can we approve of killing other humans, other Muslims? This is *our* position." I learned from that encounter that there were two positions on the war in Iraq—the "official" one and "ours"—that appeared to be mutually opposed. That year, people in different countries across the globe engaged in discussing and debating the US war on Iraq through political protests and public demonstrations. But in Uzbekistan, which was on the road to democracy, these discussions and debates could take place only in private spaces, not at a university or other public spaces. Further, in the state of surveillance, a no longer spectacular state, nonofficial views—*our* views—had to be whispered, not enunciated. The difference between what was said and what was whispered was yet another symptom diagnostic of the existing fractures in the discourse on Uzbekistan's post-Soviet democracy and freedom.

In 2011, Jahon said that she was grateful that President Karimov had "opened for Muslims the road to the hajj" (see chapter 5). She, too, wanted to perform the hajj but had to wait "to move up the list" of hajj hopefuls in her *mahalla*. The road to the hajj opened by the president had numerous checkpoints, from the *mahalla* committee's list to the federal government's exit visas to the supervision of the hajj experience itself by the representatives of the official leadership salaried by the state. Jahon also thanked the president for allowing Uzbek citizens, such as her husband, to travel overseas to make money. The post-Soviet economy of Uzbekistan apparently did not guarantee that her husband could stay in the country and earn a stable salary, which would allow them to buy a new car, remodel their house, and arrange their daughters' marriages. Thus, the claimed economic and social independence from the Soviet Union in truth did not assure individual prosperity and did not cancel out Jahon and her family's political dependence on the Uzbek state.

The "How It Is Said"

Like Erving Goffman (1956), I accept that the importance of what is said is not only in the content of the statement, but also in its presentation. Tahsir's, Tursun-oi's, Nainahon's, the taxi driver's, and Jahon's irony, their smiles, chuckles, and sarcasm exposed the unfreedom and the untruths as some of the ties that bound the Uzbek state and assured its alleged prosperity, peace, and democracy. These individuals did not resist the unfreedom and untruths in usual ways or places, either, because, in 2011, just as in 2005, the usual ways, including public protests, could endanger their lives and the well-being of their families. Rather, these women and men were laughing at their own state, at "becoming richer," or at their old president.

Unlike Goffman (1956), I contend that an ability to laugh at something, particularly at or in reference to subjects not talked about, is not just an enactment of a preexisting script. Such laughter is creative and manifests individual ability to understand, interpret, and evaluate this something. Laughing at the existing state of the Uzbek state was a form of criticism of it. For the individuals I am writing about, laughing at this state was also safer because a joke, by definition, was not to be taken seriously. Thus, laughter was among the techniques that these and other individuals used to create meaning under duress and to hold on to their dignity and faith in justice, both despite and because of the horror stories and the existence of subjects not talked about.

Therefore, the simultaneously existing praise and criticism of the Uzbek state were not expressions of false consciousness, nor were they an embodiment of an ideology imposed from outside. Rather, individuals purposefully generated this praise and criticism in the context of a state of prohibition, where dissent was suppressed and individual rights were subordinated to societal needs. Strategically, through practices of individuality that included intentional comments, silences, praise, chuckles, sarcasm, and irony, Uzbekistanis *did* talk about what was going on in their country where "nothing happens," about the place with "no events."

The Abyss of the "One-Man's-Land" Argument

In 2011, surveillance, torture, imprisonment, and intimidation were among practices of crafting the Uzbek state, a place where "nothing happens" and where subjects not talked about were commonplace (see Kendzior 2010). The practices of governmentality also included numerous police officers on the streets, traffic police on the roads, checkpoints, snipers outfitted in army uniforms on the provincial borders, the registration regime (for foreigners and locals crossing provincial boarders), video surveillance, and curfews in troubled areas (for a discussion of governmentality, see Dean 1999). These techniques in managing and administering everyday life were used to regulate security, to ensure the welfare of Uzbekistan's population, and to guarantee an ordered and predictable state—a state that worked.

One way to understand the statecraft in Uzbekistan is to consider emotions articulated as feelings, such as pride and fear, which these practices and techniques were meant to stimulate. Žižek argues that in contemporary societies the most effective form of biopolitics is a politics of fear—not just fear of the state, of the punitive consequences of breaking the law, but also fear of getting too close to and infringing on the state's space (2008, 40). This fear, Žižek contends, generates an individual desire to maintain a safe distance from others' political ideas and to stay away from the (potentially) prohibited and criticized.

Although I do not believe that fear is the only emotion (articulated as feeling) behind people's actions in Uzbekistan or elsewhere, this fear of the state's "intolerance to my over-proximity" (Žižek

2008, 41) helps to tease out the role an individual plays in statecraft. As a result of such fear, a person comes to understand someone else's intolerance of her as her fault; she violated the other's space by getting too close; she should have kept a safe distance. As in other places, in Uzbekistan this fear informed individuals' "fetishist disavowal" and active participation in maintaining "public secret(s)" and creating the unsaid (Taussig 1999; Žižek 2008).

In 2011, in referring to the massacre in Andijon in 2005, one of my acquaintances in the valley said, "They came to ask us to join, but we said 'no,' and you see, we did the right thing. [A long pause.] What did they want? Did they not have enough? Our state gave them everything. Karimov did the right thing [in giving the order to the army to fire at the protesters]. [Another long pause.] Why did they do it? Why not sit quietly and enjoy life?" The interlocutor explained the Uzbek state's action as the protesters' fault. In order for the army not to fire at them, "they" (the protesters) had to respect ("sit quietly and enjoy life") the distance that separated them from the state ("Karimov"). By violating the state's proximity limits—the state's "*right not to be harassed*" (Žižek 2008, 40–41, italics in the original)—they caused the state's fear of victimization and thus the state's punitive action.

Rapport argues that "the societies of individuals are not greater than their sum; there is nothing beyond the matter that (temporarily) constitutes the identity of the individual, and nothing beyond the force which that individual life gives onto and, in collaboration with others, adds up to" (2003, 8). If we agree with Rapport, then the state also has no life or life force of its own. In order to exist, the state has to be comprehended as such by individuals who compose it at any given time, appreciate its symbology and ideology, and find it meaningful (Rapport 2003, 26). Understood this way, any state is not excused from the politics of fear.

The state fears potential victimization because the individuals who make up the government of the state fear victimization and simultaneously create fear by defending themselves from possible victimization not only by the creation of *the unsaid*, but also through explicit acts of violence, as in the violence used to suppress the popular uprising in Andijon in 2005. The residual fallout of such violence continues to breed individual fear and create horror stories shared among everyone else, which, in turn, continue to stimulate each individual's desire to deter possible victimization. Therefore, Uzbekistan's "unique" democratic model has been built not only on love and respect or empathy that people routinely express toward each other, but also on fear; the state of the Uzbek state has been achieved daily by individuals motivated, among other desires, by the desire to deter possible victimization.

Unlike some of my acquaintances in the valley, I do not want to displace the blame for Andijon (and other mass violence in post-Soviet Central Asia) from the government onto the protestors. Rather, I want to move away from talking about the state as a metaphysical entity that exists beyond the individual. Individuals are neither completely helpless nor innocent when it comes to the state and to violence as a form of social control. Inasmuch as the state has to be understood as meaningful and necessary by the individuals who achieve it on a daily basis by appreciating, (re)articulating, and upholding its symbology and ideology, violence also has to be thought of, thought through, and enacted. The violence in Andijon did not just happen but was decided upon and enacted by individuals; the guns did not shoot without orders and by themselves.

One of the obsolete meanings of the word *craft* is "strength, power, or might." Statecraft is a process that cannot happen without individual relational existential power. Although individuals have different levels and kinds of strength and exercise different degrees of power over their lives and the lives of others, they all participate in state formation because statecraft requires more than one person. Therefore, when talking about, writing about, and analyzing Uzbekistan, it is a fallacy to reduce the state to one man, President Karimov, or to "Karimov's regime" or "Karimov's government," as if this state exists beyond the individuals creating it. Uzbekistan is really *not* a one-man's-land or a one-man's-state; it cannot be such. There should always be someone to comprehend that the land belongs both to this man *and* to somebody else to make a state. The state, in this case the Uzbek state, has a capacity to order and regulate people, to make them into the state's citizens, only as much as the people creating and achieving the state exercise this capacity (for more on statecraft, see Ferguson and Gupta 2002).

The state of Uzbekistan, like any state, is not reducible to one man or regime, one discourse or institution, one religion, one history, or one instance of human rights abuse (such as Andijon in 2005), inasmuch as being "truly" Muslim is not reducible to Islam or the Qur'an. Humans with their capacity to become, their individual desires and self-interests, their creativity and imagination, and their unique physical bodies will always assure this irreducibility. Recognizing this capacity affirms individual ability to change the state(s) of the post-Soviet states, whether through self-formation and moral evolution or revolution, and leads to a more careful and nuanced analysis as well as to more accurate generalizations about the reasons behind social complexity in Uzbekistan and elsewhere.

Despite human rights abuses, people still choose to live in Uzbekistan; even those who have amassed sufficient capital to move elsewhere find meaning in and reasons for staying there (whether we find these reasons moral or immoral). Despite violence and fear, those who populate Uzbekistan continue to believe in its future progress, whether it is articulated in terms of Islam or in other terms. Despite a lack of electricity and gas in the Ferghana Valley, people continue to have weddings, smile and joke, eat, love, and dream. They travel despite the checkpoints, feast despite ongoing criticism of conspicuous consumption, protest despite fear, learn despite the corrupt educational system, and go on living despite the pain of losing someone. Each one of them in a unique way continues trying, in F. G. Bailey's words, "to beat the system" (1969, 87) that they themselves have created, if not for the sake of larger societal transformations, then in order to satisfy self-interests. Individual expressions of irony that I discussed earlier demonstrate that social unfreedom does not cancel out our ability to laugh at others and ourselves. This ability is also an expression of individual freedom of expression, a manifestation of individual existential relational power that cannot *really* be taken away unless the self is annihilated (Rapport 2003).

Human lives in the United States, Europe, Russia, and Central Asia are different in many ways but similar in other ways. Each one of us has unique experiences. But we all need shelter, like to feel safe (even if occasionally), like to have someone to care for or something to feel passionately about, want to love or to be loved (by other humans, animals, or God), and do not want to be victimized (unless it is our own desire to feel pain). We either have or create families—different families, whether at home, at work, or online, human and nonhuman, no matter where and when we live. We experience existential vulnerability. More often than not we want to have a state that works, whether this requires changing the existing state or not challenging it. We become angry or desperate and feel happy, at least at some point in our lives. We know our body like no one else does and have relationships with our body like no one else has (unless, as some believe, this someone is God). We want to have rights, whether the right to work or not to work, the right not to be hurt, or the right to be loved and respected. We struggle, be it against or with others, the world, God, or ourselves. We create, be it by baking bread or giving birth, creating a website, building a bridge, painting, sculpting, or telling a story. Human diversity, uniqueness, and the irreducibility of human life anywhere at any time manifest the universality of human experience: they in themselves are universals. For the women and men I have written about here, this universality of human individual uniqueness is *always already there*, created and decreed by God.

Guilt: The Caucasus, August 17, 2011

I wake up in an apartment where we used to live in the Caucasus when I was about twelve years old. Dilapidated now, it has only patches of wallpaper covering the walls and worn-out linoleum covering the floor. Someone else is in the room. I know it already. I feel it. "Good morning, Svetlana." I turn my head in the direction of the sound. It is Gulnara Karimova standing at the head of the bed in what we used to call the "children's room." "Good morning," I reply hesitantly. "What the hell is she doing here?" I think. "I love the way you dress. Where do you get your dresses?" she asks. "Where?" I repeat the question, thinking about what I should say next. I do not remember where but reply, "At a secondhand store in town." "I particularly like this one," she points to a dress on the chair that reminds me of our Soviet school uniforms, a plain dark dress combined with a black or white apron depending on the occasion. "And where did you get it?" she asks and smiles. I do not know if I should take her seriously but reply, "At the same store."

She asks me to go shopping. Not sure why, I ask her if she has any money. The oldest daughter of President Karimov, a world traveler living mainly in Switzerland, wielding money and businesses expropriated from Uzbek oligarchs, should have money. "No, I do not," she answers. "People like us do not need money. Other people, like you, in order to demonstrate their respect and later ask us for favors, give us presents, treat us, and pay for us," she responds. No amount of money I have would be enough to buy a dress for Gulnara Karimova, a self-proclaimed poetess, singer, and designer of clothes and jewelry known as "Guli for Chopard"—insanely expensive creations I saw at the Tashkentskie Kuranti store on Amir Timur Square this summer. She continues, "You should have some money we could use, right? Let me call my father." The cell phone to her ear, Gulnara talks to her father. He is loud. I can hear him. "Yes," he says, "Borrow some money from her, I am busy now. Do not worry, you know what we do with people we owe money to." "Bye," she hangs up.

Even though I am afraid of the consequences of loaning money to Gulnara, I think I have no choice, and we are going shopping. Around the corner from my multistoried apartment complex, we enter what looks like an endless web of narrow streets of the Old Town district in Tashkent. Clay and brick walls are yellow and brown. The dirt roads are freshly sprayed with water and swept. Is this place inhabited? It does not look like the busy Old Town I know. We enter one of the clay buildings, a small gallery exhibiting "traditionally Uzbek" arts and crafts, including headdresses, jewelry, and hand-stitched bright silk curtains. This room leads us into another and yet another room. Finally, we enter the secondhand store. While Gulnara is looking for a dress like mine, I decide to look around. It might be my last shopping trip. She owes me some money, and, as her father said, something happens to those whom the Karimovs owe money to. I look at various brand-name shoes. They are beautiful, made of soft leather, just like I like them. But then I realize something odd. None of them has a pair. I wake up.

My dream about shopping with Gulnara Karimova could certainly be an omen that one day I will shop with her or be punished by her father. This dream could also be a reenactment of places I have visited and people I have met at different times in my life, although I have never met Gulnara Karimova. What is more likely, I think, is that in the process of consolidating my emotional memory of the time I spent in Uzbekistan in the summer of 2011, awake or asleep, I continued to selectively treat my experiences and was trying to forget those things that I was having difficulty rectifying—my failure to protect research participants and my fear.

Jared Saletin, Andrea Goldstein, and Matthew Walker suggest that sleeping promotes the "differential directed forgetting memory effect" (2011, 2534); in our sleep we can remember or recall events as well as forget them. Our unique and complex consciousness retains and discriminates information into memories we want to keep and the information we would like to forget. The episodic experiences that we find troubling are not completely erased from our memory during sleep, but they are in a sense deactivated. I certainly wanted to deactivate some of the memories of my trip to Uzbekistan in 2011. But this is not all that makes this dream significant to me.

In 2003, Jahon told me, "Even if you cut a finger, you should remember Allah. It is a sign that you missed something or did something wrong. Do not try to find out who is guilty. You should look at your actions. Usually a weak person will be looking for someone to blame. Everything is from Allah—Allah gives and Allah takes." I want to forget, and dreaming helps me to forget some of my experiences in Uzbekistan. But I continued feeling guilty, ashamed, and angry; I continued blaming myself but, despite Jahon's exhortation, did not want to accept full responsibility for my actions. To alleviate this burden, I had to find someone else to blame; my feeling of the injustice done to me and by me to others had to ascribe responsibility (such feelings are described in Solomon 1990).

At the time of this dream, my experiences of the summer of 2011 were not yet geographically or temporally distant. I wanted to blame the one-man's-state, Karimov's state. Yet I was already aware that he, the president, was not alone but had an immediate family, just like I did. I knew that his authority was not total and unchallengeable but predicated on others' (Uzbekistanis') agreement to provide for him and his family, to participate in and sponsor Gulnara's shopping expeditions. I wanted to blame him, while sensing that he made decisions in relation to his family members' needs and desires and knowing that I could exercise my relational existential power not to comply with his daughter's request. I wanted to blame him, while already knowing that there was something odd about blaming the one-man's-state. This blame did not quite add up; none of the soft leather shoes at the store had a pair.

Forgiveness: The United States, September 18 and 19, 2011

"We have guests," I hear my mother saying. My son and I are inside my mother's old apartment in the Caucasus, which she sold about twenty years ago. Jahon walks into what we used to call the "children's room," where I am playing with my son. After an exchange of the greeting niceties about our health and well-being and our children's and relatives' health and well-being, she says she brought something for me. "What is it?" I ask as her husband comes into the room. This man, short, wearing a gray suit, does not look like her real husband, who is a broad-shouldered, tall, always-smiling fellow. But she insists it is he. Jahon, dressed in a long light dress and a scarf tied in the back of her head, tells me to look at the present she brought, a white-gold ring with a huge three-karat diamond. "This

is a lip ring; it comes with piercing tools," her husband says. He adds that he is ready to pierce my upper lip. How bizarre, I think, while stating my gratitude for the present but declining his offer.

Jahon tells me that they are here to buy a puppy. Surprised, I ask why. "Because she wants one," answers her husband. My mother comes in the room. She says that in the basement there is a woman who sells "lovely puppies," but she also has many children. When we go there, we need to be careful not to trip on them.

Jahon and I go downstairs into the basement. We see many children, infants and toddlers, and about twenty puppies running erratically around the room, the only room in this woman's apartment, except the kitchen. I step into the kitchen and see pork hot dogs, which I never eat, but now I am very hungry and decide to fry a couple. When these hot dogs are done, I sit down on a stool with a soiled diaper on it. The diaper stains my beautiful silk dress. "Shit!" I storm outside.

At a distance, I see a bunch of balloons and my son running after them. The next moment I do not see my son anymore. I hope he went home. I run upstairs, inside my mother's apartment, and straight into the "children's room." My son is playing there. I am relieved to see him indoors.

Back in the corridor in front of the mirror, I see Jahon with a puppy. She says she needs sunglasses. I look through my desk and find several pairs of sunglasses and bring them back to Jahon. She chooses a pair and says that she will take my present, only if I take hers. I nod and say, "Of course."

Suddenly I am in Jahon's yard in Uzbekistan. My son and my mother are no longer with me. I am standing in front of an old metal stove, with Jahon next to me. She covers her mouth with the palm of her hand and whispers that she has been detained and has to be silent. "Come with me and you will see," she whispers. I am in the room with her and an interrogator who is eating eggs sunny-side up. She tells him that her husband is his classmate. The interrogator replies that because he knows her husband, she can go home. Jahon smiles and walks away.

Then I am back at our old apartment staring at the mirror. I look tired. I need to put on some makeup. Jahon left her cosmetics set. Maybe she meant to give it to me as a present. I put on lipstick, powder my nose, lament the wrinkles around my eyes, and go outside. Crossing the street, I see a young beautiful woman approaching me while talking to someone on a mobile phone. I think how happy this young woman must be, laughing and free. As we are getting closer to each other, I look at her and see myself. I wake up.

Tursun-oi told me that even if I do not believe in God, God still believes in me. I may not be a believer, as she is, but I am attentive to my dreams and try to interpret them to the best of my ability, as she does. This dream about Jahon, her family, Uzbekistan, my family, the Caucasus, and me was an omen, even if it wasn't sent by God.

Maria Elisabeth Louw argues that what we perceive as omens in dreams are not (just) products of our unconsciousness; they can be "hyper-real, materializations of that which has not yet materialized." These omens can be experienced "as real in a more urgent sense than the sense impressions of everyday life . . . the fear keeps sitting in one's body; the images seem like something one has seen before, even if they are images of the future" (2010, 280). Such dreams might be reflections of our past or signs of our future, which is what some call "omens."

In my case, the feelings of guilt and shame made my perceived relationships with Jahon and others morally ambiguous. My desire to clear this confusion could have generated this dream about Jahon. Or, indeed, she could have sent this dream because she too felt morally ambiguous about our relationship. Maybe Jahon hoped that I was not irreparably damaged by my experiences with the law enforcement agencies in Uzbekistan. Maybe she felt she had to send me this dream to alleviate my guilt or to ease my painful memories of fear and humiliation—or perhaps to alleviate and ease hers.

Whatever the reasons for and the origin of this dream, she and I were together in my dream populated by families, animals, trinkets, worries, fears, balloons, my desire not to feel pain (having my lip pierced), to be "beautiful and young," to be untouched by the summer of 2011, and my realization that the latter would never be because that summer already happened. All I could hope for was a promise of absolution. This dream delivered some of that absolution and helped me to regain some emotional dignity by giving me hope that I might have exaggerated the impact of my presence on the lives of others in Hovliguzar and Tashkent, by giving me hope that personal networks (such as the interrogator, Jahon's husband's friend) and the individual power to affect the lives of others have minimized the damage that an association with me might have inflicted on them.

Marranci argues that "the distinction between cultural and biological as well as psychological may be misleading"; therefore, emotional dignity "is not the result of just cultural or biological factors," but an important part of the self and of the relationships between the self and others (2009, 94). If emotions are bodily responses to external stimuli, then emotional dignity, although perceived and expressed "within the dynamics of relations," is not socially conditioned but formative of social life (94). The feeling of dignity, as an articulated emotion, swells up from within the physical body in relation to organic and inorganic others and affects the formation of our relationships with them. These relationships can inform our feeling of dignity but do not determine it.

My feelings of dignity and justice were deeply affected by the events of the summer of 2011. Through Jahon's visit—her bringing me presents, sharing her secret, involving me in purchasing a puppy, leaving me a part of herself (her cosmetics), and taking a part of me with her (my sunglasses)—this dream created a cognitive opening. By demonstrating that my fear inflated my perception of the consequences of my actions and reminding me of the importance of personal networks, this opening allowed me to alleviate my denial of self-respect in relation to her, my mother, my son, and my self.

I called Jahon in the morning on September 19, 2011. She said that she had been thinking about me yesterday at the time I was dreaming about her. I told her that, ridden by guilt, I needed to know that they—she and others—were still safe. She said that she needed to tell me that they were safe and needed to make sure that I was safe; maybe she, too, needed to regain self-respect after describing the details of our meetings to the interrogators. By sensing that we had let each other down, we housed each other in our thoughts and dreams. I did not ask and she did not tell me whether she had sent that dream. We both knew that in some way we had coauthored it. In this dream as well as during my research, she was one of my "epistemic partners" (Rabinow 2008, 65).

The Valley and I

Maybe the Ferghana Valley is my fate. Like the sandstorm described by the boy named Crow in Haruki Murakami's novel *Kafka on the Shore* (2006), it continues chasing me while changing directions. One day I loathe it, another day I miss it or feel guilty for discovering it in the first place. Maybe this storm *is* something inside me that I have to continue to experience before, while, and after writing this book. The boy named Crow claims that if I give in to this storm, close my eyes, and walk through it, step by step without any particular direction and no sense of time, I will come out of it a different person. He says that this is what such storms are about.

I am still writing down my memories, trying to put together the fragments of 2001, 2002–2003, and the summer of 2011. Although my dreams are less and less populated by the people I left in Uzbekistan, in our globalized virtually enhanced world we are never too far from each other; and if we are, then we are not so for long.

Glossary

Works Cited

Index

Glossary

ahlus sunnah. People of the Prophet's tradition.
Alhamdulillah. Thank God.
Allahu Akbar. God is the greatest.
Allahumma amen. Let it be as God wants.
Allah yo'lida. God's way.
Arabiston. A name used to refer to Saudi Arabia or the Arabian Peninsula.
ariq. A stream.
astaghfirullah. Seeking forgiveness from Allah.
atel'e. A dress shop that specializes in tailored clothing.
avom khalq. Uneducated people.
awra. Modesty.
ayat. Sign or verse.
al-Baqara. The Cow, a sura in the Qur'an.
barakat. Supernatural substance conferring the ability to grant blessings.
Bayram. A big celebration.
bazar. Market.
Bibi Mushkil Kusho. The Lady Solver of Difficulties. Also used to refer to the propitiatory ritual appealing to this female mediator for blessings.
Bibi Seshambe. The Lady Tuesday. Also used to refer to the propitiatory ritual appealing to this female mediator for blessings.
Bismillah ir-Rahman ir-Rahim. In the name of God, the Caring, and the Compassionate.
bisnesmenshi. Businesswomen.
bisplodnij. Impotent (Russian). See also *ozg'in.*
bogatstvo. Wealth.
Bojxona. Customs office.
Bol'shoe spasibo. Thank you very much.
bondo. Body.

chaixonas. Local eateries.
chelovek. Human.
cheroiliq. Beautifully.
chistki. Cleansing.
chopan. A padded robe.
communitas. Unstructured community.
dasturkhon. Meal.
dedushka. Grandfather.
deen. Faith.
delo. Case.
discoteki. Dance parties.
Dom Kulturi. Culture Center.
domla. Male religious practitioner (see also *mullah*).
do'ppi. Skull cap.
duo. Supplication; *dua* in Arabic.
ehson. A ceremonial gathering to express gratitude to God.
esenbeshniki. Agents of the National Security Service (SNB).
Farg'ona Vodiysi. Ferghana Province in Uzbekistan.
al-Fatiha. The Opening, the first sura in the Qur'an.
fiqh. Islamic jurisprudence.
al-fus-ha. Qur'anic Arabic.
gap. The rotating meetings of one's social network.
gazali. An Arabic poetic form.
Gorkom. City-level Communist Party Committee.
gumanitarnih. Humanitarian.
hadislar. The stories about and sayings of the Prophet Muhammad and his Companions.
Haid. A festival that marks the end of the month of ritual fasting; *Eid al-Fitr* in Arabic.
hajj. The annual pilgrimage to Mecca.
halal. Permitted; in the text used to mean "pure."
al-hamdu lillah. Thank God.
Hanafi mashab. The interpretive position or school of Islamic jurisprudence predominant in Uzbekistan.
haram. Forbidden.
haribi/haribki. Provincial men/women.
Havo. Eve; *Hawa* in Arabic.

hazrat. Holy person; *hadret* in Arabic.
hijab. A large scarf covering the hair, neck, and shoulders.
hikmatlar (pl.). Hymns.
Hizbut. A member of the Hizb-ut-Tahrir.
Hizb-ut-Tahrir. Party of Liberation, a party labeled as a terrorist organization in Uzbekistan.
Hoda Holasya. If God wills.
hoja. A person who has performed the hajj; *haj* in Arabic.
hokimyat. City hall.
hokimyat otin. City teacher of religion.
ibodat. Worship.
iftor. An evening meal; *iftar* in Arabic means "breakfast."
ijazah. Official authorization to transmit knowledge.
illim. Knowledge.
illim khalq. Knowledgeable people.
illimtolib. A human looking for knowledge.
imam. Male prayer leader.
Imam Azam. The founder of the Hanafi *mashab.*
imon. Faith.
Insha'Allah. If God wills.
Islom. Islam.
issiriq. A bitter herb.
jadidism. Late-nineteenth-century reformist movement in Turkistan.
jadids (pl.). Central Asian reformers.
jannat. Paradise; *janna* in Arabic.
jihad. Personal (inward) or armed struggle.
jinn. Invisible beings created by God.
Jumma namoz. Friday congregational prayer.
Ka'ba. A sacred cube-shaped building in Mecca, Saudi Arabia.
kachat' prava. Insistence on legal rights.
kalbasa. Sausage.
kalimas (pl.). The six fundamental theological principles of Islam.
karamat (pl.). Miracles.
katta savob. Great merit.
kelin. Daughter-in-law.
khalifat. A state guided by Islamic principles.
Khudoga shukur. Thank God.

khutba. Message for congregation.
kitob. Book; *kitaab* in Arabic.
kolkhoz. Collective farm.
krutie. Cool (slang).
kurpacha. Cotton-filled blankets.
kursi. Academic courses.
La ilaha illa Allah. There is no other God but God.
lyamochki. Tank tops.
madrasa. A (religious) school.
magreb. Sunset.
mahalla. Neighborhood.
maraka. Memorial service.
masala. Didactic story.
mashab. Interpretive position or school of Islamic jurisprudence; *mazhab* in Arabic.
masjid. Mosque.
maslahat. Telling stories.
mavlud. Prophet Muhammad's birthday celebration.
mazar. Sacred graveyard.
meropriyatiya. Social event with ritual components.
Mi sozdani bogom. We are made by God.
mnogozhenstvo. Polygyny.
mosolmonchiliq. Truly Muslim.
mufti. An official religious leader entitled to provide legal rulings.
mullah. Male religious leader.
murid. Committed follower.
Mustakilliq. Uzbekistan's independence from the Soviet Union.
namoz. Ritual prayer.
nasheed. Religious hymn.
nastoyashiye Musulmane. Truly Muslim.
nauka. Science.
non. Flat bread.
nur. Sacred light.
Obkom. Provincial-level Communist Party Committee.
oblastnie. Provincial people.
odat. Customs.
omonat. Someone or something lent for a period of time.

oqim. Teaching.
osh. A rice and meat dish.
otin/otinoy (pl. otinlar). Teacher; a "more respectful and official" term.
otinby. Teacher.
otincha (pl. otinchlar). Colloquial version of *otin* and/or *otinby.*
Oto. "Father," but here referring to Adam.
OVIR. Ofis Viz i Registratsiji (Office of Visas and Registration).
ozg'in. Impotent.
paranji. A form of covered modest dress that resembles a long jacket worn from the top of the head down.
pataha. Supplications.
perestroika. Restructuring.
pereval. Mountain pass.
perevyazat' trubi. Sterilize.
personal'ni dosmotor. Strip search.
pir. Spiritual leader.
po-Islamski. Islamically or in accordance with Islam.
po rabote ili otdihat'. Business or pleasure.
pravelinij Islam. Correct Islam.
pravozashitnik. A person defending human rights.
predstavitilyami pravoohranitel'nikh organov. Representatives of the law enforcement.
preduprezhdenie. A (legal) warning.
prokhuratura. Prosecutor's office.
proverka. SNB investigation of activities.
qishloq. Village.
qore (pl. qoralar). Qur'an reciter.
Rahmat. Thank you.
Ramazan. Month of ritual fasting; *Ramadan* in Arabic.
raskaz. Story.
ro'za. Ritual fasting during the month of Ramazan.
rukh. Soul.
savob. Meritorious act.
sep. Trousseau.
shahid (pl. shahidi [for men]; shahidki [for women]). Martyr.
shariat. Normative principles of Islam; Islamic law. *Shariah* in Arabic.
sheikh. Spiritual leader and scholar.

shirk. Idolatry; an opposite to monotheism.
shkolnoe obrazovanie. Education at school.
sili. Strength.
skazanie. Legend.
sluchai. An occasion.
SNB. Sluzhba Natsionalnoj Bezopasnosti (National Security Service).
sobr. Patience.
som. A monetary unit in Uzbekistan.
sotka. Mobile phone.
sovremennie. Contemporary.
spasibo. Thank you.
Spetsnaz. Russian Special Forces.
stariki. Elderly.
sunna. The Prophet's tradition.
Sunni. Those who follow the Prophet Muhammad's tradition.
sura. Chapter.
svyatie ludi. Holy people.
tafsir. Qur'anic exegesis.
tahorat. Ritual ablutions.
tajweed. Standards and rules of recitation.
tasbih. Prayer beads.
Tashkentsie. From the capital Tashkent.
taxist. Taxi driver.
toga. An honorable place at head of table.
topchan. An elevated, above-ground wooden structure.
toy. Wedding.
turamlar. Those who claim to be descendants of the Prophet Muhammad and his Companions.
udostoverenie. Badge.
ulama. Muslim legal scholars.
umma. Community or nation.
ustoz. Teacher.
varaka. Leaflets.
vazhni chelovek. Important individual.
v kommandirovku. Business trip.
Wahhabism. An understanding of Sunni Islam predominant in Saudi Arabia. In Uzbekistan, considered unauthentic to the region's religious ideology.

Wahhabist (pl. Wahhabisti). A pejorative term used in reference to a follower of any ideology considered unauthentic to the region's religious ideology; *Wahhabi* (sing.) and *Wahhabeen* (pl.) in Arabic.

Ya'seen. A sura in the Qur'an titled after the two Arabic letters *ya* and *seen.*

zikr. The process of getting closer to Allah through the repetition of a phrase or movement.

zina. Fornication.

zona. Prison camps.

zor. Great and beautiful.

Works Cited

Abashin, S. 1997. "Sotsial'nye korni sredneaziatskogo islamizma (na primere odnogo seleniya)" (Social roots of Central Asian Islamism [exemplified by one village]). In *Identichnost' i konflikt v postsovetskikh gosudarstvakh* (Identity and conflict in post-Soviet states), edited by M. B. Olcott, V. Tishkov, and A. Malashenko, 447–67. Moscow: Carnegie Endowment for International Peace.

Abbott, N. 1942. *Aishah, the Beloved of Muhammad*. Chicago: Univ. of Chicago Press.

Abramson, D. 2000. "Socialism's Bastard Children." *POLAR: Political and Legal Anthropology Review* 23, no. 1: 49–64.

———. 2010. *Foreign Religious Education and the Central Asian Islamic Revival: Impact and Prospects for Stability*. Washington, DC: Central Asia–Caucasus Institute & Silk Road Studies Program.

Abramson, S. M. 1962. "Otrashenie protsessa sblizhenia natsij na semejnobitovom uklade narodov Srednej Azii i Kazahstana" (Reflection of the process of increased contact of a nationality in daily life among Central Asian peoples). *Sovetskaya Etnographia* 3:18–34.

Abu-Lughod, L. 2010. "The Active social Life of Muslim Women's Rights: A Plea for Ethnography, Not Polemic, with Cases from Egypt and Palestine." *Journal of Middle East Women's Studies* 6, no. 1: 1–45.

Adams, L. 2002. "Globalization in Central Asia: Notes of Centrality and Marginalization." *Journal of Central Asian Studies* 6, no. 2: 2–12.

———. 2010. *The Spectacular State: Culture and National Identity in Uzbekistan*. Durham, NC: Duke Univ. Press.

Afsaruddin, A. 2002. "Reconstituting Women's Lives: Gender and the Poetics of Narrative in Medieval Biographical Collection." *Muslim World* 92, nos. 3–4: 461–81.

Ahmad, S. 2006. "Al-Huda: The Story of 'Islamic' Revivalism amongst Urban Pakistani Women." PhD diss., Syracuse Univ.

Akiner, S. 1997. "Between Tradition and Modernity: The Dilemma Facing Contemporary Central Asian Women." In *Post-Soviet Women: From the Baltic to Central Asia*, edited by M. Buckley, 261–305. Cambridge: Cambridge Univ. Press.

Akiner, S., and Central Asia–Caucasus Institute. 2005. *Violence in Andijan, 13 May 2005: An Independent Assessment.* Washington, DC: Central Asia–Caucasus Institute & Silk Road Studies Program.

Alimova, D., and N. Azimova. 2000. "Women's Position in Uzbekistan before and after Independence." In *Gender and Identity Construction: Women of Central Asia, the Caucasus, and Turkey*, edited by F. Acar and A. Gunes-Ayata, vol. 68 in the series Social, Economic, and Political Studies of the Middle East, 293–306. Leiden: Brill.

Almond, I. 2007. *The New Orientalists: Postmodern Representations of Islam from Foucault to Baudrillard.* New York: St. Martin's Press.

Asad, T. 1999. "Religion, Nation-State, Secularism." In *Nation and Religion: Perspectives on Europe and Asia*, edited by P. van der Veer and H. Lehmann, 178–97. Princeton, NJ: Princeton Univ. Press.

Ashur, S., and F. Najibullah. 2011. "'Most-Famous Uzbek' Almost Invisible in Uzbekistan." *Eurasianet*, July 10. At http://www.rferl.org/content/uzbekistan_comedian_obid_asomov_blacklisted_/24259693.html.

Ashwin, S. 2000. "Introduction: Gender, State, and Society in Soviet and Post-Soviet Russia." In *Gender, State, and Society in Soviet and Post-Soviet Russia*, 1–29. London: Routledge.

Atayeva, N., and D. Belomestnov. 2011. *The System of Torture and Extrajudicial Execution in Uzbekistan.* Le Mans, France: Association for Human Rights in Central Asia.

Babadzhanov, B. 2002. "Central Asia: A Gathering Storm?" In *Islam in Uzbekistan: From the Struggle for "Religious Purity" to Political Activism*, edited by B. Z. Rumer, 299–333. New York: M. E. Sharpe.

——— 2004. "Debates over Islam in Contemporary Uzbekistan: A View from within." In *Devout Societies vs. Impious States? Transmitting Islamic Learning in Russia, Central Asia, and China through the Twentieth Century: Proceedings of an International Colloquium Held in the Carré des Sciences, French Ministry of Research, Paris, November 12–13, 2001*, edited by S. P. A. Dudoignon, 39–60. Berlin: Schwarz.

Badran, M. 2009. *Feminism in Islam: Secular and Religious Convergences*. Oxford: Oneworld Publications.

Bailey, F. G. 1969. *Strategems and Spoils: A Social Anthropology of Politics*. New York: Schocken Books.

Bakhtin, M. M. 1981. *The Dialogic Imagination: Four Essays*. Austin: Univ. of Texas Press.

Barrett, J. 2008. "Gender and Sources of Religious Information in Uzbekistan." *Cognitie Creier Comportament* 11, no. 2: 417–36.

Behar, R. 1993. *Translated Woman: Crossing the Border with Esperanza's Story*. Boston: Beacon Press.

Berdyaev, N. 1943. *Slavery and Freedom*. London: Geoffrey Bles.

Bogner, M., and Human Rights Watch. 2003. *Uzbekistan, from House to House: Abuses by Mahalla Committees*. New York: Human Rights Watch.

Bringa, T. 1995. *Being Muslim the Bosnian Way: Identity and Community in a Central Bosnian Village*. Princeton, NJ: Princeton Univ. Press.

Bruce, S. 2000. *Fundamentalism*. Cambridge, MA: Polity Press.

Bush, George W. 2002. Address before a Joint Session of the Congress on the State of the Union, Jan. 29. At http://www.presidency.ucsb.edu/ws/?pid=29644.

Butler, J. 2004. *Precarious Life: The Powers of Mourning and Violence*. London: Verso.

Carrithers, Michael, Steven Collins, and Steven Lukes. 1985. *The Category of the Person: Anthropology, Philosophy, History*. Cambridge: Cambridge Univ. Press.

Cavarero, A. 2007. *Horrorism: Naming Contemporary Violence*. New York: Columbia Univ. Press.

Charlick-Paley, Tanya, with P. Williams and O. Oliker. 2002. "The Political Evolution of Central Asia and South Caucasus: Implications for Regional Security." In *Faultlines of Conflict in Central Asia and the South Caucasus: Implications for the U.S. Army*, edited by O. Oliker and T. S. Szayna, 7–40. Santa Monica, CA: RAND.

Chaudet, D. 2008. "Islamist Terrorism in Greater Central Asia: The 'Al-Qaedaization' of Uzbek Jihadism." *Russie.Nei.Visions* 35:1–29.

Chiseri-Strater, E. 1996. "Turning in upon Ourselves: Positionality, Subjectivity, and Reflexivity." In *Ethics and Representation in Qualitative Studies of Literacy*, edited by P. Mortensen and G. Kirsch, 115–32. Urbana, IL: National Council of Teachers of English.

Chodorow, N. J. 1999. *The Power of Feelings: Personal Meaning in Psychoanalysis, Gender, and Culture.* New Haven, CT: Yale Univ. Press.

Cohen, A. 1994. *Self-Consciousness: An Alternative Anthropology of Identity.* London: Routledge.

Conley, J. M., and W. M. O'Barr. 1998. *Just Words.* Chicago: Univ. of Chicago Press.

Constantine, E. A. 2007. "Practical Consequences of Soviet Policy and Ideology for Gender in Central Asia and Contemporary Reversal." In *Everyday Life in Central Asia: Past and Present*, edited by J. Sanadeo and R. Zanca, 115–26. Bloomington: Indiana Univ. Press.

Corcoran-Nantes, Y. 2005. *Lost Voices: Central Asian Women Confronting Transition.* London: Zed Books.

Damasio, A. 2000. *The Feeling of What Happens: Body, Emotion, and the Making of Consciousness.* New York: Vintage.

Davies, C. A. 2008. *Reflexive Ethnography: A Guide to Researching Selves and Others.* New York: Routledge.

Dean, M. 1999. *Governmentality: Power and Rule in Modern Society.* London: Sage.

Deeb, L. 2006. *An Enchanted Modern: Gender and Public Piety in Shi'i Lebanon.* Princeton, NJ: Princeton Univ. Press.

Denber, R., and I. Levine. 2005. *"Bullets Were Falling Like Rain": The Andijan Massacre, May 13, 2005.* New York: Human Rights Watch.

DeWeese, D. A. 1994. *Islamization and Native Religion in the Golden Horde: Baba Tukles and Conversion to Islam in Historical and Epic Tradition.* University Park: Pennsylvania State Univ. Press.

Dr. Dre, with Eminem. 1999. "Forgot about Dre." By Andre Young, Melvin Bradford, and Marshall Mathers. On *Dr. Dre.* Santa Monica, CA: Aftermath/Interscope. Lyrics at http://www.azlyrics.com/lyrics/drdre/forgotaboutdre.html. Accessed Nov. 10, 2013.

Dr. Dre, with Eminem and Skylar Grey. 2011. "I Need a Doctor." By Marshall Mathers and Alexander Junior Grant. On *Detox.* Santa Monica, CA: Aftermath/Interscope. Lyrics at http://www.azlyrics.com/lyrics/drdre/ineedadoctor.html. Accessed Nov. 10, 2013.

Dumont, L. 1994. *German Ideology: From France to Germany and Back.* Chicago: Chicago Univ. Press.

Dunlop, J. B. 2006. *The 2002 Dubrovka and 2004 Beslan Hostage Crises: A Critique of Russian Counter-Terrorism*. Stuttgart: Ibidem.

Durkheim, E. 1915. *The Elementary Forms of the Religious Life: A Study in Religious Sociology*. London: Allen & Unwin; New York: Macmillan.

Dzhumaev, A. 1996. "'Turkestanski Starets' hodja Ahmed Yassavi i musulmanskie duhovnie pesnopeniya" (Turkistan's elder holy man Ahmed Yassavi and Muslim spirituals). *Muzikal'naya Akademia (Sovetskaya Musika)* (Musical Academy [Soviet Music]) 3–4:125–31.

Ellis, C. 1993. "'There Are Survivors': Telling a Story of Sudden Death." *Sociological Quarterly* 34, no. 4: 711–30.

Emerson, C. 1990. "Russian Orthodoxy and the Early Bakhtin." *Religion and Literature* 22–23:109–31.

———. 1997. *The First Hundred Years of Mikhail Bakhtin*. Princeton, NJ: Princeton Univ. Press.

Eminem. 1999. "My Name Is." By Labi Siffre. On *Slim Shady*. Santa Monica, CA: Aftermath/Interscope. Lyrics at http://www.azlyrics.com/lyrics/eminem/mynameis.html. Accessed Nov. 10, 2013.

———. 2000. "I Am Back." By Andre Young, Eric Collins, Michael A. Elizondo, and Marshall Mathers. On *The Marshall Mathers*. Santa Monica, CA: Aftermath/Interscope. Lyrics at http://www.azlyrics.com/lyrics/eminem/imback.html. Accessed Nov. 10, 2013.

Farhadi, S. 2010. "Uzbekistan Combats Polygamy: Women Asked to Have a Pre-nuptial Contract." *Central Asia Online*, Oct. 30. At http://centralasiaonline.com/en_GB/articles/caii/features/main/2010/2010/2030/feature-2002.

Fathi, H. 1997. "Otines: The Unknown Women Clerics of Central Asian Islam." *Central Asian Survey* 16, no. 1: 27–43.

Felgenhauer, P. 2011. "Russia Begins Tsentr 2011 Military Exercises." *Eurasia Daily Monitor* 8, no. 169. At http://www.jamestown.org/single/?no_cache=1&tx_ttnews%5Btt_news%5D=38404#.U2uW5a0dAYE. Accessed May 7, 2014.

Ferghana News Agency (Moscow). 2007. "Uzbek Authorities Are Using Islam to Promote 'Development of Society and Prosperity of the Country.'" Mar. 21. At http://enews.fergananews.com/articles/1883.

Ferguson, J., and A. Gupta 2002. "Spatializing States: Toward an Ethnography of Neoliberal Governmentality." *American Ethnologist* 29, no. 4: 981–1002.

Fitz Gibbon, Kate. 2005. "A Central Asian Cinderella: The Tale of Bibi Seshambe. SSRN, Feb. 18. At http://ssrn.com/abstract=1628847 or http://dx.doi.org/10.2139/ssrn.1628847.

Flueckiger, J. B. 2006. *In Amma's Healing Room: Gender and Vernacular Islam in South India.* Bloomington: Indiana Univ. Press.

Forgas, J. 2001. "Affective Intelligence: The Role of Affect in Social Thinking and Behavior." In *Emotional Intelligence in Everyday Life: A Scientific Inquiry*, edited by J. Ciarrochi, J. Forgas, and J. Mayer, 46–64. New York: New York Univ. Press.

Foucault, M. 1960. *Madness and Civilization: A History of Insanity in the Age of Reason.* Translated by R. Howard. New York: Vintage.

———. 1972. *Archaeology of Knowledge.* New York: Vintage.

———. 1980. *Power/Knowledge: Selected Interviews and Other Writings, 1972–1977.* Edited by C. Gordon. New York: Pantheon Books.

Garfield, J. L. 2007. "Educating for Virtuoso Living: Papers from the Ninth East–West Philosophers' Conference." *Philosophy East and West* 57, no. 3: 285–89.

Geertz, C. 1968. *Islam Observed: Religious Development in Morocco and Indonesia.* New Haven, CT: Yale Univ. Press.

Gergen, K. J. 2009. *Relational Being: Beyond Self and Community.* New York: Oxford Univ. Press.

Gharib, A. 2011. "Herman Cain Laughs Off 'Ubeki-beki-beki-stan-stan' Gaffe, Blames Belafonte and 'Colonel' West." *ThinkProgress*, Center for American Progress Fund, Oct. 11. At http://thinkprogress.org/security/2011/10/11/340669/herman-cain-laughs-off-ubeki-beki-beki-stan-stan-gaffe-blames-belafonte-and-colonel-west/.

Gillette, M. 2000. *Between Mecca and Beijing: Modernization and Consumption among Urban Chinese Muslims.* Stanford: Stanford Univ. Press.

Gilsenan, M. 2012. "Religion and Society in the Modern Arab World." In *The Anthropology of Islam Reader*, edited by J. Kreinath, 51–64. London: Routledge.

Goffman, E. 1956. *The Representation of Self in Everyday Life.* New York: Doubleday.

———. 1971. *Relations in Public.* New York: Harper and Row.

Gomberg-Munoz, R. 2010. "Willing to Work: Agency and Vulnerability in an Undocumented Immigrant Network." *American Anthropologist* 112, no. 2: 295–307.

Gorshunova, O. V. 2001. "Otyncha." *Etnoragraficheskoe Obozrenie* (Ethnographic review) 3:134–40.

Greenberg, J. 2011. "On the Road to Normal: Negotiating Agency and State Sovereignty in Postsocialist Serbia." *American Anthropologist* 1:88–100.

Gudkov, L. D., B. B. Dubin, and N. A. Zorkaya. 2008. *Postsovetskij chelovek i grazhdanskoe obshchestvo* (Post-Soviet human and civil society). Moscow: Moskovskaya shkola politicheskih issledovanij.

Hafez, S. 2011. *An Islam of Her Own: Reconsidering Religion and Secularism in Women's Islamic Movements.* New York: New York Univ. Press.

Haraway, D. 1988. "Situated Knowledges: The Science Question in Feminism as a Site of Discourse on the Privilege of Partial Perspective." *Journal of Feminist Studies* 14, no. 3: 575–99.

Hardy, N. 2010. "Foucault, Geneology, Emergence: Re-examining the Extra-discursive." *Journal for the Theory of Social Behavior* 41, no. 1: 68–91.

Hay, M. C. 2010. "Suffering in a Productive World: Chronic Illness, Visibility, and the Space beyond Agency." *American Ethnologist* 37:259–74.

Heathershow, J., and N. Megoran. 2011. "Contesting Danger: A New Agenda for Policy and Scholarship on Central Asia." *International Affairs* 87, no. 3: 589–612.

Hegland, M. E. 1997. "A Mixed Blessing: The Majales—Shia Women's Rituals of Mourning in Northwest Pakistan." In *Mixed Blessings: Gender and Religious Fundamentalism Cross Culturally*, edited by J. Brink and J. Mencher, 179–96. New York: Routledge.

Hensel, C. 1996. *Telling Our Selves: Ethnicity and Discourse in Southwest Alaska.* Oxford: Oxford Univ. Press.

Hirschkind, C. 2006. *The Ethical Soundcape: Cassette Sermons and Islamic Counterpublics.* New York: Columbia Univ. Press.

Hjellum, T. 2000. "Features of Capitalism and the Restructuring of Ruling Classes in China." *Copenhagen Journal of Asian Studies* 14:105–29.

Hoodfar, H. 2001. "Reproductive Health Counseling in the Islamic Republic of Iran: The Role of Women Mullah." In *Cultural Perspectives on Reproductive Health*, edited by C. M. Obermeyer, 154–74. Oxford: Oxford Univ. Press.

Horvatich, P. 1994. "Ways of Knowing Islam." *American Ethnologist* 21, no. 4: 811–26.

Horwitz, E. P. 1993. "Just Stories of Ethnographic Authority." In *When They Read What We Write: The Politics of Ethnography*, edited by C. B. Brettell, 31–43. Westport, CT: Bergin and Garvey.

Hourani, G. F. 1985. *Reason and Tradition in Islamic Ethics*. Cambridge: Cambridge Univ. Press.

Human Rights Watch. 2007. *Nowhere to Turn: Torture and Ill-Treatment in Uzbekistan*. Human Rights Watch Report, vol. 19, no. 6(D). New York: Human Rights Watch.

———. 2011. "Uzbekistan: Government Shuts Down Human Rights Watch Office." May 16. At http://www.hrw.org/news/2011/03/15/uzbekistan-government-shuts-down-human-rights-watch-office.

Hunter, J., and J. F. Blumenbach. 2011. *The Anthropological Treatises of Johann Friedrich Blumenbach: With Memoirs of Him by Marx and Flourens, and an Account of His Anthropological Museum by Professor R. Wagner, and the Inaugural Dissertation of John Hunter, M.D., on the Varieties of Man by John Hunter and Johann Friedrich Blumenbach*. Elibron Classics. London: Adegi Graphics.

Huntington, S. 1996. *The Clash of Civilizations and the Remaking of World Order*. New York: Simon and Schuster Press.

Ibn Sina. 1945. "Risala fil 'ashq" (A treatise on love). Translated by E. Fackenheim. *Medieval Studies* 7:211–12.

———. 1974. *Irat al-shaykh al-ra'is* (The life of Ibn Sina). Albany: State Univ. of New York Press.

Ilkhamov, A. 2002. "UP FRONT—Controllable Democracy in Uzbekistan." *Middle East Report* 32, no. 1: 8–10.

———. 2006. "The Phenomenology of 'Akromiya': Separating Facts from Fiction." *China and Eurasia Forum Quarterly* 4:39–48.

Ingold, T., and E. Hallam. 2007. "Creativity and Cultural Improvisation: An Introduction." In *Creativity and Cultural Improvisation*, edited by T. Ingold and E. Hallam, 1–24. Oxford: Berg.

International Crisis Group. 2011. "Joint Letter to Secretary Clinton." Sept. 27.

Irigaray, L. 1993. *Je, Tu, Nous: Toward a Culture of Difference*. New York: Routledge.

Issoupova, O. 2000. "Motherhood: From Duty to Pleasure?" In *Gender, State, and Society in Soviet and Post-Soviet Russia*, edited by S. Ashwin, 30–54. London: Routledge.

Jackson, M. 2010. "From Anxiety to Method in Anthropological Fieldwork." In *Emotions in the Field: The Psychology and Anthropology of Fieldwork Experience*, edited by J. Davies and D. Spenser, 35–54. Stanford, CA: Stanford Univ. Press.

Kalmbach, H. 2008. "Social and Religious Change in Damascus: One Case of Female Islamic Religious Authority." *British Journal of Middle Eastern Studies* 35, no. 1: 37–57.

Kamp, M. 2005. "Gender Ideals and Income Realities: Discourses about Labor and Gender in Uzbekistan." *Nationalities Papers* 33, no. 3: 403–22.

———. 2006. *The New Woman in Uzbekistan: Islam, Modernity, and Unveiling under Communism*. Seattle: Univ. of Washington Press.

Kandiyoti, D. 1998. "Rural Livelihoods and Social Networks in Uzbekistan: Perspectives from Andijan." *Central Asian Survey* 17, no. 4: 561–78.

———. 2007. "The Politics of Gender and the Soviet Paradox: Neither Colonized, nor Modern?" *Central Asian Survey* 26, no. 4: 601–23.

Kandiyoti, D., and N. Azimova. 2004. "The Communal and the Sacred: Women's Worlds of Ritual in Uzbekistan." *Journal of the Royal Anthropological Institute* 10, no. 2: 327–49.

Karagiannis, E. 2006. "Political Islam in Uzbekistan: Hizb ut-Tahrir al-Islami." *Europe–Asia Studies* 58, no. 2: 261–80.

Kendzior, S. 2010. "A Reporter without Borders: Internet Politics and State Violence in Uzbekistan." *Problems of Post-communism* 57, no. 1: 40–50.

Khalid, A. 1998. *The Politics of Muslim Cultural Reform: Jadidism in Central Asia*. Berkeley: Univ. of California Press.

———. 2003. "A Secular Islam: Nation, State, and Religion in Uzbekistan." *International Journal of Middle East Studies* 35:573–98.

———. 2007. *Islam after Communism: Religion and Politics in Central Asia*. Berkeley: Univ. of California Press.

Khamidov, A. 2008. "Uzbekistan: Having Weathered Winter, Authorities Brace for Spring." *Eurasianet*, Feb. 27. At http://www.eurasianet.org/departments/insight/articles/eav022808f.shtml.

Kon, I. S. 1995. *The Sexual Revolution in Russia: From the Age of the Czars to Today*. New York: Free Press.

Krakovsky, M. 2006. "Frequent Readers of Fiction Score Higher on Tests of Empathy Than Do Readers of Nonfiction." *Psychology Today* 36, no. 6: 52–53.

Kramer, A. 2002. *Geistliche Autoritat und Islamische Gesellschaft im Wandel: Studien Äber Frauenlteste (otin und xalfa) im Unabhangigen Usbekistan* (Spiritual authority and Islamic society in transition: Studies of religious women [*otin* and *khalfa*] in the independent Uzbekistan). Berlin: Schwarz.

Lahoud, N., and A. H. Johns. 2005. *Islam in World Politics*. New York: Routledge-Curzon.

Laidlaw, J. 2010. "Social Anthropology." In *The Routledge Companion to Ethics*, edited by J. Skorupski, 369–83. London: Routledge.

Lear, J. 2006. *Radical Hope: Ethics in the Face of Cultural Devastation*. Cambridge, MA: Harvard Univ. Press.

Louw, M. E. 2007. *Everyday Islam in Post-Soviet Central Asia*. London: Routledge.

———. 2010. "Dreaming Up Futures: Dream Omens and Magic in Bishkek." *History and Anthropology* 21, no. 3: 277–92.

Lyon, S. M. 2010. "Motivation and Justification from Dreams: Muslim Decision Making Strategies in Punjab, Pakistan." *History and Anthropology* 21, no. 3: 263–76.

Maffesoli, M. 1996. *The Time of the Tribes: The Decline of Individualism in Mass Society*. London: Sage.

Mahmood, S. 2001. "Rehearsed Spontaneity and the Conventionality of Ritual: Disciplines of Salat." *American Ethnologist* 28, no. 4: 827–53.

———. 2005. *Politics of Piety: The Islamic Revival and the Feminist Subject*. Princeton, NJ: Princeton Univ. Press.

———. 2006. "Secularism, Hermeneutics, and Empire: The Politics of Islamic Reformation." *Public Culture* 18, no. 2: 323–47.

———. 2008. "Feminism, Democracy, and Empire: Islam and the War of Terror." In *Women's Studies on the Edge*, edited by J. W. Scott, 81–115. Durham, NC: Duke Univ. Press.

Marranci, G. 2006. *Jihad beyond Islam*. Oxford: Berg.

———. 2008. *The Anthropology of Islam*. Oxford: Berg.

———. 2009. *Understanding Muslim Identity: Rethinking Fundamentalism*. New York: Palgrave Macmillian.

Massell, G. J. 1974. *The Surrogate Proletariat: Moslem Women and Revolutionary Strategies in Soviet Central Asia, 1919–1929*. Princeton, NJ: Princeton Univ. Press.

Massicard, E., and T. Trevisani. 2003. "The Uzbek Mahalla: Between State and Society." In *Central Asia: Aspects of Transition*, edited by T. Everett-Heath, 205–18. London: Routledge Curzon.

Masylkanova, A. 2010. "Ferghana Valley, Home for Terrorists?" *The Morning Post*, Columbia School of International Public Affairs, June 23. At http://www.themorningsidepost.com/2010/06/23/ferghana-valley-home-for-terrorists/.

Mattson, I. 2008. "Debating Form and Function in Muslim Women's Leadership." In *The Columbia Sourcebook of Muslims in the United States*, edited by E. E. Curtis, 252–63. New York: Columbia Univ. Press.

Mauss, M. 1954. *The Gift: Forms and Functions of Exchange in Archaic Societies*. Glencoe, IL: Free Press.

McBrien, J. 2009. "Mukadas's Struggle: Veils and Modernity in Kyrgyzstan." *Journal of the Royal Anthropological Institute* 15:S127–S144.

McBrien, J., and M. Pelkmans. 2008. "Turning Marx on His Head: Missionaries, 'Extremists,' and Archaic Secularists in Post-Soviet Kyrgyzstan." *Critique of Anthropology* 28, no. 1: 87–103.

McGlinchey, E. 2007. "Divided Faith: Trapped between State and Islam in Uzbekistan." In *Everyday Life in Central Asia: Past and Present*, edited by R. Zanca and J. Sahadeo, 305–18. Bloomington: Indiana Univ. Press.

———. 2011. *Chaos, Violence, Dynasty: Politics and Islam in Central Asia*. Pittsburgh: Univ. of Pittsburgh Press.

McNamara, P. 2009. "Feminist Ethnography: Storytelling That Makes a Difference." *Qualitative Social Work* 8, no. 2: 161–78.

Megoran, N. 2010. "The Background to Osh: Stories of Conflict and Coexistence." *oDR: Post-Soviet World*, Oct. 11. At http://www.opendemocracy.net/od-russia/nick-megoran/background-to-osh-stories-of-conflict-and-coexistence.

Metcalf, B. D. 2009. "Telling the Story of Islam in Asia: Reflections on Teleologies and Timelessness." *ASIANetwork Exchange* 16:2–23.

Miklashevsky, A. 1924. "Sotsialnye dvizheniya 1916 g. v Turkestane" (Social movement in 1916 in Turkistan). *Byloe* 27–28:238–74.

Milton, K., and M. Svasek, eds. 2005. *Mixed Emotions: Anthropological Studies of Feelings*. Oxford: Berg.

Mohanty, C. T. 2003. *Feminism without Borders: Decolonizing Theory, Practicing Solidarity*. Durham, NC: Duke Univ. Press.

Muminov, A., U. Gafarov, and R. Shigabdinov. 2010. "Islamic Education in Soviet and Post-Soviet Uzbekistan." In *Islamic Education in the Soviet Union and Its Successor States*, edited by M. Kemper, R. Motika, and S. Reichmuth, 223–89. London: Routledge.

Murakami, H. 2006. *Kafka on the Shore*. Translated by P. Gabriel. New York: Vintage International.

Najmabadi, A. 1998. "Crafting an Educated Housewife in Iran." In *Remaking Women*, edited by L. Abu-Lughod, 91–126. Princeton, NJ: Princeton Univ. Press.

Nalivkin, V., and M. Nalivkina. 1886. *Ocherk bita zhenshini osedlago tysemnago naseleniia Fergani* (A sketch of the everyday life of women of the sedentary population of the Ferghana Valley). Kazan, Russia: Tipografiia Imperatorskago Universiteta.

Narayan, K. 2007. "Tools to Shape Texts: What Creative Nonfiction Can Offer Anthropology." *Anthropology of Humanism* 32, no. 2: 130–44.

Naumkin, V. V. 2005. *Radical Islam in Central Asia: Between Pen and Rifle*. Lanham, MD: Rowman & Littlefield.

Navaro-Yashin, Y. 2008. "'Life Is Dead Here': Sensing the Political in 'No Man's Land.'" In *Ethnographica Moralia: Experiments in Interpretive Anthropology*, edited by N. Panourgia and G. Marcus, 168–88. Bronx, NY: Fordam Univ. Press.

Nikolski, A. 2011. "Rossia i ee souzniki otrabatibaut bor'bu s povstantsami" (Russia and its allies prepare to fight against popular uprisings). *Vesti* (The News) (Moscow), Sept. 15.

"Nord-Ost Ten Years On." 2012. *oDR: Russia and Beyond*, Oct. 23. At http://www.opendemocracy.net/od-russia/irina-borogan-andrei-soldatov/nord-ost-ten-years-on.

Northrop, D. T. 2004. *Veiled Empire: Gender and Power in Stalinist Central Asia*. Ithaca, NY: Cornell Univ. Press.

Olcott, M. B. 2007. "The Shrinking U.S. Footprint in Central Asia—Many Central Asians Prefer Doing Business with Countries, Like Russia and China, That Do Not Bring Up the Subject of Political Reform." *Current History* 702:333–39.

Papas, A. 2005. "The Sufi and the President in Post-Soviet Uzbekistan." *International Institute for the Study of Islam in the Modern World (ISIM) Review* 16:38–39.

Pedersen, M. A. 2012. "Proposing the Motion: Morten Axel Pedersen." *Critique of Anthropology* 32, no. 1: 59–65.

Peimani, H. 2002. *Failed Transition, Bleak Future? War and Instability in Central Asia and the Caucasus.* Westport, CT: Praeger.

Peshkova, S. 2005. "Family, Sacred Places, and Islamic Law: Islamic Approaches to Reproductive Health in the Ferghana Valley." *Anthro-Globe*, Sept. 23. At http://anthroglobe.info/docs/Reproductive_Health_in_Ferghana.htm.

———. 2009a. "Bringing the Mosque Home and Talking Politics: Women, Space, and Islam in the Ferghana Valley (Uzbekistan)." *Contemporary Islam: Dynamics of Muslim Life* 3, no. 3: 251–73.

———. 2009b. "Muslim Women Leaders in the Ferghana Valley: Whose Leadership Is It Anyway?" *Journal of International Women's Studies* 11, no. 1: 5–24.

———. 2014. "Teaching Islam at a Home School: Muslim Women and Critical Thinking." *Central Asian Survey* 33, no. 1: 80–94.

Peyrouse, S. 2007. "Christians as the Main Religious Minority in Central Asia." In *Everyday Life in Central Asia: Past and Present*, edited by J. Sahadeo and R. Zanca, 371–83. Bloomington: Indiana Univ. Press.

Poliakov, S. 1992. *Everyday Islam: Religion and Tradition in Rural Central Asia.* New York: M. E. Sharpe.

Privratsky, B. 2004. "'Turkestan Belongs to the Qojas': Local Knowledge of a Muslim Tradition." In *Devout Societies vs. Impious States?* edited by S. Dudoignon, 161–212. Berlin: Schwarz.

Rabinow, P. 2003. *Anthropos Today: Reflections on Modern Equipment.* Princeton, NJ: Princeton Univ. Press.

———. 2008. *Marking Time: On the Anthropology of the Contemporary.* Princeton, NJ: Princeton Univ. Press.

Rapoport, A. 1998. "Spatial Organization and the Built Environment." In *Companion Encyclopedia of Anthropology*, edited by T. Ingold, 460–502. London: Routledge.

Rapport, N. 2003. *I Am Dynamite: An Alternative Anthropology of Power.* London: Routledge.

———. 2010. *Human Nature as Capacity: Transcending Discourse and Classification.* New York: Berghahn Books.

Rasanayagam, J. 2010. *Islam in Post-Soviet Uzbekistan: The Morality of Experience.* Cambridge: Cambridge Univ. Press.

Reeves, J. 2012. "Uzbek Man Pleads Guilty in Plot to Kill Obama." Associated Press, Feb. 10.

Reeves, M. 2005. "Locating Danger: *Konfliktologiia* and the Search for Fixity in the Ferghana Valley Borderlands." *Central Asian Survey* 24, no. 1: 67–81.

Rouhani, A. 2008. "An Investigation into Emotional Intelligence, Foreign Language Anxiety, and Empathy through a Cognitive-Affective Course in an EFL Contex." *Linguistik* (online) 34 (Feb.): 41–57. At http://www.linguistik-online.de/34_08/rouhani.pdf.

Rouse, C. 2004. *Engaged Surrender: African-American Women and Islam.* Berkley: Univ. of California Press.

Roy, O. 2000. *The New Central Asia: The Creation of Nations.* New York: New York Univ. Press.

Sahadeo, J. 2011. "The Accidental Traders: Marginalization and Opportunity from the Southern Republics to Late Soviet Moscow." *Central Asian Survey* 30, nos. 3–4: 521–40.

Said, E. 1988. *Orientalism.* London: Penguin.

Saktanber, A. 2002. *Living Islam: Women, Religion, and the Politicization of Culture in Turkey.* London: I. B. Tauris.

Saletin, J. M., A. N. Goldstein, and M. P. Walker. 2011. "The Role of Sleep in Directed Forgetting and Remembering of Human Memories." *Cerebral Cortex* 21 (Nov.): 2534–41.

Salvio, P. 2007. *Anne Sexton: Teacher of Weird Abundance.* Albany: State Univ. of New York Press.

Schielke, S. 2010. "Second Thoughts about the Anthropology of Islam, or How to Make Sense of Grand Schemes in Everyday Life." *Working Papers* 2:1–16.

Seigel, J. 2005. *The Idea of the Self.* Cambridge: Cambridge Univ. Press.

Sells, M. 1999. *Approaching the Qur'an: The Early Revelations.* Ashland, OR: White Cloud Press.

Slingerland, E. G. 2007. "Chinese Thought from an Evolutionary Perspective." *Philosophy East and West* 57:375–88.

Sluka, J., N. Chomsky, and D. Price. 2002. "What Anthropologists Should Know about the Concept of Terrorism: A Response to David Price." *Anthropology Today* 18, no. 2: 22–23.

Snesarev, G. P. 1974. "On Some Causes of the Persistance of Religiocustomary Survivals among the Khorezm Uzbeks." In *Introduction* to *Soviet Ethnography*, edited by S. P. Dunn and E. Dunn, 215–38. Berkeley, CA: Highgate Road Social Science Research Station.

Sokefeld, M. 1999. "Debating Self, Identity, and Culture in Anthropology." *Current Anthropology* 40, no. 4: 417–48.

Solomon, R. 1990. *A Passion for Justice: Emotions and the Origins of the Social Contract*. Reading, MA: Addison-Wesley.

Speer, S. A. 2005. *Gender Talk : Feminism, Discourse, and Conversation Analysis*. London: Routledge.

Stowasser, B. F. 1994. *Women and the Qur'an: Traditions and Interpretations*. New York: Oxford Univ. Press.

Sugarman, J., and J. Martin. 2011. "Theorizing Relational Agency." *Journal of Constructivist Psychology* 24:283–89.

Sule, B. B. M., and P. E. Starraff. 1991. "Islamic Leadership Positions for Women in Contemporary Kano Society." In *Hausa Women in the Twentieth Century*, edited by C. Coles and B. Mack, 29–50. Madison: Univ. of Wisconsin Press.

Sultanova, R. 2000. "Qadiryya Dhikr in Ferghana Valley." *Journal of the History of Sufism* 1–2:531–38.

———. 2011. *From Shamanism to Sufism: Women, Islam, and Culture in Central Asia*. New York: I. B. Tauris.

Tabishalieva, A. 2000. "Revival of Traditions in Post-Soviet Central Asia." In *Making the Transition Work for Women in Europe and Central Asia*, edited by M. Lazreg, 51–57. World Bank Discussion Paper no. 411. Washington, DC: World Bank.

Taussig, M. 1999. *Defacement: Public Secrecy and the Labor of the Negative*. Stanford, CA: Stanford Univ. Press.

Taylor, C. 1992. *Sources of the Self: The Making of Modern Identity*. Cambridge, MA: Harvard Univ. Press.

Thomson, K. O. 2007. "The Archery of 'Wisdom' in the Stream of Life: 'Wisdom' in the Four Books with Zhu Xi's Reflections." *Philosophy East and West* 57, no. 3: 330–44.

Tokhtakhodjaeva, M. 1996. *Daughters of Amazons: Voices from Central Asia*. Lahore, Pakistan: Shirkat Gah.

Tomson, W. 1950. "Free Will and Predestination in Early Islam." *The Muslim World* 40, no. 3: 207–16.

Troitskaya, A. L. 1929. "Zhenskij Zikr v Starom Tashkente" (Women's zikr [spiritual exercise] in Old Tashkent). *Sb. Muzeja Antropologii i*

Etnografii (Collections of the Museum of Anthropology and Ethnography) 7:71–99.

Tudge, J. 1991. "Education of Young Children in the Soviet Union: Current Practice in Historical Perspective." *Elementary School Journal* 92, no. 1: 121–33.

Turner, V. W. 1969. *The Ritual Process: Structure and Anti-structure*. Chicago: Aldine.

"Uzbekistan's Health Care Reality Belies Official Cheer." 2011. *Eurasianet*, Nov. 14. At http://www.eurasianet.org/node/64509.

Varisco, D. M. 2005. *Islam Obscured: The Rhetoric of Anthropological Representation*. New York: Palgrave Macmillan.

———. 2007. *Reading Orientalism: Said and the Unsaid*. Seattle: Univ. of Washington Press.

Von Doorn-Harder, P. 2006. *Women Shaping Islam: Reading the Qur'an in Indonesia*. Chicago: Univ. of Illinois Press.

Wadud, A. 2007. *Inside the Gender Jihad: Women's Reform in Islam*. Oxford: One World.

Watt, W. Montgomery. 1948. *Free Will and Predestination in Early Islam*. London: Luzac.

Weber, M. 1978. *Economy and Society*. Berkeley: Univ. of California Press.

Whitlock, M., prod. 2010. *Through the Looking Glass: Andijan Massacre*. London: FactionFilms.

Wiktorowicz, Q. 2005. *Militant Islam Rising: Muslim Extremism in the West*. Lanham, MD: Rowman & Littlefield.

Yaniseyev, M. 2011. IMU Lacks Popular Support. *Central Asia Online*, July 15. At http://centralasiaonline.com/en_GB/articles/caii/features/main/2011/07/15/feature-01.

Yemelianova, G. 2010. *Radical Islam in the Former Soviet Union*. New York: Routledge.

Ye'or, Bat. 2002. *Islam and Dhimmitude: Where Civilizations Collide*. Translated by Miriam Kochan and David Littman. Madison, NJ: Fairleigh Dickinson Univ. Press.

Zanca, R. 2004. "'Explaining' Islam in Central Asia: An Anthropological Approach for Uzbekistan." *Journal of Muslim Minority Affairs* 24, no. 1: 99–107.

Zhilina, A. N., and T. N. Tomina. 1993. *Narody sredneĭ Azii: Traditsionnoye zhilishche narodov Srednej Azii XIX–nachalo XX vv* (Peoples of

Central Asia: The traditional dwellings of Central Asian peoples in the 19th–early 20th centuries). Moscow: Nauka.

Žižek, S. 2002. *Welcome to the Desert of the Real: Five Essays on September 11 and Related Dates*. New York: Verso.

———. 2008. *Violence*. New York: Big Ideas, Small Books.

Zuvaidov, R. 2011. "Angliskaya Mata Hari s Rossijskim passportom" (English Mata Hari with Russian passport). *Tadjiksie Trudovie Immigranti* (Tajik Labour News), Aug. 21. At http://tajmigrant.com/anglijskaya-mata-xari-s-rossijskim-pasportom-v-fergane.html.

Index

Svetlana Peshkova is an assistant professor in the Department of Anthropology at the University of New Hampshire, Durham. She is a sociocultural anthropologist with interdisciplinary teaching and scholarship. Her publications explore a wide range of topics, including Muslim women's leadership, nonliberatory desires and discourses, Islamic education, reproductive health, and spatial dynamics of Islamic renewal. Her recent interests include personal life histories, natural architecture, emplacement of the feminine divine in Central Asia, and performative anthropology.